ABOUT THE AUTHOR

ROBERT COLES is a professor of psychiatry and medical humanities at the Harvard Medical School and a research psychiatrist for the Harvard University Health Services. His many books include the Pulitzer Prize–winning five-volume *Children of Crisis* and the bestselling *The Moral Intelligence of Children* and *The Spiritual Life of Children*. He is also the James Agee Professor of Social Ethics at Harvard. He lives in Massachusetts.

The Moral Intelligence of Children

Children of Crisis, I: A Study of Courage and Fear

Still Hungry in America

The Image Is You

Uprooted Children

Teachers and the Children of Poverty

Wages of Neglect (*with Maria Piers*)

Drugs and Youth (*with Joseph Brenner and Dermot Meagher*)

Erik H. Erikson: The Growth of His Work

The Middle Americans (*with Jon Erikson*)

The Geography of Faith (*with Daniel Berrigan*)

Migrants, Sharecroppers, Mountaineers (*Volume II of* Children of Crisis)

The South Goes North (*Volume III of* Children of Crisis)

Farewell to the South

Twelve to Sixteen: Early Adolescence (*with Jerome Kagan*)

A Spectacle Unto the World: The Catholic Worker Movement (*with Jon Erikson*)

The Old Ones of New Mexico (*with Alex Harris*)

The Buses Roll (*with Carol Baldwin*)

The Darkness and the Light (*with Doris Ulmann*)

Irony in the Mind's Life: Essays on Novels by James Agee, Elizabeth Bowen, and George Eliot

William Carlos Williams: The Knack of Survival in America

The Mind's Fate: Ways of Seeing Psychiatry and Psychoanalysis

Eskimos, Chicanos, Indians (*Volume IV of* Children of Crisis)

Privileged Ones: The Well-off and the Rich in America (*Volume V of* Children of Crisis)

A Festering Sweetness (*poems*)

The Last and First Eskimos (*with Alex Harris*)

Women of Crisis, I: Lives of Struggle and Hope (*with Jane Coles*)

Walker Percy: An American Search

Flannery O'Connor's South

Women of Crisis, II: Lives of Work and Dreams (*with Jane Coles*)

Dorothea Lange

The Doctor Stories of William Carlos Williams (*editor*)

Agee (*with Ross Spears*)

The Moral Life of Children

The Political Life of Children

Simone Weil: A Modern Pilgrimage

Dorothy Day: A Radical Devotion

In the Streets (*with Helen Levitt*)

Times of Surrender: Selected Essays

Harvard Diary: Reflections on the Sacred and the Secular

That Red Wheelbarrow: Selected Literary Essays

The Child in our Times: Studies in the Development of Resiliency (*edited with Timothy Dugan*)

Anna Freud: The Dream of Psychoanalysis

Rumors of Separate Worlds (*poems*)

The Spiritual Life of Children

The Call of Stories: Teaching and the Moral Imagination

Their Eyes Meeting the World: The Drawings and Paintings of Children (*with Margaret Sartor*)

The Call of Service: A Witness to Idealism

Doing Documentary Work

FOR CHILDREN

Dead End School

The Grass Pipe

Saving Face

Riding Free

Headsparks

Lives of Moral
Leadership

ROBERT COLES

Lives of Moral Leadership

Men and Women Who
Have Made a Difference

RANDOM HOUSE
TRADE PAPERBACKS
NEW YORK

Library of Congress Cataloging-in-Publication Data
Coles, Robert
Lives of moral leadership: Men and women who have made a difference/Robert Coles
p.   cm.
Originally published: First ed. New York: Random House, 2000.
ISBN 0-375-75835-6 (pbk.: alk. paper)
1. Conduct of life—Case studies.   2. Leadership—Moral and ethical aspects—
Case studies.   I. Title.

BJ1547.4.C64   2001   170′.92′2—dc21   2001031625

Book design by J. K. Lambert

In loving memory of Jane, Mom to her family;

and to them: Bob, Renée, young Robert; Danny,

Juliana, young Sean; and Mike

Preface to the Paperback Edition

In the pages ahead, readers will have an opportunity to meet certain individuals whose behavior has demonstrated moral leadership: a willingness to say and do what needed to be expressed—or further, to be given the life of action. All books, of course, for better or for worse, stand for themselves, but their later editions, such as this paperback one, do give the authors a chance to have another go at things, say what might amplify (or rectify) a particular subject matter. Here, then, I have a valuable opportunity to let past readers of this book offer their comments, their observations, their remembered experiences to readers who come to these pages.

I have been especially impressed, and often quite touched, by the high school and college students who have written to me, come to see me, or whom I have met in the course of visits to the institutions where they have been studying. Indeed, when this book's publisher suggested an introductory essay for this edition, I immediately recalled the remarks of a freshman college student who, like her fellow American citizens, had weathered the hard-fought presidential election of 2000, and had wondered during its course what to think of the candidates, needless to say, but also, as she put it, what to think of "all the rest of us, looking for someone to be a good leader."

After that comment, she spoke of the public confrontations between Vice-President Al Gore and Texas governor George W. Bush—and of the efforts each made to claim for himself the loyalty of millions of Americans. She also allowed herself, memorable for me, to take up the central theme that runs across the chapters ahead: "They both were telling us that they knew the best answer to all of our troubles—that they were the best (that to vote for them was the best we could do). My friends and I, we were going back and forth! One was telling us, in so many words, that he was the really honest and strong leader, who would do what should be done; and the other was telling us that *he* was the one, so don't listen to *him*! I was moving back and forth, listening to them, watching them, and for a while I convinced myself that the problem was mine: If I really knew what a good leader is, then I'd know who to pick and vote for! My mom and dad said each one was trying to convince as many people as possible to stick with him, but I said that if they were really the best kind of leader, they'd put themselves on the line, no matter if they lost some votes, because they one hundred percent believed one thing. I think each of them does have strong beliefs, but they were both going back and forth, I thought, and that's when I wondered if you can be a moral leader and at the same time keep watching the polls out of the corner of your eye!"

In fact, she was prepared to take on her own doubts, misgivings; she wanted to "clear her mind," she averred, so that she might see what both candidates were trying to do—declare their points of view, and, too, gain the agreement, the support, of an attending television audience. Hence this further avowal about the question this book poses, through presentations of certain lives: "I guess that if you're going to be a leader, you have to want to go someplace, take people with you! Otherwise you're someone who wants to win an election, or win an argument, but you're looking every which way for direction (the polls, the looks people give, the opinions of the experts)—and that way, you're truly a follower, not a leader (I think), and it's too bad for you, and too bad for everybody else. My folks keep reminding us that you have to be your own person, and I guess if you want company, you'll meet people halfway. If you're a leader, people come toward you. I was thinking of my folks, what they'd say to us when we watched those [television] debates: There are the leaders, and then the followers who could be leaders in their own lives, maybe, or they could be followers, depending on who they are."

She stopped, this perceptive and thoughtful college student; she paused for a long stretch of musing, remarked upon the ambiguity and complexity of American politics, and then queried her listener on this book's "contents," as she called the pages that await the reader. Most of all, she wanted to know whether there are others who might belong here, "plain folks," she called them, even as she declared her interest in those ordinary men and women who do get mentioned, and whose moral leadership mattered a lot to her, and certainly, to this book's author.

"Sometimes I get really tired of these politicians," she declared—a response, obviously, to the close election (nearly a tie) she and the rest of us in this nation had just followed in the newspapers, on radio, and on television. Thereupon, she made note of the bus driver, the teacher, the newspaper editor, the writer, the social activist who make appearances here. She wanted to take these individuals to heart, learn from them (a reader's intense yearning to embrace others she meets through a book's presence in her life), but she also wanted to assert her own authority as a person who responds to certain others as a follower or a leader, depending on the given occasion.

The more she spoke, the more I realized that readers can become followers, but as well, some of them, some of the time, distinct moral leaders! "Let me run down the field a little," this basketball athlete as well as capable and discerning student, said. And soon enough she was covering a substantial amount of territory with these comments: "There will be times when a teacher talks, and lots of us just shrug our shoulders and are counting the minutes until she clams up. Another time, she catches us off guard, and we're hanging on her every word! The same with my folks—I'll feel one way [about them] one time, another way another time. I was talking with my [school] friends and we decided that this leadership thing, it's partly up to your *mood*. I don't think you get into that [right she was!], but I think that happens. I mean, one day you're ready for someone to take your hand and show you the way, and another day you're into yourself, or you have things to do other than pay attention to someone who is calling the shots, preaching her head off. The same with any day, because your mind shifts around, depending on what time it is, and what you've got to do—and depending on how the world's treating you, what's going on in the world."

She had put so much on the table with those reflections and self-observations—a host of "variables," some social scientists might claim, which in their sum remind us that moral leadership draws on human needs (to assert, to be told, to be helped along), and also on the world's needs—the favoring circumstances that elicit our responsive thoughts, actions, or the distinctly unfavorable circumstances that dampen various possible initiatives of mind and heart. Moreover, a young person who had left home for schooling, for courses to attend, books to read, films to see, friends to know, had reminded herself and her listener of the early roots of moral leadership—in our home life and in our young experience in neighborhoods, in classrooms. In a sense, she was wondering not only about the moral leadership of some political and spiritual and intellectual individuals, but that of children, who have their own early reasons to figure things out, and so doing, win others over.

I thought of that student many months after I'd been fortunate to hear her speak, hear her vigorous examination of moral leadership (as others exert it, in life, in history) get connected to her own memories of growing up. Indeed, her words came to my mind after I'd seen a documentary film, *Daring to Resist*, given us by Martha Lubell, a gifted psychological investigator as well as an artist with the camera.

Ms. Lubell's film presents three elderly Jewish women who recall vividly, compellingly, their childhood experiences in Holland, Hungary, and Poland during the Second World War, when Nazi troops and terror dominated those countries, among others, in Europe. The women's stories are brought home to us through the use of family photographs and home movies as well as personal statements—a narration of words and pictures. We learn of children who realized full well the purposes of the Nazis, their overall genocidal intent, even as the parents of those children tried hard to ignore what was there, all around them, to be seen and heard. In a sense, the film tells of children becoming moral leaders—able and willing to take stock of a looming murderous tyranny, and, very important, determined to take action, whatever the danger, the ultimate cost. This astonishing, enormously instructive documentary, this witness of elderly survivors of totalitarian brutality, reminds us that the young can occasionally lead their elders—that girls under ten could not only read clearly the writing on the walls around them, but take up arms, do their best to deter in all possible ways those bent on the destruction of them, their kin, and their neighbors. This moral tale of a youthful resistance, taken up with no encouragement from parents and relatives and nearby friends and families, all bent on day-to-day survival, reveals an extraordinary kind of moral leadership—in the film's title, the young "daring to resist" hence become survivors while their mothers and fathers, and others with them, all perish.

As I watched this film I was again mindful of Erik H. Erikson's words, which appear later in this book: "We have to pay attention to what children can offer us, as much as to what we can offer them," he once told us—and then this topsy-turvy insistence: "We're the ones being brought up so often—a child can make us see what we try so hard not to see." He then added this: "Children will sometimes play the game 'follow the leader,' and I think their parents sometimes play that game, as the followers!" In *Daring to Resist*, certain children left their homes, left all they had learned to take for granted, rely upon and treasure, in an effort to confront rampant (and heavily armed) injustice, thwart its predominance through all sorts of breathtakingly ingenious strategies, plays, maneuvers: a knowing moral confrontation of devilish power on their part, and a story from over half a century ago that ought to live in any chronicle of moral leadership as it has been enacted under the least encouraging circumstances imaginable.

Books can become our companions, and those who figure in them can sometimes take up long-term residence in our minds and hearts, bent as they both are on finding some valuable reasons in this life. When the American novelist Walker Percy was once testily asked about "the point" of his first novel, *The Moviegoer*, he replied with disarming candor: "I wrote the book to find my way, and I sure hope it might help some others a little bit to find their way, on their journey toward meaning." Those last three words struck all of us hearing them with *their* meaning, mighty indeed: books, with the words they feed us through our eyes (or for the blind, through their fingers), a big assist in the travels we take during our time allotted us here, a "journey" toward some understanding of this life, its significance or its hazards, and a "journey" we take with others, some of them leading us on, some of them companion followers whom we occasionally spur, stir, lead, with their eyes glued on us—the moral leadership we find in this world, receive from certain people, and also ourselves give to this world every now and then.

Contents

Introduction:
Stories of Moral Leadership

The pages ahead are meant to tell of moral leaders I have known, and of moral leadership of various kinds as it has figured in particular lives—leadership exerted by individuals well-known and influential, and also by ordinary folks, people young and old who have responded with moral energy to a crisis or challenge in a way that has meant a lot to others.

I hope through these accounts of moral leadership to show how each of us plays a role in the moral drama of the world around us, and show by implication how we can play an even greater one, at one time or another, in the course of our lives. We need heroes, people who can inspire us, help shape us morally, spur us on to purposeful action—and from time to time we are called on to *be* those heroes, leaders for others, either in a small, day-to-day way, or on the world's larger stage. At this time in America, and in the rest of the world, we seem to need moral leadership especially, but the need for moral inspiration is ever present.

Over the years I have tried to understand the development of moral understanding in children: how character is shaped and young people are led to develop moral awareness. Here I want to address the moral life of adults, as it, too, gets shaped by and in turn shapes others, a continual and mutual process: the moral leadership we provide or are inspired by in public life, in schools and universities, in our cultural, civic, and religious lives, in our homes, and at critical moments in our personal life, when (to draw upon Walker Percy's phrase at the end of *The Moviegoer*) "we hand one another along."

Moral Witnesses

I summon here as moral witnesses certain individuals I've been lucky to know, and I mean for the stories I tell to be representative of moral leadership, even as I try to talk about the qualities that make for it. I attempt here to describe those people, and to render what I have observed and tape-recorded and remembered about them. Some of the men and women in this book are well known (Robert Kennedy, Dorothy Day), others are less familiar to most readers, still others are ordinary folks, or people known only to their students (teachers such as Werner Jaeger and Perry Miller) or readers. I call upon my work, take up the much-neglected matter of "moral psychology" through the example of Erik Erikson's reflections on the actions of a Boston bus driver. I also call upon a moral tradition as I have learned it and heard it translated by teachers in elementary schools and universities. The truth is that, complain as we might about the absence of moral behavior in life today, we have to work to advance it. We need to hand one another along through the moral leadership we show, or through how we support it in others.

I also want this book to show how literature can be a living moral catalyst and presence for many people, for a leader such as Dorothy Day, who constantly turned to Tolstoy or Dostoyevsky, and for Robert Kennedy, who found enlightenment in one of Shakespeare's characters, Henry V. In that spirit I try to connect these and other moral leaders to certain morally awake writers, such as Ralph Waldo Emerson and Joseph Conrad.

The book starts with my first meeting with Robert Kennedy, in 1965, when I was thirty-five years old. I had testified before the Senate Ribicoff Committee, which was looking into the racial problems of urban America; Robert Kennedy, a senator from New York at that time, talked with me at some length. Soon thereafter, I accompanied him on some of his field trips to the Mississippi Delta, to Appalachia, where I'd also worked. Early on he asked me this: "How did you get to where you are in life?" This book is in part an answer to that question. The upshot of Kennedy's query was a long moral conversation on both our parts—and in a way, that encounter, and his pointed, searching question with its obvious personal meaning for him at that moment in his own life, set the thematic tone for this book as well: the how, the why, the whither of our introspective journeys as men and women, as citizens, and as teachers of one another as we, all of our lives (no matter our stations or situations), hand one another along morally—the moral connectedness that matters so much in our minds and hearts.

No wonder, then, I write about Yale Kneeland, a great physician teacher of mine at medical school, his dignity and decency a big example for us, who watched him so closely; and I recall a class I audited at Union Theological Seminary while a medical student, the teacher, Reinhold Niebuhr, telling us what it meant to him to know Dietrich Bonhoeffer—indeed a teacher inspiring us morally even as he was inspired by Bonhoeffer's resistance to Hitler. I write, too, about ordinary people who became heroes of mine—their ethical strength a stirring witness for the regions in which they lived.

The Lives of Moral Leaders

Here, accordingly, are lives of moral leadership—incidents in them, moments of them, chronicles of their unfolding, the turns of fate and chance and circumstance that visited particular persons, the responses they dared to make in the course of their time spent on this earth. I write in the documentary and narrative tradition, offering accounts of social or political or religious or spiritual or economic leadership as it has been demonstrated and observed by others, me included. The work mentioned here has taken me to homes, churches, schools, neighborhoods, soup kitchens, and offices in our nation's capital: a collective witness of moral leadership provided by the rich and influential and powerful, by the unknown and quite vulnerable. I have tried to bring out the qualities that make for moral leadership—qualities such as courage and idealism, and a capacity for effectiveness, an ability to get something done.

The point of this book is to say what moral leadership is, to show varieties of it: to indicate how a range of individuals can bring us all up morally, can become part of a nation's moral fiber—a child, an adult, a person in politics, or one quietly trying to get through a seemingly quite ordinary life. Suddenly and surprisingly we can become an example to others—or those others to us: they hand us along, become a source of moral encouragement to us, arouse us and stir us, move us to do things when we might otherwise not be provoked, and they have the will to act in pursuit of purposes we have come to regard as important.

These are people whose acts, ideals and ordeals, ideas and thoughts, whose affirmed, visible commitments, have in one way or another had meaning and worth to others, have enabled others to see their own aspirations and dreams brought to life. A six-year-old child, Ruby Bridges, once put it well, I think, as she pioneered school desegregation in the South of the early 1960s. I have written about Ruby at some length elsewhere; she had no political, ideological, moral, or philosophical goals that she could spell out, but she knew to say the following as she reflected upon the consequences of her attending a previously all-white school, against the daily opposition of a vociferous mob: "I try to get there, and I figure if I do, then other kids might say they're willing to try and go, too, and pretty soon, it could be better for us here."

This child had no specific notion of herself as a leader, but she did "know something," she once declared, and she did place the resonance of that discernment in her "bones." She placed herself, her life, literally on the line, and in the hands of "luck"—moral leadership was something that she felt deep down within herself and was willing to enact as part of her daily life. Maybe her own self-description can be of help to those of us who seek definitions of moral leadership: "I got picked by accident, because we live here and it all happened! When Lady Luck comes and visits, you do your best, Granny says, and then you know in your bones that no way you should let them win over you, because there is all the folks, they're in this with you, the other kids."

In a different vein, I once heard moral courage characterized at a meeting with my colleagues held in the course of a symposium sponsored by the American Psychoanalytic Association. The speaker, Erik Erikson, whose thoughts come later in this book, stirred many of us younger psychiatrists when he spoke of the leadership young people can provide to their elders, their parents, and teachers: "Courage is leadership affirmed."

We Hand One Another Along

Finally, there are these words from a New Orleans elementary school teacher of Ruby's, whom I also came to know when that city was struggling with racial antagonisms as they became a moral crisis: "You have a real honest talk with yourself and find out who *you* are and what you really believe is right, the correct choice, and why that's it, and then, with your values figured out, the reasons you have why you are ready to do something. That means you have to act, act on your beliefs, and you have to behave right, not just talk right, and you have to convince others to go in the direction you're going, where you're headed, convince them that they should join with you, take your hands in theirs, a go-along party of folks, that's how I'd say it: a leader is someone who knows how to persuade others to keep others company, to stand for what she believes in, the good, the one hundred percent right thing to do—and so they're all walking like a strong family does: all on a walk together, and keeping tune with each other, and getting strong on account of each other. That's what you do for yourself and for other folks: you keep each other going, you give each other reason to keep going. If you're going to lead, you have to win people over to what you believe is the truth, the way to truth, and that means they're willing to put their trust in you, and that's a gift, you know—the leader is given trust because the ones he's leading (or it can be a she!), they believe it's right to follow, right for them and right for what they think is right."

This teacher had tried to connect morality and activity in her off-the-cuff remarks. She was getting at the enactment of leadership in the daily theater of a life lived in a place of residence, of work. "I tell my children," she averred, "that the first thing you need to know is where you want to go, and why; then you need to know if you want company, if you're willing and able to tell others what you believe, and by golly, win them over. That's what some children already do, especially in sports. They go talk with some folks young like them, and they win them over, get them going, and they 'walk them through' what's ahead, what needs to be done, for the glory of the school, a victory."

In 1963, my wife, Jane, one day wrote the phrase "moral leadership" on a piece of paper, her term for what she had seen and heard in the South during the civil rights era. Moral leaders, Jane had begun to recognize, can be people in high places or quite humble people, can be of this, that, the other background, can be established in life or just starting out in it. In the following pages, moral leadership is to be found both in "high and low places," as back then she knew to remind me—and I try to tell now how such leadership works, how certain individuals manage with others, and to what effect.

I include here profiles of moral leaders, as I have come to know them, who gave moral instruction and leadership to others in the public scene, in the classroom, in the course of lives lived as they connect with one another—travelers all, who have meant something to me and to others, even as they themselves searched hard for meaning, purpose, and moral direction. I try to analyze and convey what makes for moral leadership in its various affirmations and expressions—large and small—as it is exerted in politics or in cultural or intellectual life, as well as in so-called ordinary life. By more than implication, I hope hereby to offer a sense of what matters morally—how what matters can, in fact, come alive in the way we live with others, hand one another along.

One last note, speaking as I just did of those who have meant something to others—I want to acknowledge my wife, Jane, and our children (and grandchildren), as I did in the dedication. I also want to acknowledge gratefully the considerable help for this book I was given by Kate Medina, by Amanda Urban, by Ed Gerwig, by Patrick Yachimski, and by Trevor Hall. Finally, I mention two good friends: Dorothy Day, whom I met well before my work in the South, when I was a volunteer in a soup kitchen of hers in New York City's Bowery; and Danilo Dolci, the extraordinarily decent, thoughtful community worker and social and political worker in Italy whom I was most privileged to get to know and interview in the 1960s, and whose qualities of mind, heart, and soul as a leader I have tried to describe in this book.

Lives of Moral
Leadership

An Effective Moral Leader:
Remembering Robert Kennedy

How to exert a certain kind of leadership—moral leadership—and be effective, get something good done: this was the lesson a group of us doctors learned in 1967 from encounters with Robert Kennedy— a lesson about how a moral purpose gets applied to the world in a practical way.

We were a group of physicians who had spent time in the Mississippi Delta doing medical examinations of children. We were surprised at what we'd found—that in the United States there were still children suffering from malnutrition, vitamin deficiencies, and the diseases associated with them: beriberi, scurvy, rickets. We were more than surprised; at times we were stunned: American boys and girls, here in the second half of the twentieth century, presented medical histories and symptoms of illnesses that we associated with the Third World, that we believed long gone from our country and had ourselves never seen in the hospitals and clinics where we had trained or were working. Some of us had gone to Alabama, eastern Kentucky, and West Virginia, where we also saw children, and came to conclusions about their health. All of those children were poor, the sons and daughters of tenant farmers or jobless people who lived up the Appalachian hollows, and many of them were in poor health.

In the late spring of 1967 we wrote up a substantial documentation of our observations, and with the help of the Field Foundation, which had initially dispatched some of us to the South and Appalachia, we were put in contact with high government officials whose responsibilities, so we thought, included the health of American citizens. We wanted to spur them to action. Soon enough we were walking those long bureaucratic hallways in Washington, those corridors of American power. We met with the secretary of agriculture, the secretary of health, education, and welfare, and the head of the Office of Economic Opportunity (OEO, as it was called then—a sixties echo, that abbreviation, of various New Deal agencies). We presented our findings to those men, and to their associates, and returned to our hotel deeply discouraged.

Again and again we had been asked *why* we were bothering—what was it we hoped to *accomplish,* and for what *purpose.* The issue seemed to be *us,* rather than the children whose lives we had witnessed and tried to describe in all their jeopardy and vulnerability.

The oldest of us, Milton J. E. Senn, then in his late sixties, a pediatrician and the head of the Yale Child Study Center, was dispirited enough to want to return to New Haven, and as he put it, "never go near this befouled city again."

That adjective, "befouled," got us all going as we had dinner and tried to digest the experiences we'd had: indifference at best, and outright reprimands—as if we were trying in some way to make things worse, to upset the proverbial apple cart. We were reminded that the one federal program that had some impact on the people we had interviewed was a "food surplus" initiative under the control of the Agriculture Department, and ultimately, under the control of the senators and congressmen of states such as Mississippi and Alabama—men hardly interested in advancing, as it was constantly put to us, our "agenda."

By then we were eating with no great enthusiasm while we discussed the daily hunger of others, and we wondered what more there was for us to do; Dr. Senn's disenchantment and disgust had turned infectious, had prompted in us doubts and fears. We felt ourselves sinking into a moral morass; we prepared to leave the capital city with a growing melancholy, and I have to say in candid retrospect, with no small amount of wounded pride, which took the form of insistent self-pity.

We had talked with big shots, and they uniformly had given us the back of their respective hands. Though we were speaking on behalf of humble fellow citizens, we ourselves were not so humble, and I fear we not only knew it but suffered on that count: how dare these federal officials treat *us* so cavalierly!

We were packing our bags when a phone message asked us to be in touch with Senator Robert Kennedy's office. Unbeknownst to us, individuals of the Field Foundation and of the Southern Regional Council (an interracial group long dedicated to undoing the social and economic consequences of segregation, and more broadly, racism) had been in touch with the junior senator from New York and had told him of our findings, had sent him our report;* most important, they had informed him of what we had just tried to accomplish in those office visits, to no apparent effect (other than our own quite evident disenchantment). The senator wanted to meet with us, and would arrange his schedule to fit our needs. But most of us had teaching to do, patients to see, and so had to leave Washington. Two of us, Dr. Senn and I, were persuaded to make a quick initial visit to the senator's office, and indeed he volunteered to see us right away so that we could be on our way home midday.

When we met Senator Kennedy he wasted no time with pleasantries. He had read what we had written, he told us; he had heard of our efforts to inform various government officials of our impressions and, too, of our collective sense that we'd been dismissed out of hand, even chastised. He wanted to know from us what we now intended to do. Dr. Senn, a tall, plainspoken man who for decades had learned from

---

* "Hunger in America," *New Society,* January 2, 1968.

children how important it is to be open and honest, immediately replied with a brief, blunt statement: "We've done all we can do." I will always remember those six words, because the senator repeated them quietly. He seemed to be musing—even as, for a moment, I wondered whether he intended irony, or meant to be sardonic and implicitly to reprove us. Dr. Senn sat there, awaiting words other than his own from the senator. Instead, an awkward silence ensued, to the point that I found myself searching for something to say, to no avail. Dr. Senn had clearly decided to refuse further comment, and seemed edgy, ready to leave. He had both hands on the arms of his chair, and I could feel him getting set to lift himself up. Finally, this remark from the senator, as a response to Dr. Senn's statement: "I'm not so sure."

Those words were meant to stir us up, spur us on, begin a conversation. But we were unresponsive—awed, yes, in the presence of this senator, this former attorney general, this brother of a recently slain president, this man who himself seemed then like the waiting heir to the presidency. We were also silent, I now realize, out of our considerable ignorance and innocence. We were voters, of course, and we had been involved before in what get loosely called "public issues" or "social issues." We had written articles, given speeches in universities and at professional meetings—especially Dr. Senn, who had been for many years a pediatrician who very much wanted to alert the general public to the burdens and troubles millions of unlucky children virtually inherited as a birthright. Senator Kennedy knew that; he clearly admired Dr. Senn, wanted to draw him out, learn more, be of help to us. We seemed, though, at a standstill, if not an impasse. The silence had lasted too long—finally, Dr. Senn did what he seemed so poised to do: he stood up, then pushed the matter further by announcing that he had to leave to catch a plane.

I sat there wondering: ought I now get up or ought I say something that would keep us all talking, no matter the evident desire (and practical need) of one of us to depart? In a second the senator moved decisively, paradoxically. He stood up straight and tackled directly the impending breakup: he asked Dr. Senn if he might stay on a bit longer, catch the next plane—and offered to get him a reservation and have him driven to National Airport. A second's hesitation on Dr. Senn's part, a look of doubt on his face—and the senator, sensing reluctance, maybe a despair or disgust that prompted a wish to withdraw, spoke again: "It's important—we can do something." A pause, and then, "This should be the beginning, not the end."

This is one of the hallmarks of a leader—having the courage to speak up despite others' moods or discouragement. Warily but obligingly Dr. Senn yielded, sat down, but said nothing. I spoke on his behalf and said we'd done all we could do, but added that we certainly welcomed any suggestions Senator Kennedy had to offer.

The senator was not immediately forthcoming. He glanced away from us and looked out the window—a common occurrence with him, I would realize. He was clearly figuring out what to do, even as Dr. Senn's body language was telling his story: he squirmed in his chair, gave me a look that indicated frustration, a sense of futility. The senator's silence persisted—to the point that I anxiously wanted to say something to break the tension. Finally, yet another terse remark from Robert Kennedy: "Okay, there's work to do." A plan, and action.

In no time he was on the phone, while we sat and waited. After a few calls, he suggested that we ask our fellow physicians to return to Washington. He wanted to meet them, hear from each of us what we'd learned, plan with us the steps that might be taken to make our observations about the children, as he put it, "available to people." Both Dr. Senn and I were slow on the pickup, and we registered our naïveté, our innocence, by reminding the senator that we'd already written our report, handed it to our colleagues in professional organizations, shared it with government officials, and even (at the suggestion of Field Foundation officials) briefed some reporters on what we had witnessed and concluded. A smile from the senator acknowledged our effort, and then yet another of the senator's brief rejoinders—a mix, once again, of the tentative and the forceful: "I think we can do a little more."

"I Think We Can Do a Little More":
Listening in Order to Act

I believe Kennedy saw that our moral leadership was foundering on frustration—the unfortunate mix in us of high ideals not backed up by an understanding of how to get things done in the politics of the world.

Days later we all met for lunch with Robert Kennedy and his aide Peter Edelman, and one by one we spoke. The senator listened with unremitting attentiveness—he was listening in order to act.

Later we would all remark upon the sense we had that he was both glued to our words but constantly trying to estimate how others would react to them: the larger social and political significance, and how to get our message across. After each of us spoke, he whispered to Peter Edelman and made notes to himself, brief sentences hastily scribbled.

Dr. Raymond Wheeler, a prominent internist from Charlotte, North Carolina, and the president of the Southern Regional Council, was sitting beside me, and at one point he passed me a piece of paper on which he'd written, "Those eyes, they don't let go of you!" I folded the note and kept it, because at the time, and almost word for word, that thought crossed my mind, and Dr. Wheeler's statement seemed to move the matter from my subjectivity to an undeniable objectivity.

In fact, Senator Kennedy had paid special attention to Dr. Wheeler for good and important reasons that we would later find instructive. He was a gracious, kindly, white southerner whose medical credentials were impressive; he was the kind of person senators and congressmen would listen to. He spoke in a soft, appealing drawl, and he spoke fluently, easily. He could be gentle and retiring one moment, self-possessed and precisely knowledgeable the next. Each time Dr. Wheeler spoke, Senator Kennedy whispered something to Peter Edelman. Finally, when we had all had our say, the senator politely thanked us, and with a grave look on his face remarked, "I think the American people would like to know what you doctors have observed." An understated, unexceptional opinion, with which, of course, we heartily agreed! A second afterward Dr. Wheeler was being singled out to represent us. For the first time a smile, albeit a thin one, crossed the senator's face—and with it came these words: "I'm sure it would be helpful if Dr. Wheeler told this story."

Yes, yes, we all agreed; yes, for a white southerner to speak from the mind and heart about the medical observations he'd made; but we had no idea how to accomplish it. Nor did the Senator tell us then what he had in mind.

Rather, he thanked us for coming to Washington, for having lunch with him, for what we tried to do in the course of our several research trips across the Deep South and Appalachia, and, not least, for, as he put it, "being willing to work with me and others in the Senate."

As we left the room we wondered what that last comment meant.

The senator and his aide quickly departed—after a brief handshake was offered each of us by both of them. They were behind schedule, Peter Edelman told us, and we were anxious to depart Washington as soon as possible. So doing, in our taxis, we felt pleased, even honored, to have been given so much time and consideration by this eminent and influential legislator. But we had a sense of conclusion rather than anticipation as we made our farewells before seeking our various gates at National Airport. Here, after all, was a very busy U.S. senator, who seemed quite morally and politically engaged with us but who had come up with no specific recommendations, and who had, actually, left us with no announced hope or plan to see us again, and with no mention, even, that he'd be in touch with any of us at any time.

Dr. Senn, our senior physician and a man of long administrative as well as clinical experience, was once again inclined to outspoken, blunt skepticism: "A nice, cordial blow-off!" That was hard to hear—one person's disappointed take on a man, a meeting. We weren't all sure we agreed, but we all nodded, maybe out of a wish to placate or please our most elder colleague, whose pediatric brilliance we had found to be a crucial necessity in the course of our medical survey work.

Days passed with no word from Washington. We were busy writing up our "fieldwork" for possible publication in a medical or a pediatric journal. We assumed that a compassionate, morally aroused senator

had very much wanted to rise to the occasion that our reported findings had seemed to offer, and mobilize help for those children, but that
he had been diverted by more pressing issues and had second thoughts
about what, if anything, might be done in Congress or elsewhere.

One morning, however, my wife, Jane, picked up the phone at
home and was asked if I might be available. She was speaking to Senator Robert Kennedy's secretary, and a second or two later I was talking
with him.

I had met Robert Kennedy before this recent journey south with my
colleagues. I had testified, the year before, in 1966, before the Ribicoff
subcommittee that was investigating America's urban problems.
Robert Kennedy had just been settling into the Senate then. After I testified, he had asked questions, asked what the government could do to
improve some of the conditions I had described.

Now he was remembering that day and for a good reason. He asked
if my colleagues and I would consider testifying before another special
subcommittee he was trying to get going, whose purpose would be to
investigate thoroughly and across the nation exactly what we had been
trying to explore about the medical and nutritional conditions of children in a few states of the Southeast.

High-Up Enablement—and Moral Leadership—at Work

In late July 1967 we all were in Washington again. We each had prepared statements for the subcommittee, and together we met with Senator Kennedy twice informally so that he would be able to learn what
we hoped to set forth, and most important, recommend on behalf of
the children we'd met and others like them. During those two meetings, and others that I had with him at that time, Robert Kennedy's political energy became thoroughly evident. Single-handedly he arranged
for Dr. Wheeler not only to testify before a Senate committee, but to
appear on all the television evening news programs and especially, at
great length, on the *CBS Evening News* with Walter Cronkite.

Knowing how to use Dr. Wheeler meant that Dr. Wheeler's message, and manner of delivering it, decisively influenced the eventual shaping of a food stamp program for poor families. Moreover, Robert Kennedy's attention to us, as we tried to formulate our ideas and present our clinical studies, was critically enabling—it was also, as Dr. Senn would put it to me in a letter months later, "an education in itself as to how this country works high up."

That education was, of course, connected to politics: we doctors learned how a determined legislator who knew his way around the executive branch of our government as well as Congress, and who had the ear of newspaper writers and television reporters, did his work; how he began to awaken the country to the possible import of some newly gathered medical information. We also learned how a politician could turn into quite something else—how he could lead a group of doctors, prompt them to stop complaining about how *they* had been treated by certain federal officials, and instead to start telling their elected representatives and fellow citizens what was happening in certain families, and with what consequences down the line. Not least, we learned how a politician's canny, assertive, knowing political energy becomes, at a certain point, a passionate but also measured and astute exertion of moral leadership.

In particular, I have in mind the three meetings I had with Robert Kennedy during that summer: what he said, how he said it—his manner of being. Once, for instance, I had spent some time with him discussing the particular children we'd met. I explained the symptoms of various vitamin-deficiency diseases. I showed him photographs of the boys and girls who were suffering from those diseases. He immediately commented on how fat some of the children were.

I was surprised by that response. I knew in my medical bones the reason: poor people don't have the money to buy fruit and vegetables and lean meat; moreover, they don't have the educational, cultural background that stresses the importance of such foods—rather, they buy cheap food that assuages hunger, supplies energy, and adds fat aplenty to those who consume it, such as soft drinks, "streak-'o-lean" meat, potato chips. Put differently, one can be overweight and undernourished. I told the senator that, at length. He listened carefully, then explained to me, quite bluntly, why he had brought up the matter: he hadn't been thinking, at that moment, about the children—rather, he was concerned about what ordinary, middle-class people would think when they saw (on television, in newspapers, and in magazines) pictures of hungry children who are also quite heavy in appearance.

Political Reality and Moral Leadership

Senator Kennedy could see a look of perplexity crossing my face, and behind it some disappointment (the latter not yet explicitly acknowledged by myself to myself). He pulled no punches—he said it was his job to anticipate the reaction of other senators to what we'd observed, and as well, to think of the way "ordinary people" (a phrase he often used) would "come down" on the issue (another phrase he favored). We were now in the midst of politics, I knew, even as he could see my growing discomfort as a result.

I said nothing. I tried to go back to my medical and social knowledge—why poor children end up malnourished but overweight. He decided he had to be tough with me.

He explained to me that there were plenty of people who had no great interest, to put it mildly, in the children we had examined; and that unlike the poor, those people were "well-represented" in Congress and elsewhere—growers, for example, who wanted to pay low wages for lots of work, and who decried welfare payments from the government while they themselves received quite substantial farm subsidy payments from that same government.

He pushed things further, spoke of the importance of language in politics (I remember thinking of George Orwell's essay on that subject, "Politics Versus Literature," as I listened): one person's "welfare" (an aspect of "socialism") is another person's "subsidy" (an aspect of the "free enterprise system"). A smile crossed his face as we contemplated the basic irony of wealthy, conservative planters in Mississippi denouncing "handouts" to the poor, while accepting them as lifesaving for themselves—a kind of socialism for the rich, free enterprise for the poor.

Still, I wasn't sure where we were headed with this discussion, which struck me either as an interesting distraction or at best a side issue. We doctors, after all, had our medical information, and we were now pleased that a senator had rallied to our support and was trying to bring attention to our findings.

Kennedy did not want to change the subject, however. He noted that *perception* really matters in politics, and seemingly he knew that such a comment came across to me as an unexceptional and irrelevant piety—hence a brief but pointed reminder and explanation: we had "gone south" not only as physicians but as "citizens anxious to make a persuasive statement, a plea, even, to our fellow citizens." When those people saw hungry children who looked anything but emaciated and ailing, what were they likely to think?

He answered his own question—they'd conclude that some parents don't know how to feed their boys and girls the right food: hardly a good reason for a major legislative effort.

I sat there worried, puzzled. How had we gotten off on what I thought to be a tangent? Indeed, some of "our" children looked quite thin, even scrawny, and some skeletal. Yes, I saw the potential source of bafflement—that plump would mean well-fed for certain people. But we could always explain to them what I had just explained to him. Couldn't we?

I addressed the problem that way to the senator, told him I was sure that people would understand—once they were given some clarification or interpretation. But Kennedy wasn't so sure.

He pointed out to me that in our report we had made no mention of what we'd just been discussing—either the "anomaly," he called it, of paunchy youngsters who were being called by us malnourished or hungry, or our account of why that development happens.

He agreed with me that such an explanation on our part would be helpful, but he also warned me that we ought be very clear, at the start, with respect to the matter: "up-front" was the phrase he used. He also let me know he understood I might be unhappy with this sudden turn in our conversation. "Look," he said at one point, "you folks can ignore this [political reality] now—but it'll come home to haunt you." He could see on my face that I hadn't the slightest idea how that "haunting" would take place—even as I scribbled hard to attend his remarks.

How Politics Works

He gave me what was for him, who was usually laconic, an extended description of the way politics in general works, and in particular of what we physicians ought to expect. I can still hear his voice as he did so, and one or two sentences will always be in my head: "Mississippi has two United States senators, and neither of them has a reputation for any great interest in the people you visited when you were there." Moreover, he reminded me, many of the people we had met didn't vote or, if they were black, had never been allowed to vote.

He now shifted to a general statement, again unforgettable: "Politicians remember who supports them, or if they don't they go out of business."

He gave me a small lecture then, a rare, lengthy discourse. He told me that it is true that each United States senator represents all the people of his or her state, but that most senators have "a clear idea of the makeup of their constituency." When he used that last word my face must have registered a blank, or bewilderment, because he proceeded to let me know which groups of people were his keen political allies, which were cool to him, or stayed clear of him, turning either to Republicans or other Democrats—and why.

He did the same kind of analysis for Mississippi's senators, and Alabama's, and West Virginia's and Kentucky's, the very states we'd visited.

He also warned me, memorably (and accurately, it turned out), that we'd have to deal face-to-face with those senators; that after we testified (indeed, I was meeting with him to discuss our testimony) we'd have to submit to close questioning by those whose states we'd gone to visit. Another striking observation: "I doubt they'll be as favorably impressed as I suspect a few of us from the Northeast will be."

He wanted me to realize that, as he kept putting it, there is a "routine" side to politics; that many in politics have figured out whom to please, and why—have worked hard at developing their "population base," and accordingly can "count on the hard work and free flow of cash of lots of individuals." I winced. I asked whether there weren't senators who "struck out on their own," took their stands on the basis of what they believed was right, even if some of their friends and allies disagreed. Yes, yes, of course there were; he was noticeably impatient with my willfully idealistic insistence—my version, perhaps, of *Mr. Smith Goes to Washington.*

He picked up on my language, playing with it when he said, "They may end up 'striking out,' period."

Challenging Moral Smugness

I found those minutes troubling; they made me anxious and showed me the pragmatic, politically astute side of him that in my gross naïveté I hadn't been prepared to see. Yet in truth he was being protective of us by warning us of reality, of what to expect: he was bringing us down from our highfalutin innocence and idealistic moral high ground. He had, from the start, spotted a certain smugness in a few of us, a conviction on our part that we knew exactly what we were talking about and that accordingly we ought to be heeded, the sooner the better. Hence his polite assault on our self-pity (itself an aspect of our lack of experience in politics), our failure to look realistically at why we'd been fended off, our inclination to take the whole matter personally, whether by impugning the motives of others or threatening to pull back from our initial lobbying effort amidst declarations of our inadequacy, our failed mission. The point, rather, he kept insisting, was to understand politics, to steel ourselves for a tough fight; again his propensity at times to use language playfully—to be "enough above the fray that you won't be knocked out in it."

This call for distance, for careful calculation of our prospects, for preparatory zeal, for a prudent estimate of one's utterly expectable adversaries, was not what we'd expected of him, of anyone—hence his felt need (I only later realized) to speak as he did. He had accurately taken the measure of our privileged innocence, and with it, perhaps, an unwitting self-importance, or in Dr. Senn's case, a certain stubborn integrity—his obvious, lifelong interest in children and his efforts on behalf of them. But that elderly physician's life and personal demeanor had also become a challenge, even a provocation to this senator who had his own occupational hazards to confront, even as he had so shrewdly pointed to our blind spots.

Dr. Senn wanted us to proceed, to "go ahead and publish our findings," in the expectation that they would eventually "give some politicians second thoughts." He added a second thought of his own: "The country will listen to us, to our reports. That is our job, to speak up loud and clear about what we observed." Here was a man in his sixties, the proverbial elderly children's doctor, who had seen so very much, who had done so very much, who was no stranger, surely, to politics; the head of a university center, with all *its* manipulative sides, the guile *it* demanded of various professors become administrators, individuals of influence as well as responsibility, power as well as accomplishment—and now, his expressed annoyance with the cautionary advice offered by a senator and his staff.

Not that Dr. Senn had been disrespectful. He had not declared a reluctance to huddle with political advisers, nor had he failed to understand why we'd been fended off as we went to various government officials, and why we had to prepare ourselves for our critics, and yes, watch our words as we made our case. Rather, he stood apart, watching, sometimes silently glowering. When he spoke, his words were wry and ironic (and often not unlike those of the senator!). Dr. Senn was, however, gravely worried that we'd surrender our medical alarm, our moral exasperation, to the requirements of a carefully qualified, didactic presentation, as it was being suggested to us by the senator and his staff. At a certain point, he feared, we'd come across as "technically minded epidemiologists apologizing for the inadequacy of their research, and wringing their hands in public." But he had no patience, finally, with what he felt to be an unfair caricature of an intended course of action—the request that we emphasize our credentials and indicate the "methodology" we'd used, the "quantitative research" we'd done. Never mind "figures and numbers," he was unashamedly a clinician; he was ready to uphold the legitimacy of brief, exploratory clinical research—in contrast with a "long-term study" in which thousands of children would be examined, their families, too (and comparisons made with what was found elsewhere, in "comparative populations" similarly studied).

For Dr. Senn, for all of us, our observations mattered much, medically and morally. But for our newfound political advisers, there were possible dangers ahead, and *they* mattered—what some experts other than ourselves, mobilized by *other* political advisors, might want to say about us and our manner of doing our work: the conclusions to which we'd come, our motives (and how they might have helped shape our claims). Dr. Senn could, at a certain point, shrug—fall back on his evident self-respect: here I am, a clinician with decades of experience who came to certain southern towns, met and examined children brought to me in church basements, in obscure, humble homes, and saw, indisputably, signs and symptoms of certain diseases that in turn told of inadequate or faulty nutrition—without need for elaborate laboratory confirmation. Let others come and survey thousands of children, do blood tests and urine tests galore, take chest X rays, EKGs, and journey to counties across the land for comparative evaluations. He knew what he'd seen; he knew why he was alarmed; he knew what the children he'd met urgently needed; and, not least, he felt he knew why our simple, direct, pediatric examinations would be challenged—out of political and economic convenience rather than a true scientific anxiety, let alone any ethical concerns.

Being One's Own Kind of Leader

By no means did Senator Kennedy want us to retreat into a maze or haze of jargon. In a way, he wanted us to be more effective, our own kinds of leaders, with our own moral messages on our tongues. He wanted us to speak the truth as we had found it—but he wanted us to be *careful* about what we claimed on behalf of our inquiries, about where we wanted to go with them, and to anticipate what others less sympathetic to our intentions would make of our efforts.

Moreover, he was concerned about how we presented our work— *not only its matter, but our manner.* Kennedy had once wondered aloud what some pediatricians from Mississippi and Alabama might find if they went north to, say, New Haven and Boston, strolled through certain neighborhoods, used their stethoscopes in certain kitchens or living rooms or churches, as we had in the South, and described their findings in an urgently worded public document, as we had—one not shared beforehand with local doctors or medical-school authorities or political figures responsible for that community's public health.

Such a suggestion of redressed balance did not in the least knock Dr. Senn off balance; he would welcome, he made clear, any and all medical investigations, done in any and all parts of the nation. If there was beriberi and scurvy and rickets in New Haven, a half a mile from the Yale Child Study Center, and a pediatrician from, say, Greenwood, Mississippi (where we'd been), had found evidence of those and other diseases, then it was "great," Dr. Senn would say, that the medical documentation had been done, and "more power," he would insist, to such a medical deed.

How to Win a Moral Victory Rather Than a Pyrrhic One

All of us doctors quickly agreed with Dr. Senn, though we also saw what the senator was trying to suggest: we were in the middle of a complicated political struggle, and we'd best try to figure out how to negotiate ourselves successfully through it—how to win a moral victory, rather than a Pyrrhic one. We hadn't, after all, yet written up all of our fieldwork for a medical journal, or given a talk about it to our fellow physicians at a medical meeting. Rather, we'd addressed our fellow citizens through the news we'd made, through interviews we'd had with reporters. We'd also visited certain elected or appointed federal officials, and one of them was urging us to take care, do more research, frame our findings in such a way that we protected ourselves from any number of criticisms, be they outright political in nature, or masked in the language of science.

As I talked with Robert Kennedy, I began to understand that Dr. Senn's moral earnestness had touched a nerve in the senator—had, in fact, reminded him of a similar inclination in himself: his own lively desire to change things, make the world better. Dr. Senn wanted us to say that we had not only made certain medical diagnoses but that we were dismayed by what we'd seen, and that we wanted everyone to know how it could go for certain children, in the hope that such shared medical information would stir an immediate response—programs to address the problem. Dr. Senn, that is, was unashamedly a moralist, ready to have his public say immediately and vigorously, whereas Senator Kennedy and his aides were trying to estimate how that presentation would work best so that (here is the convergence) what Dr. Senn wanted *would actually take place.*

At one turn in our talk the senator smiled and said that he was glad that Dr. Senn was maintaining his position, arguing on behalf of a strongly moral statement on our part.

I was surprised—Kennedy had just been less than approving of such an approach, made clear to me the risks, argued on behalf of a "low-key" series of remarks that would, he hoped, gradually persuade his fellow senators that they at least ought to hold substantial hearings, learn at some length, for themselves, what we'd hastened to report. He saw my surprised look and right away explained his abrupt shift of attitude; so doing, he launched us both into a long discussion of moral leadership—how it ought best be exerted, how it can be put in jeopardy.

A Talk About Moral Leadership:
Moving from Argument to Action

"I know Dr. Senn's instincts," the senator said, a broad smile on his face. He went further, wondering whether Dr. Senn might not only be right substantively but politically as well! Perhaps a full-fledged, medically sanctioned, "politically vigorous" assault on the social and economic system whose consequences we'd witnessed would "get something going," no matter the criticisms that might arise in doctors, researchers, and others who would demand elaborate, quantitative, and laboratory-based surveys. That, he made clear, is what he wanted to see happen—"something lasting longer than your words and mine."

Speaking of words, I was struck then by the memorable simplicity of his language and the moral energy that informed it. He worried about "effect," he kept saying; he wondered whether we'd "ever move from argument to action." Maybe, he mused, all of us, himself included, ought to follow Dr. Senn's lead, and then this, spoken with yet another broad smile: "We can charge up the hill, our guns blazing with our outrage, and hope that the other side beats a wild retreat."

The Politics of Survival

He wasn't so sure, though—even as he worried about his own hesitations and vacillations. Still, that was his job—he was there, he reminded himself and me, to stand back and try to look around corners, look ahead, lest we get nowhere fast despite our honorable intention, and as he put it, despite "the important cause" we were trying to represent. Politics, he remembered, is not only, alas, "the pursuit of the just," through speeches made, votes cast, laws enacted. Politics, he pointed out with patience but not patronizingly, is constant compromises made, and "above all, survival is important." He amplified: "You folks are going after people with this report of yours, people who want to defend the status quo, even medical people in those places you visited as 'outsiders'—you shouldn't forget that, if you want to get through this with your heads above water." A minute or so later, he tellingly amplified his major point: "You guys won't just be holding up your stethoscopes; you'll be wagging your fingers—and I guess we have to figure out how you do both." A brief pause, and then: "I suppose you *do* have two hands, each of you."

That moment of recognition with respect to us was more than echoed as we discussed in detail what ought happen, what might happen once the Senate hearings got going. After a sustained spell of political skepticism, of realpolitik described and pronounced as inevitable and as the arbiter of all things, the standard to which everyone must repair, the senator suddenly did an about-face; he drank a full glass of water, and with it seemed to be differently disposed toward our mission. He became less sure of himself, more open to life's unpredictability, even the life of the hide-bound, rule-bound Senate: "Surprises can happen, something can get started and take on a life of its own"—such conversational pieties became mere starting points for an awakened moral and narrative momentum in him.

For the first time, Senator Kennedy talked about Congress as not only a place where laws were considered, debated, and passed, but as a "public forum," a setting in which citizens can be given a chance to express their yearnings, their worries. He personally was impatient with a lot of the procedural inertia he had to confront, he acknowledged, and he found some of the discussion and argument on the floor of the Senate "tedious, uninspiring at best." But he very much enjoyed certain committee hearings—under those circumstances he could listen and learn: he met all sorts of people who could testify on one subject or another, yet who also were men and women he regarded as teachers. After many a committee's hearings were over, he found himself better educated than he had been before. He even ventured to become a bit psychological (not his inclination!), to make this categorical distinction: "In committee hearings the emphasis is on this *issue,* the next one; on the floor [of the Senate] the emphasis is on what *we're* saying, on *us*—we all stoop to showing off, we're all egotistical. That is why in committee hearings there is more leeway." That was why a persuasive witness, or a series of lively, compelling questions put to a witness who was otherwise retiring or withholding, could "make a difference."

Moral Passion

We carefully prepared our remarks, and ourselves, for the "cross-examination" Senator Kennedy warned us was forthcoming from James Eastland and John Stennis, Mississippi's influential senators. I had, as mentioned, testified before Senator Kennedy, so I knew how thoroughly prepared he was likely to be—but now he was *there* in an extraordinary way: his moral passion a force in itself, and a huge boost to us, as we tried to find our individual and collective voices. I remember with particular clarity Dr. Senn's response to the senator—the surprise and gradual admiration that emerged from an elderly doctor who had almost walked out on our planned effort to testify. "He's really giving himself to this," Dr. Senn kept saying—and as a result, he himself strengthened his testimony, made it more personal; he spoke as a physician, yes, but also as a citizen, as someone who (he put it) hoped "for more for our country," hoped that it would "prove itself worthy of our national ideals." Those sentiments may now, in retrospect, seem unexceptional, the worn pieties we all recite at certain moments. But we were physicians speaking before U.S. senators, and we had initially hoped to make our statements as dispassionate and "scientific" as possible—to give our medical accounts, with no social, let alone moral, afterthoughts.

Robert Kennedy met with us after the first round of testimony, thanked us and reassured us, and told us we were on our way: "A good job," he said to each of us as he shook our hands and gave us that thin smile, while looking right into our eyes. "This is a slow process," he also told us, a reminder and an apology both. He became quite candid at that point, letting us all know that he could become impatient, that he was constantly trying to "speed things up," frequently to no avail. In fact, he had wondered, as we spoke, whether some of the children whose medical condition we described ought have been asked to tell of their lives.

We all remained silent, each of us wondering whether such a presentation—us with those youngsters—would have been appropriate, would have worked. He sensed our ethical reservations, our practical concerns; he had felt them, too. Still, he kept wondering whether the presence of those boys and girls would have been desirable, no matter their fearful shyness and the consequent utter silence that would probably have descended on them as questions were posed to them, and no matter, too, the awkward feeling on the part of many that this was a maneuver, a ploy, an indulgence in sentiment at the cost of privacy to a group of young Americans who already had quite enough trouble with which they daily had to contend.

In this regard, Dr. Senn was the only one of us who was willing to reply to the senator's thoughts—he shared with us an aside, but now a topic of explicit discussion. No, Dr. Senn, remarked, he didn't think we'd have been right doing that—and then a brief but cogent presentation of his reasons: the children would be traumatized, and it would be manipulative of us to arrange for that outcome, not to mention wrong.

Those words got something going in Robert Kennedy—a lot: his face turned grim, he lowered his head for an instant, and then abruptly confronted Dr. Senn with a silent stare. I recall thinking: they're at it again, the two of them! Finally, this from the senator: "We certainly wouldn't want to do anything to make matters worse for those children"; and after the briefest of pauses, "I only hope we can end up being of help to them."

Those last words were spoken with gravity but had an edge of irony, and even anger—a legislator expressing his concern, his apprehension, too, his awareness of the obstacles ahead.

The following day, I was again in the senator's office. He'd asked me to spend a half hour or so going over the next steps we might take on behalf of the children I'd met, and others like them across the nation. There were more hearings to be held, of course, but he had no great faith in them, as he'd already indicated through his remark to Dr. Senn the day before, and as he declared with greater, more explicit emphasis at the start of our conversation. He called the hearings "goings-on," a strange way of referring to them. He was stressing, I slowly realized, the show of it all—a public performance—and he was indicating a certain contempt for what was unfolding. Ordinarily, he continued, he could put up with it all—it was part of the job. But in this case he had no stomach for the endless delays he foresaw, as senator after senator made statements and asked questions, and as the various discussions and disagreements and sanctioned arguments unfolded. He understood Dr. Senn's concerns and reservations, but he wondered whether "the good doctor" understood how likely it was that "we" would, in fact, get nowhere—unless in some manner we took certain initiatives. He had "all the respect in the world," he had to say, for the "capacity of this town to shrug its shoulders at anything."

He let me know the depth of his feeling by waiting a second, repeating that word "anything," now with some vehemence. Thereupon, he turned his head, looked out the window—as if he was surveying all that "anything," doing a census in his mind of the various urgent issues that had, finally, been ignored or treated insensitively by federal lawmakers in the capital city. When his eyes returned to the room, his voice was ready to announce another kind of departure: "I wonder whether we ought to go visit the people you doctors went and saw—I wonder if we should have our hearings in Mississippi or Appalachia, or in my own state [New York], if that's where hungry children are—*wherever.*"

He hit that last word hard, and as if to make clear his intentions, he raised his right hand and moved it across an imaginary arc that must have encompassed in his mind the entire span of the fifty American states. He stood up, and I began to follow his lead.

But with a gesture of his right hand he told me to stay seated, and then courteously went back to his own chair. He looked at his desk, picked up a letter opener, twirled it for a few seconds, put it down, spoke. It was important, he'd concluded that "we" figure out a way of moving beyond the Senate and its hearings; they were a first step, an important one, and in the long run, a necessary one, but other steps were also necessary—that is, if "we're to get anywhere."

At that juncture, he took note of my face, which must have radiated the ignorance and confusion of the mind behind it. I had thought that these hearings were a big breakthrough—only weeks earlier we'd all been rebuffed by high government officials, and now senators were listening to us, and reporters were asking us questions, and television cameras were whirling as we spoke in corridors of the United States Capitol, no less. Now the country was beginning to learn, through news stories generated by our testimony, of the medical conditions we had encountered and tried to document. Now, to paraphrase the senator, we were surely getting somewhere.

Yet he felt otherwise, felt we were "fooling ourselves" if we mistook all the coverage being accorded "this story" as a decisive victory and mistook the hearings—which, ironically, he had single-handedly arranged—for an all-important sign of headway. To my consternation, he delivered this verdict: "These hearings can mark the end of all this—strange as it may seem, the end."

He wanted me to understand his line of reasoning; certainly he understood mine, hence that phrase, "strange as it may seem." He wanted me to realize that politicians, "many of them, maybe most of them" were occasionally inclined to "stand for the status quo—it's what brought them [to Washington], and it's what keeps them here." One way to maintain things as they were was to refuse to acknowledge any need for any change—but many in politics didn't really believe everything was perfect; and besides, to be "tough about it," there was no better way to keep that status quo than to appear ready, at any moment, to discuss social problems as they came to light. Looking directly at me, he repeated these words for my tape recorder, now out and playing as I write this, words which I've kept hearing in my head over the years, especially when I've been called to speak before legislators: "You can talk these issues into the ground. You can heat them up, by being unwilling to discuss them—but you can also bring in all the parties, give them all the time they want, and they'll leave so talked out they're quiet: case closed."

I was quite troubled by that statement; I didn't really believe in its truth—a kind of nihilism, I began to think. I could understand what he was trying to say, but I felt he was pushing his sense of things too far, exaggerating in order to make the obvious argument that canny politicians, trying to disguise themselves as statesmen, were always ready to stall, to pretend—to say what they didn't mean, and vice versa. What did it indicate, I wondered, that a prominent senator, who himself had initiated hearings on behalf of a cause we doctors were championing, was now sounding skeptical of all we were trying to do? I didn't then have any inclination to speak up, voice concern or alarm, question the reasons behind what I'd just heard. I kept silent, and so did Senator Kennedy—until, at last, he picked up a memo, read it, asked me a few questions (the answers to which he needed to know for the next day's hearings), and abruptly ended our meeting by thanking me for coming to his office.

I have memories of taking a long walk thereafter, of wondering whether I'd said or done something wrong, of feeling hurt and worried and downcast, and gradually irritated and angry. If he felt we were wasting our time, then dammit, we ought to go home. Why this sudden gloomy and cynical appraisal of hearings that seemed to be going quite well—hearings whose substance was being amply put on the record?

I had an appointment to see the senator the next morning to discuss with him what we doctors planned to present later that day, and to discuss with him, also, any future investigative projects that might be useful. (We were planning visits to Native American reservations out West, and possibly Eskimo villages.) I was not up early that next day, or all that eager for the scheduled meeting. I did come to the Senate Office Building ahead of my appointment, walked a wide circle or two, and will never forget seeing a car, with Robert Kennedy sitting in the rear, pull up near the Capitol. I watched, waiting for him to get out. But he didn't. His head was bent, as if he was reading something. I stood there looking—looking and looking. About ten minutes later he got out of the car, holding a black briefing book in his hand. He smiled at his driver, thanked him, and made for his office. I followed at a distance—I was to meet him five minutes before, but had held off going to his office because I had seen firsthand where he was. When I did get there, I was told I'd need to wait, and I did, for a half hour or so.

When I was shown into the senator's office he was still reading that briefing book. He looked up, thanked me for coming by, and immediately remarked upon all the "homework" he'd been doing. I was tempted to say "Yes, I know," but instead offered only a tentative smile clumsily meant to express a firm gratitude for all the time and attention he'd been giving to us in recent days. He told me, right away, that he hoped "you doctors aren't discouraged"—and I understood, at once, a reference to our previous conversation. I said no, but promptly contradicted myself by stating my belated realization of the *many* issues crying competitively for his notice and that of other senators. By implication I was indicating a certain worldly resignation, at last: we with our medical report were but a few of hundreds who had claimed the attention of our country's executive and legislative officeholders, and so there was no point expecting too much. Indeed, to do so, to pester others, was to uphold one's self-importance, all right—and to risk an eventual letdown (which I was unwittingly experiencing).

What I'm now writing Robert Kennedy more than realized. He had taken our psychological measure. I hadn't the knowledge of his daily work, nor the political and moral imagination to put myself in his shoes. I was only beginning to fathom what it meant to be a senator, and in this instance a national political figure. In no time I heard this: "There *are* a lot of issues out there, but it's our job to decide which ones matter most." I nodded, glad to be told such, because I was really being told that our particular "issue" was among those this senator surely considered highly important. Then a surprising turn—the senator stood up and began aloud a new train of thought: he wondered sometimes whether he had the "right temperament" for the job he presently had; he could be "impatient, very impatient" under certain circumstances—"such as those now before us." I was struck by his use of that pronoun: his willingness, to include himself in our company. He laughed, as if he, too, had taken notice of what he'd just indicated through casual resort to a two-letter word.

He pointed out that there were no physicians in his family. Perhaps one of his children would become a doctor! It was a tough, demanding occupation, he knew. The same with politics, of course—"very grueling," and ultimately less satisfying, so he judged.

On the other hand there were "opportunities" in what he termed "the political arena"; and as he recited them, I recall thinking that this was a somewhat abstract and not especially surprising (or interesting) recitation. I wondered what the point of it all was—yes, of course, a senator or a governor or, Lord knows, a president, can "move things along," "help people who otherwise have no one to turn to," "highlight problems." Maybe, I thought, the senator was trying to persuade *himself* with that language, not me—maybe he was picking up where he had left off the day before; amidst a lot of talk and more talk (the stuff of hearings, as he reminded me, as well as Senate business "on the floor") there were still, nevertheless, those various "opportunities." He used that word enough for me to notice, to feel a bit queasy—a cliché, a somewhat slippery, even calculating, word, a contrast with the high-minded language he (and his older brother) had so often used in speeches or even off-the-cuff comments to reporters.

For a few seconds he returned, still standing, to his briefing book. I was trying to think of what to say that would enable me to leave. The phone rang and—speaking of "opportunities"—I stood up, ready to leave, and sure that with a gesture or two on his part and mine the morning encounter would be thankfully ended. But he motioned for me to sit down, and in seconds he was off the phone.

Now I heard a memorable series of remarks. Now I heard that phrase *moral leadership.* Now I heard a declaration of what ought be, what might be—a powerfully introspective but by no means lengthy description of "civic life" at its best.

Most of the time, he had to admit, his job was "humdrum"—but that was life "for all of us." Even the presidency, I ought to know (from someone who certainly did know!), could involve a lot of "tedium and detail," a not very attractive description, an awkwardly related one, and hence, ironically, one that I couldn't help keeping in mind. On the other hand, there were moments when "whether you're in the White House or here [in his office] or wherever you are in the country," you still could make choices. It was truly important to know that, he said, to keep reminding yourself of that: "You can go one way, or you can go the other." This question of hunger in America, for instance: there were plenty of excuses that would enable any of us to turn away or go after some other issue. To do so, however, would be "unconscionable"—that is what he had decided.

He had just been reading that briefing book, he reminded me; he had closed it once, closed his eyes, had tried to imagine some of those children whose diseases had been described, had tried even to have a conversation with them, in which he asked them about their lives (what they did with their time, what subjects they liked in school, what they wanted to be, to do, when they got older), and had tried to imagine their replies. The trouble was, in this attempted encounter those little ones hadn't been able to tell him much. Mostly they hung their heads low. No, they weren't black—I had queried him on that score. They were, in fact, white—he had "forgotten" that most of the children we had met in, say, the Mississippi Delta were, unsurprisingly, black and poor, whereas the "kid or two" he'd conjured in his thoughts, attempted to address, were (he had to admit) "probably living in some suburb up here."

Shrewdly and with a terse eloquence, he let that "failure" on his part—his mind's incapacity to evoke a certain truth that, as a matter of fact, he (of all people) knew well (after exposure to all those briefing books!)—become a moral prod of sorts: "There it is—not only me, but all of us! There's only so far you can go in your mind." He stopped, seemingly to let his mind reflect upon what he'd said about it; then he admonished himself: "I just hope I can do better after all this is over! If I really get the picture—what's happening to these children you doctors visited—then I can help others do the same. That's my job."

As I heard him speaking, I finally recognized that he was speaking to himself as much as to me, the ever-willing, fast scribbler, who now and then, with his permission, switched on a tape recorder. He was speaking out loud, as it were, thoughts he'd tried to pose for his own consideration as he read what his aides had written, and listened to what some of us had been declaring as medical observers. He was becoming stirred to a degree of commitment that he could only selectively permit, so he had already made sure I understood. Though once he'd let that frame of mind develop, that motion of the heart get under way, there must not be a "turning back," or even the conventionally applauded and applied caution, circumspection of the seasoned politician, or for that matter, statesman.

Not that such caution need or ought be tossed dramatically at the proverbial winds. On the contrary, the greater the connection to or immersion in a particular struggle, the "more challenging and important" it becomes to figure out a proper political and moral stance in relation to it, so the Senator repeatedly emphasized. "I have to watch myself on this [issue]," he declared, and that morning he was especially anxious to explore the matter more closely. He spoke of his routine obligations, how he'd learned to deal with them—the putting on of a face, really, that so many of us know to do at times. Then there were more demanding moments, when he had to "bear down" with considerable energy, and prudence and vigilance. But every once in a while "something grabs your heart"—and then, more vigorously engaged, "you have to be watchful," lest you "go overboard," and "harm the very thing you care the most about."

A not surprising irony, I thought, as we talked—yet I could sense how worried he was, and wary, how "watchful" he felt he had to be with respect to his own moral passion, now aroused. I heard from him at this moment a lesson or two about the way a politician, stirred to action, "must proceed." Of course, that very word *proceed,* used and used, told of his more cautious and controlled side, never absent. Indeed, he often appeared tensely coiled, moved to great feeling on the one hand but also very much constrained by what was, really, a mandate calling him from within—that it was best to stay within certain limits, keep an eye out for the wolves waiting around any corner of a political life, rely on "proper procedures" as a means of proceeding, lest disaster strike in an unguarded moment.

At one point, a most telling moment, he spoke of us doctors, but he was really saying something about his own sense of how he ought to act, with what hopes and aims and purposes: "I would think that you'd all be pleased, coming out of this, if you got a lot of your colleagues involved, and if the subject became discussed—by the American people, more and more of them." I nodded, naturally—an unexceptional sentiment. I was, to be honest, not all that impressed: he was clearly quite awakened, bestirred by what he'd heard and seen (through the photographs we presented), and yet his blandly stated comment more or less offered the obvious—what any politician would call desirable when addressing any issue that required a public airing. I was, though, missing something, and later I came to understand. He was, with that unobjectionable attribution of intent and desire (*you'd* be pleased if *you* got a lot of *your* colleagues) declaring his own mission's goal. *He* would set out, go here and there, try very hard to draw others to pay heartfelt heed— hence the trips he took to the rural South and Appalachia, where we'd been, and to similarly impoverished places out West, and to certain neighborhoods in his own state, New York, as well. To do so required time, energy—and involved risks. If supporters would rally, detractors would find a way to be heard, or more worrying to him, maybe, would do their work silently. In that last regard, he had several times already tried to help us comprehend the ways of politics, the manner in which power can be wielded in retaliation or self-defense as well as (our hoped-for experience) on behalf of a given cause.

Early on, during one of our meetings, at lunch, he had whispered a caution, a warning, too: "You're stepping on toes—people will move, and they'll move to protect themselves." Another of his brief homilies, not especially remarkable or revealing, so we doctors thought at the time—the kind of offhand comment all too quickly overlooked or dismissed by us as we clamored for his powerful attention in the expectation that he would open doors and vault our reported concerns into a suddenly receptive public arena. In truth, he'd been intimate and instructive with us, and early on, when he'd offered that adage. It was as if (I belatedly came to know) he'd tried to grab us, alert us to the smell of danger, tell us something like this (though the words are mine, a cumulative response to his behavior, his gestures and appearance as I came to observe them, his frowns, his occasional brief comments as they shaped my personal sense of him): "Hey, you guys, this is no cakewalk. You can keep on being properly proud of yourselves for what you've done (I hope you won't become smug, a bit too self-satisfied!), but I tell you, there are lots of folks out there who aren't going to welcome your conclusions and your criticisms with open arms. I could spell it all out for you, the way the White House [President Lyndon Johnson] will interpret this, especially my connection to it, and the way extremely influential senators will react, men who have been here in Washington for decades and know one hundred levers to pull that you never dreamed to exist—so pay attention, keep your eyes wide open, and if you hold your heads up high, don't get carried away, keep in mind, rather, what may be coming at you any which way. Remember, even in a moral or spiritual vein, that 'pride goeth before the fall'—and in ordinary politics, my pals, there are plenty of legs out there, waiting to trip you (and I'll let you in on something: no one will ever know who owns a lot of those legs)."

That morning in his office his eyes conveyed the foregoing message, I thought, or imagined—especially when they reached through the window for the world outside, a contemplative reflex of his that spoke volumes. He hinted in platitudes, and I slowly caught on—a wise protection and act of prudence on his part in front of a stranger, though I had the feeling that in company with his closest cronies he'd never have had to say or imply any of the above (nor allude to it through the truisms he'd been sending our way).

There was, however, one flash of political abandon, of political revelation (if not moral self-evaluation) in that morning's time I spent on Capitol Hill. The senator had just about finished going over the testimony that had been given, the further testimony anticipated. He was letting me know about what he collectively called "press," the inquiries his office had received from various journalists, and the initiatives he'd personally made—calls direct and indirect to summon interest, to alert individuals about specifics, or what he called "the larger picture." He had picked up a paperweight from his desk, held it briefly, put it down firmly. He looked right at me and began talking with a touch of formality: "I want you to know . . ." He stopped for a second or two, a noticeable, even lengthy pause under such circumstances, and then got himself going again with some difficulty, I thought at the time, because the words came forth just a mite more slowly than was usually the case. (In retrospect I realized he was speaking with emphasis.) "I want you to know," he repeated, "that I'll give this all I've got." A moment's pause, and then: "I'll tell you now, it'll seem easy at first—there'll be a lot of attention and interest. But it'll get hard, really hard—we'll have a fight, here [in the Congress] and elsewhere. You guys will be out of it by then, but it'll continue, and I expect . . ." He stopped again, for longer than a few seconds. He was more than thinking. He was calculating the entire struggle and its outcome, I would decide later as I wrote down what I remembered hearing, and as I took note of a somewhat dramatic spell of silence that, at the time, had me bewildered, increasingly doubtful, and anxious. At last, this brief avowal: "Well, I expect we'll get through this struggle, and I expect that if we do, some children will eat better than before."

A modest, concrete, oddly compelling way of putting it, I thought then, and still do. My wife, Jane, when told of the above, loved the simplicity of that statement, the commanding assurance of the verb "expect" that delivered the forecast of what would eventually happen. I have to admit, though, that at the time I wasn't all that cheered. We had been fed a lot of medical, nutritional, economic information, "advice," a lot of statistics and "projections" and social or political "analysis": stories, really, in the abstract of what was going on, and what would happen in the future to the children whose condition we had, in part, viewed and documented. To say (after a struggle he himself had warned me, at the very least, wouldn't be easy) that "some children" would end up having enough food so that things would be "better than before" struck me as no great promissory stride into a just future.

I guess I wore my feelings on my face or, rather, let my body show them through a slight, unplanned tilt of the head downward. Senator Kennedy caught the movement, the glum signal, and before I had the slightest idea of what I'd felt or, in a slight gesture, done, he was ready with an aphoristic try at reassurance that, if it did nothing else, awoke me to my own mood and state of mind: "We have to start somewhere—this will be a strong start, I expect." I can still recall myself

noticing, especially, that last word again—thinking that it had resonance, that it implied a lot, that it told of this man's barely controlled
determination, of his conviction and backbone, and so ought be more
reassuring to me than I'd allowed.

Soon enough, he was on the road and a bunch of us were in tow,
watching and listening, sometimes pointing something out, more often
attending what he had noticed and felt to be important. He had a way
of holding himself back, a cool, reserved, calculating side, ever taking
the measure of people, places, things, ever estimating costs and bene-
fits; he also had a tentative, tender side, suddenly apparent, open and
artless, fun-loving and mischievous—and that part of him connected
quietly, almost wondrously with children, as I kept observing. He visited the humble people of humble counties in Mississippi, in West Virginia; to see him sitting on the floor with the young, or bending over,
or on his knees as they showed him something—shyly whispering
their words of greeting to him, their answers to his queries, their decla-
rations of desire or worry—was to see great influence and privilege also
humbled. To be sure, intent was always present, as was guile and
scheming and the contained, stagy gestures that political performers
and their advisers have known to remember as they go about their
thoroughly public business. Still, at times I felt that this national big
shot (hugely influential, yearning for that final, presidential power he'd
witnessed in its execution so intimately a few years earlier) had suddenly lost it, turned into a smitten child, anxious to draw out another
child. He would get lost in a moment, forget his schedule, exasperate
all those waiting on him, those watching his various moves. His eyes
would be locked into those of a child, or of an adult, a fellow human
being who was, for that moment, not black or white, poor or vulnerable or hard-pressed or at wit's end, but a parent, trying hard to get food
for a child, trying to make sense of the world for that child.

"What do you say," he asked one man, a dad, like him, "when your
girl here wants more to eat and it isn't there?" The father replied lacon-
ically, with no evident bitterness, with an almost biblical resignation,
and yes, with a remarkable loyalty to Freud's "reality principle," never

mind ordinary, common sense: "That there isn't more now." He added the following, his stated subjectivity—a bonus for the senator's ears: "I try to be calm when I speak, and sometimes I'll say tomorrow will be coming soon, and with it some food, and sometimes I'll hold the little one tight, and she'll feed off that, you know—the closeness." At that point the senator raised his right arm, put his hand on the man's right shoulder, kept it there a long few seconds, while he said this: "I'm sorry. We can do better in this country. We will—we ought to." Then, as he withdrew his arm, himself shaken, frail, hurt, downcast, he repeated his last words with emphasis, as if they were the lines of a chorus in one of those Greek tragedies that he so favored reading: "We *will*—we *ought to.*"

Later that moral refrain kept coming at him, and through him, to any of us within hearing distance. He would switch his response, saying, "We've got to do something," pronouncing "got" as "gut," an insistence that was not spoken to an audience but, rather, uttered out of a seething impatience that couldn't be restrained. His clenched right fist often gave it all away—it sought surfaces for rest and expression both: he'd move the hand, thus clenched, back and forth across a table, the arm of a chair, his right knee, and his upper leg. Somehow that father's fatalism had merged with his own—and ignited a firestorm of moral intensity, political savvy, cunning. The hand eventually unfolded so that he could write notes, kept for himself or passed to his aides. His slanted written hand, the clipped, sometimes elliptical comments, the snappy underlined suggestions, the abrupt endings with a dash rather than a period (as if to say more, to say it all was impossible yet ultimately necessary) all fitted his mood.

Once, as he left a tenant farmer's cabin in the Mississippi Delta, the hot, humid day enveloping him, wilting his shirt, bringing sweat out of his forehead and his neck and his arms, he again clenched that fist; he used it to hit the hood of the car that was waiting to carry him off, a punctuation mark that could easily be explained by the weather or the exhaustion of a field trip, a road show, but also as an explosive moment in a wrenching moral journey that had brought him close, indeed, to those long ago Athenian playwrights, to that contemporary French existentialist novelist, Camus, whose words he was so wont to summon as he traversed the luckier roads, the campuses and convention halls, of midcentury America.

Back in Washington, he had to forget all that, and did forget, and could not forget. I won't forget the last time I saw him, in his Washington office, in the autumn of 1967. By then he was on his way to that long-anticipated leap, that announcement, that meeting with the fate, the destiny, the awful circumstance of which his Attic poets and playwrights sang so implacably, sonorously. We had our substantive talk. "Here's where we are, where we stand," I can still hear him declaring—and then the concise, even curt legislative summary, with a slight inkling, thereafter, of his political judgment, his guess as to what was likely to happen and why, all wrapped into a wryly allusive comment: "There will be problems from the same quarters, but we're moving along—and it's hard to be in favor of hunger in children, even if you think of yourself as representing well-fed grown-ups."

Toward the end of our meeting the senator got up, but not to show me the door. He shook his head, and worried out loud yet again about "the slowness of things" in Congress and, too, about the "real need" of the families whose homes he'd visited and whose memory he very much also visited from time to time. He was able to "go along to get along" only so much—every once in a while a "moral buzzer," as he called it, sounded in his head, he often knew not why. "Strange," he remarked, "I'll be in a [committee] hearing, or on the [Senate building] train, or making a call, waiting for someone to answer, and I'll think of one of those kids in Mississippi, or their mom, or their dad." He didn't seem to want the kind of glib, explanatory response people like me have learned to offer all too commonly. He wasn't really as mystified by the occurrence he'd just described as the initial word "strange" might suggest. Rather, he was glad that his memory was still working—he only feared the day when it stopped, and he had no relief from "all this stuff," by which he meant (he pointed out) the memos and marked-up legislative bills and background papers piled on his ample, imposing desk.

"To Justify Himself, Each Relies on the Other's Crimes"—Albert Camus

With a sweeping glance at it all, he turned away toward that always inviting window, and then quickly came back to the here and now. Did I know this line of Camus: "To justify himself, each relies on the other's crimes"? No, I did not. I was about to ask the usual academic (or cocktail party) question—whence that quote? But I felt ashamed, really, at the thought of doing so—the stoop that would make the words securely mine, to be used confidently on some future occasion. Anyway, he had more to say. He kept hearing in the Senate about leadership; all the time the word was spoken, as he put it, "leadership this, leadership that." He was "sick of the word"—sick of the "phoniness" he detected in its use, the self-flattery more than implied by the user. He belonged in the company of those he had just mentioned, he wanted to make clear—in case I didn't know it. By then, I knew him well enough not to demur.

How to Exert Moral Leadership—and Be Effective

This was serious business, he kept remarking, in what for him was a monologue of sorts—"how to exert a certain kind of leadership." Then a second's hesitation, before the added qualification, "moral leadership," and then the final, all-important phrase, "and be effective." I was the last person to have a ready answer for a question asked, though rhetorically. But his subsequent silence made me nervous, and I heard myself mumbling something slippery and reassuring (a mannerism of the clinic, maybe)—"Just to bring up the subject, ask the question, is a step in the right direction." I received back a stare, with no assenting nod or crack of a smile: a dissatisfaction that wouldn't yield to banal politesse.

A phone call put an end to a difficult conversational turn. I sat there trying to come up with some clever and concrete statement that would prove me a worthy respondent. When he hung up, I thought I had what it takes: "I think the people we met in Mississippi, they'll keep us honest." He wouldn't buy it, though; he immediately rephrased my remark: "They *are* honest, but I'm not sure they'll keep us that way!" By then I was prepared to protect myself by going on the psychological attack against him, in the silence of my thoughts: he was being all too self-accusatory, and that was, at best, self-defeating. Fortunately he had other things to bring up, hastily: an account of what was pending before Congress in the way of legislation meant to help needy families obtain food otherwise beyond their financial reach. As he recited the status of such efforts, he certainly made it clear that my unspoken characterization of "self-defeating" was—well, a self-defeating one on my part.

Now his secretary was letting him know that our time was decidedly up. He told me that it was hard, this life of constant activity, of scheduled appointments and obligations and votes and more votes on the Senate floor, and trips back and forth from New York State to Washington. It was hard "just being an adequate senator"—he had no idea how the "leaders" of the Senate, with their "national responsibilities," managed to do their jobs adequately. (He was, then, as mentioned, actively contemplating a run for the presidency, and would soon jump into the race.) Ever so graciously, he walked me out of his office, down the corridors, and toward the elevators. He was being mischievous, I was told; he was "playing hooky" from his office for a few minutes. He spoke of his children, the first time he'd done so with me at any length. He *so* missed them sometimes! The other day, in Manhattan, he'd almost canceled his meetings and flown back to have supper with his wife, sons, and daughters. But he'd remained—"I was slumming on Park Avenue." I caught the musical reference, and we chatted briefly, amiably, about Irving Berlin songs. There were days, he mused, summoning the composer, that he was "reaching for the moon"—but that was his job. He hoped he could keep reaching, and he hoped he would encourage others to reach—even as he himself was encouraged to do that reaching by the people he met in the South, in Appalachia, in his home state of New York: young and old, of all backgrounds, who lived such "marginal" lives, and yet who had their own moons to scan, even to hope one day to touch. Finally, this: "The moon is out there for all of us. A senator, a leader may hold it up to his constituents—promise them the moon!—but you should remember that they've got their own eyes, and they've got their own needs, and they matter, what they're seeing (and why)."

The Living of Leadership

So much for the subject of inspired and inspiring leadership, I recall thinking as we stood there, a last chewing of the fat before the stairs, the elevator. I remarked that, "hard" as his work was, he "seemed to be enjoying it," a pleasant cliché that was meant to help us end the conversation—help return him to his job. "Yes, sometimes," he both averred and demurred—and then his way of signing off: "I'll hope things get better for those folks we met on the trip [to the South, to Appalachia]—they have it a lot harder than you or me." My turn to say yes—after which, this comment: "We'll see what happens. I've learned by now that there's no predicting too far in advance." With that, of course, silence. I thought we'd ended our meeting—and he did begin to turn around, to go back to that busy, busy office of his. He offered one more remark, though: "You learn what's ahead through the living of it—and what to do, the same way." I nodded, and he said what was customary, that he hoped we'd be in touch soon, and I sure agreed, and then I stood watching as he walked away in no great rush. *The living of it,* I kept hearing in my head: the living of leadership, the living of an effort to do some good in this world, and prompt others to follow along; *the living of it* as exemplified by someone who had done lots of living in his forty-three years, and who at that time had less than twelve months left of his life to enjoy.

II

On Robert Kennedy
and Shakespeare's *Henry V*

Shakespeare's creation, the character of Henry V in the play by that name, figured in a conversation we doctors had with Robert Kennedy at a moral crossroads in our campaign to get legislation passed that would feed hungry children in the South. Robert Kennedy and one of us, Dr. Milton Senn, were both given thought by Shakespeare's king. The occasion was a meeting in which the senator was urging on us a show of conviction, of unity, of moral energy and assurance. "I would not quibble," he warned us, for obvious reasons, about our coming testimony, our public behavior before inquiring senators—a means, for him, of putting a good deal of human tragedy on the table for Americans to consider. In reply, several of us agreed with the obvious: that we need not disagree about medical judgments or conclusions, since we had no real argument going on among us, only some doubt about what might work best to make things better for the hurt, bewildered families we'd met. The senator, for good reason, wanted more food in the bellies of the children and their parents but gave worried voice with respect to some "problems" we'd noted—that the issue wasn't only food but the nature of food, as it is in turn chosen, cooked, prepared, and served. Some parents, we remarked, were interested in food that did neither themselves nor their children much good. We pointed out a repeatedly observed irony: migrants gathering healthy, nutritionally valuable food, but then turning to soda pop and fried, starchy food, whereas fruit and vegetables (which they themselves had harvested and could offer their families) were readily ignored, firmly set aside. We were troubled, not only about medical matters but about the education needed by impoverished, down-on-their-luck people.

"I understand your concerns," the senator told us, but he wanted a more clear-cut, less ambiguous presentation—a forthright plea on our part for the medical and nutritional lives of these families. Yet we hadn't thought about the hazards of a public discussion on our part—hadn't realized that the victims would eagerly be blamed (with words such as "Why don't they get smarter, take better care of their kids, feed them better!") by those who cared little or not at all for the individuals whose problems and plight we were trying so hard to document. "I understand your desire to talk all this out," Robert Kennedy, who had become our leader, said—after which a political sermon was sent our way: people would misunderstand us, or fail to get our message if we complicated it; moreover, those who cared not a whit about the fate of the children we'd observed would revel in the complexities of our discussion, and in no time weaken the possible impact and consequences of our testimony, much to their political satisfaction.

Yes, we understood; yes, we said, we wanted to achieve some medical and legislative initiatives. But we began, some of us, to demur—Dr. Senn in particular, already at moments the senator's critic. Milton Senn had no inclination to forsake a certain skepticism about various political ideas. Immediately he spoke up and insisted that we make our case "as it is," not worry about hiding any of it, or about any possible misunderstanding. "We can explain this matter to the public," he was sure, and as for politicians who wanted to "confront us or distort our findings," or "use them for their own purposes," he had "faith in the ability of people to find the truth, to see through those politicians who want to misconstrue what we learned in our work."

Right away, a lecture from the senator (not the first) on politics, public opinion, and the way things work in Congress with respect to its relationship to news, to the printed version of news, the visual presentation of news on television. Clearly, he hoped (as he put it in words customary for him) that we would "proceed," "move along, so that this issue is resolved in favor of the poor," an outcome we all desired to see. Dr. Senn, though, was not easily persuaded by that unarguable declaration of aspiration. He was grimly intent on having his full say in that room and, ahead, in any other room where he'd be speaking. The senator chose not to disagree with him over details; instead, politely but wryly, and with some irony, he shifted the conversation, making mention of Shakespeare's play *Henry V.* In a gesture of amity, he quoted from Act Four, the famous evocation of the king that clearly meant so much to this mid–twentieth century legislator: "We few, we happy few, we band of brothers; for he today that sheds his blood with me shall be my brother . . ."

We were surprised, and those of us who knew that play reasonably well were perplexed. To be sure, that part of the play puts the young king in an arresting role; he stirs and excites his listeners to attend the several dramas of a ruling (and royal and military) order. For understandable reasons, the young Kennedy brothers, upon their early 1960s ascension to American political power, would find such rhetoric appealing—as a means of appealing to others. Yet to remember that moment of young, futurist confidence in a ruler bent on consolidation of power, in persuasion of those at home, and not least in military victory abroad, is also to hold in mind the shrewd inclination of a playwright to go beyond the tingling suasion of Agincourt—to remind his audience that rulers or leaders can be attractively winning but also quite something else: compromised by the deceptions, the outright lies, the constant deceitful calculations to which they are heir, and, not rarely, bound by their own acts of commission, so often willfully overlooked, or if not, unmentioned. Put differently, a playwright has a ruler sound engaging, even seductive—yet *Henry V* is about Agincourt, an ultimate scene of carnage and cruelty, of suffering meant to bolster the trappings of royal bombast, of a young king's sway and that of his chosen "happy few, we band of brothers."

Actually, the reference to *Henry V* by Kennedy, a political leader, got Dr. Senn and me going; we talked for hours that very day about Shakespeare's rulers, the attractive side to some of them, such as Henry V, but also the base and vulgar and even criminal side to others—the betrayals and deceits and conceits that Shakespeare, their tough-minded and wide-ranging moral and psychological architect, puts forth so unrelentingly. The king who is young Harry, the fifth Henry on the throne, takes pains to investigate the political world, the double-talking pretentiousness of his would-be and ever-so-ingratiating court followers. The clergy and the officials of state and of the military, parade before him, beseech his favor, and reveal successively their craven desires, their falseness of manner, of being. If a young ruler can at first be innocent and well-intentioned, he eventually learns the score—what those who seem to hang on his every word are intent on getting. An outspoken, alluring moral call to arms turns into a display of self-interest, revealed in a kingdom—the king as the eventual recipient of the commitment of his subjects, and, too, the beneficiary of such as it is carried out and (into battle) forth.

We are asked to contemplate, finally, an ostensible display of moral leadership as it attracts legions of followers, soldiers—and so we, the observers of history, become a playwright's students, wonder about the apparently credible, the all too dangerously false, the misleading: the assertion of moral heroism sounds brightly summoning, but deep down it is blindly indifferent to the blunt truth available, the human degradation forthcoming (slaughter on the field, lies, and human pretenses of various kinds around the bend of time, of events at home, and across the English Channel). A moral appeal, grounded in nationalism as the road to gain and worse, with crookedness of various kinds everywhere, covers in vain a crass opportunism of a leader, his court, his country. Shakespeare aims to embody this kind of ultimately bogus moral leadership, wave it before history's thoroughly eager followers—before any of us who may be tempted to join their lot and exult in noble language, while letting go of the base facts ironically, sardonically concealed. When the poet William Butler Yeats turned to that play, that story, that inviting rhetoric of a leader's, a ruler's, moral arousal, he was constrained to describe the young king this way: "He has the gross vices, the coarse nerves, of one who is to rule among violent people." But Shakespeare goes further; as Yeats puts it, the play *Henry V* gives this ever-so-seductively arousing, well-spoken young ruler, who knows his way with words, "a resounding rhetoric that moves men as a leading article does today." Moreover, "his purposes are so intelligible to everybody that everybody talks of him as if he succeeded, although he fails in the end, as all men great and little fail in Shakespeare."

So it is, in "ideas good and evil," that one lyrical master nods over the centuries (and across the Irish Sea) to another: an alert, subtle moral scrutiny of a moral leadership that is evoked and portrayed in its various dimensions. I think it fair to say that Dr. Senn's scrutiny over the days, as a reader of both Shakespeare and his critical respondent, Yeats, supplied us with the determination we needed to stand up for what we believed to be right, to be *our* right, in conversations with a young, sometimes movingly articulate contemporary leader who would, weeks later, smile at us while we discussed with him more openly and directly a play of Shakespeare's and, too, our own worries— even as we tried to take his senatorial lead, make common cause with him. Indeed, I can still hear Dr. Senn's comments on *Henry V,* call back in my mind my own words, prompted by my wife, Jane, who knew that play so well and taught it in her high school classes yearly. After Dr. Senn spoke on behalf of all of us, and as a Shakespeare critic, the senator smiled and told us generously and tactfully not to worry, "you Shakespeare fans," and then added that "the beauty of great writing is how it reaches so many, all so different": a moral leader reaching out to embrace others, yielding in such a way that a possible disagreement became a show of support, of solidarity that went across a room; and very important, a moral leader tacitly acknowledging the echoing significance today of a play's long-ago cautions. "Yes, sir," we felt eager to say, because he had given us plenty of room to be together with trust and self-confidence, his spoken, ethically sensitive leadership now a welcome sign to us as we all closed ranks and tried to make clear what we believed ought be done, politically, legislatively, medically, and educationally, and why.

In retrospect, some of us realized that Robert Kennedy, ever the leader anxious for a consensus that would achieve certain goals (now a consensus among himself and the doctors in his presence), had called upon *Henry V* to further a moment of moral introspection. A senator was urging clear-cut moral exhortation in the name of fast expediency upon some doctor-citizens who (through Dr. Senn, certainly) were holding out for a qualified moral insistence. So it once was, a leader's desire to mobilize potentially reluctant or uncertain followers, grasp victory, and so it was, then, with us, a leader's desire to "proceed," no matter reservations or worries. We were not headed for Agincourt, Senator Kennedy knew, but he had, with Shakespeare's assistance, brought all of us to some thought, even to some second thoughts—and in the end all of us, in unison, had our candid say in public hearings initiated and sponsored by New York state's junior senator.

III

Conrad's *Typhoon*

In story after story, Joseph Conrad, the one-time seaman, the morally awake writer, explored the nature of leadership, its various opportunities, and its considerable risks. His sea captains, in *Typhoon* and *Heart of Darkness* and *Lord Jim,* are trying to do their work, remain loyal to their obligations, yet are tested not by their degree of competence so much as by fate, chance—what occurs in their experience as leaders: the arrival of a crisis or a potential disaster, and thereafter the need not only to fulfill their occupational duties but to act in such a way that their beliefs and principles allow them to keep on being leaders.

Often in Conrad the leader doesn't *look* as if he's up to the job—he's not good with words or fancy in other ways. But when the typhoon hits, his moral grounding enables him to act, to lead, to prevail. The mystery of who will prove to be a moral leader is at the heart of Conrad's story.

Indeed, one begins to know about Captain MacWhirr of *Typhoon* not by his moral outspokenness or sensibility, given repeated expression in the course of his seafaring life, but, rather, as a consequence of fate—an ocean's terrible threat to his ship and to all the life aboard it, hence the title of the tale.

Yet while *Typhoon* explores a leader's response to a major threat, the story's teller has other fish to fry—he wants to warn us about our own possible notions, what we may be disposed to think about the prerequisites of good leadership, how it is *supposed* to look, its favorable antecedents.

On the steamer, *Nan-Shan,* a captain navigates, and with him are a chief engineer, Solomon Rout, and a chief mate, Jukes. The three are English, and in the boat's hold are dozens of Chinese, so-called coolies, clutching their hard-earned money, packed in on their bottom-of-the-boat journey. Well before the climactic moment, when a turn of weather will challenge everyone on the *Nan-Shan* in a life-threatening manner, we learn that the one on top of things is, in fact, very much on bottom in terms of what sometimes connotes a leader—social position, educational polish, place in the pecking order.

Captain MacWhirr is a modest Belfast grocer's son (the Polish-born novelist Conrad had learned his sociology) and he is silent, hard to figure out, distant in his own fenced-off world. In contrast, those below him in rank, in the fixed hierarchy of a ship's administrator, are portrayed as the captain's superiors intellectually—the mate, Jukes, and the chief engineer, Rout, are articulate, observant, and introspective, precisely the kind of individuals many of us would fancy ourselves to be or wish we were: marked off to be leaders, to be followed by others of superior privilege.

Jukes has a name out of Dickens, and Rout's name is not altogether promising, and yet they are lively, imaginative, and thoughtful, whereas MacWhirr, the captain, whose name seems to have destined him for the turbulent ups and downs of life as well as of the Pacific, comes across as impossibly cut-off and laconic—as a stolid fellow, yes, but one whose mumbling bashfulness bespeaks of an absence of "class," of its occasional insistence upon education as an adornment. In that regard, the more Jukes and Rout write letters, show themselves able to express themselves, to speak thoughtfully, to reflect upon their given lives and register their distinct distance from MacWhirr ("He never talks"), the more we wonder, as they surely did, whether a coming typhoon will endanger them as it will others—the abundant coolies for whom they have no great concern. The captain is of limited intelligence, yet his orders mean everything under the tough, demanding laws of the sea.

Much of *Typhoon* explores, in a sense, the "above" of the seamen against the background of the "below," the coolies—and, of course, with nature, in its unpredictable, punishing possibilities, a constant presence. Who will confront the sea, the weather, in all of nature's enormous unpredictability? Who will act effectively as nature threatens a boat that we soon enough are asked to see as a microcosm of our earthly life as it happens in this or that nation or society?

Right at the start, by his third paragraph, Conrad tips his hand, makes clear his interest: "Yet the uninteresting lives of men so entirely given to the actuality of the bare existence have their mysterious side."

That broadly reflective comment, with both psychological and philosophical undertones, is connected to Captain MacWhirr, to his modest origins (his grocer father is described as "petty")—and in a short time, through his bright mates, he is given to us with no great favor: " 'For my part,' Solomon was reported by his wife to have said once, 'give me the dullest ass for a skipper before a rogue. There is a way to take a fool; but a rogue is smart and slippery.' This was an airy generalization drawn from the particular case of Captain MacWhirr's honesty, which, in itself, had the heavy obviousness of a lump of clay."

Here is a warning not only about an approaching storm of great danger but about our inclination to stir up in our minds our own kind of storms—intellectual, analytic, paradigmatic storms; hence the joining of the word "airy" to "generalization," the latter the common, even necessary ingredient that enables our reputations as "thinkers."

Here is a novelist defiantly resisting the temptation to a conclusive cleverness. He will not give us a cut-and-dried leader, whose psychology and social antecedents nicely, conveniently suit our expectations or possible requirements—rather, it is as if he wanted to encourage us to calculate *chance* (the title of another one of his fictions) as a hugely elusive variable, beyond our quick grasp. Flannery O'Connor similarly warned in a cultural broadside, *Mystery and Manners,* a warning to herself, as well as to so many of us: "The task of the novelist is to deepen mystery, and mystery is a great embarrassment to the modern mind."

Such admonitions from writers are, of course, self-directed. Conrad, approaching a tale of irony and paradox, knew how important it was for him to avoid giving us a setup in *Typhoon,* so as to allow us room to wonder about the mystery that O'Connor wrote about. And mystery he won't stop preparing us to behold—even as he has Solomon speak airily rather than wisely, and as we learn from the voluble and thoroughly shrewd, ambitious, quick-witted, and discerning Jukes about the "jolly innocent" Captain MacWhirr.

But *Typhoon* is meant to surprise us, maybe confuse or even provoke us. A moral intelligence emerges dramatically in this man who has been so patronized, dismissed in the more refined or cultured minds of his crew. The crew at times verges toward the not rare smugness that goes with self-importance. Conrad wants us to contemplate a moral heroism that is quite adequate to a fierce storm's threat of chaos, wherein so often the survival of the fittest (those with power, rank's perquisites) becomes the ruling principle. We aren't quite prepared for MacWhirr's moral leadership, but we learn to appreciate his humble tenacity, his thoroughgoing refusal to come up with convenient psychological and social strategies that will make his decisions seem sane, sensible, salutary. Instead, he is doggedly fair-minded, almost instinctively so, we come to realize. He is the unperturbable leader whose conscience won't buckle under the weight of quick-coming ideas that might serve his own interest in survival, and certainly that of his very bright underlings, Jukes and Rout, who now become, for us, newly edified, ethically awakened reporters and documentarians: they let us know about a leader who won't panic morally. Quite the contrary, MacWhirr wants the storm of sorts within his ship—the coolies, who might go wild with fear—to be calmed, even as he awaits the arrival and eventual abatement of the coming storms in nature.

For Conrad, then, moral leadership has to do with a rock-bottom decency that is (as Ruby Bridges said) in someone's bones—in his very being, in a human nature that stands up to nature in all its threat of the topsy-turvy, of a disastrous denouement.

For Conrad, too, moral leadership, when confronted with the "actuality" he mentions—when presented face-to-face with life's threats, alarms, opportunities, and possibilities—becomes a quality revealed in its awesome emergence rather than as something eminently predictable. Hence the mounting narrative tension in the hands of a novelist and thinker who ironically means to put thought in its place.

MacWhirr does not win us over with ideas, or through an affecting expressiveness; he proves to be, however, responsibly considerate of others as well as of himself—those close to him by virtue of race, nationality, or status. The man who is bereft of appealing language, who doesn't easily use inviting words, is the man who leaps over the barriers of language, who manages to enable an important communication between himself and his two mates on the one hand and a boat full of Chinese-speaking passengers on the other. Conrad, thereby, has reminded us that moral leadership can draw on the depths of our lives, on something deep down within heart and mind, something real and important to us that is reflexive rather than necessarily related to the easy come, easy go of the intellect's habits. A daunting one for us, that terrifying typhoon of Conrad's—those of us who want to tame so very much in this life, to subdue various storms and surprises with our mind's calculations put to words.

By the end of *Typhoon* we are asked to feel the emotions of surprise, of wonder. Moral leadership is displayed by an unpretentious person who comes through extraordinarily well—his keen levelheadedness, buttressed by the guarantees and traditions of his position, afford him the will and the savvy that are elicited in full measure by an accident of weather, and become his great chance: he follows through on his humble if limited humanity, which finally emerges as quite adequate to the tasks at hand to make him, in their completion, a fine moral protagonist.

Conrad's Moral Heroes in the Everyday

No wonder, then, that Jane and I, during the civil rights era, when we got to know so many activists, kept going back to Conrad, and most especially to *Typhoon*. Here in the South of the 1960s, after all, were modest men and women, not especially adept at fancy or highfalutin talk, or anxious so to be. Often they were individuals who were trying hard to "do the right," as they frequently said, and to prove themselves worthy of their "situation," a word also frequently used. A yeoman farmer, a sharecropper, actually, referred in this way to himself, to his "situation," he kept calling it: "I wasn't born to be the first, to lead my neighbors to the [voting] registrar's so we all can be allowed to vote. I'm not sure how to answer those people when they question me. All I know is I'm the one who's eligible to vote, and I've lived all my life, but never with the right to have a choice over who's to be my mayor or some other politician over us. It's hard for me to read. Words don't come easy to me. But this is my duty now, before our Lord, to show Him I'm His 'good servant,' like they say in church, and to prove something to myself: when there was a time for some of us colored folks to raise our hands, to stand up and walk up those [courthouse] steps, to prove we can pray and we can speak, ask for our rights as citizens—then, with God's help, I came through. That means I did what was the right to do, and that helped others to do the same, because you want and need company when you're standing with all your might up to people trying to scare you half out of your mind, make you a coward, up to your eyes.

"Why, this morning, as I got myself dressed, I said to my missus, 'There's a bad storm coming, a tornado out of that dark sky, the winds mounting higher, and they could take us all afar, sweep us all the way out of here.' She was scared as could be, the missus, but she reminded me we've not yet let the winds get their own way, and she kept saying we should show the world that no wind can blow us away—can stop us from thinking good, from being true to our God and our own people, and our families. If you're true to who you are and what you believe, if you've lived like you've learned, do what you know it's right to do, then you're true to God, and no tornado in the whole of the Lord's creation will pull you, carry you away from yourself, here, and 'ain't that the truth,' my momma would say, and listening to my missus, I knew I'd stand fast, and I could depend upon what I'd a long time ago heard—and so we all did."

So those two, he and she, did—a social and political "tornado" of sorts came their way, yet they could, indeed, "depend upon" no less than what they had learned to become, what they knew to do, knew ought be done; and in time they got others to join with them, and consequently the "tornado" that threatened to put them in dire jeopardy got nowhere with them; it was a "hard breeze," all right, they once called it, but it could not budge their sense of what they should go about doing, and their determination to bring along others in a similar vein. Here were, after a fashion, Conrad's moral heroes; unlikely as could be in some respects, until their spontaneous moral resourcefulness was *there,* for them a perfectly expectable, necessary response to adverse weather, from whatever direction. Moral grounding was theirs for the asking, the doing, the enacting.

Like Captain MacWhirr, they weren't "ones for talking high and mighty," only "folks who walked when walking had to be done": each step up the county courthouse a stride toward a proper citizenship, "an up-front vote for what's good," as they put it—so that their moral leadership itself helped keep in motion the biggest storm of all, a "tornado" that blew away ("please God, at last") all the tug and pull of a melancholy past.

Not that moral leaders only await the call of history, as in the civil rights struggle. A college student of mine, Don, worked one summer as a clerk in a grocery store. He was then in high school, but he began to feel tired, apathetic, just before he was to return to the classroom. Soon enough Don was in a doctor's office, then the hospital, with a diagnosis of leukemia. Soon enough, too, he was in need of blood transfusions. Don had worked well that summer with one of the store's salespeople, a middle-aged woman who had a son his age. When she learned of the youth's illness she went to the hospital to visit him, but while there she also went to the blood bank. She did not have the kind of blood he needed, but she had blood that others could use, and she resolved to find additional donors in order to help Don and others similarly afflicted. She phoned friends. She initiated conversations with neighbors—with customers both Don and she had attended that summer. Eventually, Don would call her his "blood friend," a humble working woman who tried so hard to assist a youth whose educational future once had her in awe, and then prompted in her a rallying effort: over and over she told Don that he'd "make it," to the point that her efforts on his behalf, her visits to his bedside, much touched and even inspired him. "I didn't want to disappoint her," he told me as he looked back at what turned out to be his medical success story—but also a moral, even spiritual experience: "She worked so hard to help me when I was down—and on my way out, I thought for a while! The doctors told me she got an army of people mobilized to help me and others who needed transfusions. I joked with her; I told her she was 'a general of a blood army,' something a doctor had said. She gave a big laugh, and then she told me it was the least she could do. 'You did the *most*'—I told her back. My folks called her our 'angel.' I guess you never know where good will come from when you need it, where good is in this world—that was the big lesson I learned when I got sick back then."

IV

Moral Integration: Four Stories

From 1960 to 1965, I observed the onset of school desegregation in the South. I met the African-American children who pioneered that effort, in New Orleans, Atlanta, Charlotte, Jackson, and Birmingham. In Atlanta, two of the ten teenagers who led their race into previously all-white high schools had also begun to work with the Student Nonviolent Coordinating Committee, known popularly at the time as SNCC, and one of the major civil rights groups. Soon enough, I was working at the SNCC offices myself and participating in various political initiatives undertaken by the young people of both races who came together during those tumultuous civil rights years. Most especially, I was involved from start to finish with the Mississippi Summer Project of 1964—a critical moment in the struggle to enfranchise over a third of the citizens of an American state who, in the second half of the twentieth century, still could not vote. In Freedom Houses across the Delta students took their then quite dangerous stand. Three of them died. Scores were injured. The Voting Rights Act of 1964 was surely, in part, a political testimony to that effort—a consequence of the aroused public notice those Freedom Houses secured across the nation (because of all the activity taking place in and near them). At great personal danger, hundreds of youths of both races and from all parts of the United States planted themselves firmly on Delta soil, confronted Dixie's bastion segregationist state, and thereby set in motion a great deal of social and racial change in a state hitherto immune to such a development.

Over the years much has been written about the civil rights activists, the students who pioneered school desegregation, the young SNCC leaders who envisioned and then made real the Mississippi Summer Project. In the first volume of *Children of Crisis,* I wrote at some length on the children who endured threats and mob action in order to go to school with other (white) Americans; I wrote, too, about a number of the SNCC members who, in their teens and twenties, took on sheriffs and state policemen and, not least, armed terrorists who set fires, shot rifles and pistols, and used dynamite—a day-by-day attempt to prevail over Freedom Houses, raze them to the ground, scare and injure and kill those inhabiting them. I tried, as well, to learn through interviews how ordinary white people viewed a moment of dramatic racial confrontation; and to learn how ordinary African-American men and women responded to what was a risky call to arms by a relatively privileged cadre of outsiders, whose ideals were, indeed, tested strenuously that summer of 1964 but who knew that at any point they could simply leave, take up with honor a life elsewhere, and be remembered, celebrated for the bravery they had demonstrated under quite dangerous circumstances.

When I did my writing, I relayed the events I observed through the eyes of (the voices of) the various protagonists; whether the court-appointed children who were to initiate "integration," that much disliked word among the South's white people in the early 1960s; or the SNCC members, who set up those Freedom Houses and set in motion the activities planned and sponsored by them: voter registration drives especially, but also, health care and tutoring programs. I myself worked with those medical and educational efforts, and thereby met a number of African-American Mississippians who weren't in the civil rights struggle as combatants—were, rather, meant to be the beneficiaries of what had been started, as one tenant farmer in McComb County put it, "for our sake," but then he quickly added this: "We could get hurt a lot, of course, on their account, before it gets any better hereabouts."

What follows calls upon those days; and here in this chapter I have protected the privacy of individuals through changes in names, locations, and personal characteristics (a contrast with the rest of the book, whose protagonists are publicly well known).

1. MORAL SUPPORT: THE THOMASES AND THE TOMASELLOS OF MISSISSIPPI

I still remember that man using the phrase "on their account"—a clear split intended: "us colored folks," as he often put it, against (in several senses of that expression) "the SNCC people" who were doing their best to "stir things up," a phrase not only used by the white people of that county and others across the Magnolia State. That tenant farmer was younger than many of the veteran leaders of SNCC. At twenty-seven he was a husband, a father of four, a man who had been working the land since childhood, and who expected to do so until the Lord "called" him—a time, a moment he'd many times tried to imagine: the ascent and arraignment before Almighty God. He summoned impressive descriptive powers as he related what he thought was awaiting him: "They'll check me in, one of the angels, maybe, who lives up there. They'll call my name: 'Andrew Thomas, you be the one here?' 'Yes, sir,' I'll answer them. 'Okay, tell us why you think you should be tapped by the Lord, and allowed "life forever after," tell us!' That's when I hope I have something to say. You come up there empty-handed, and you're a goner right away. That's the big test, and your whole life is your case you're putting before the Lord, and He's the judge of it, and your future life is what's to be decided. I try to tell my little ones, it's important to be good, because there's a record you make down here, and you carry it up there, and it's in your soul, written on it, and they must have some way of looking it all over and coming up with their decision, and it's *yes* or *no,* it comes down to that. You pass or you flunk. Your life's been good (pretty good—no life is perfect, for sure); or you've fallen down bad, really bad, and they can't overlook it, no sir."

Such a way of thinking (and talking) was his by virtue of a devout religious life. Every week he and his wife, Ruth, and their children went to a "tabernacle" church, to listen and pray and sing and exclaim and, not rarely, cry worriedly or shout joyfully. Neither Andrew nor Ruth Thomas could read, but they had committed to memory parts of the Old Testament, and, of course, the New Testament, and they owned a Bible, which occupied a shelf all its own in the humble rural cabin they lived in, at the edge of the land they both worked.

Not that they were too far from McComb. Ruth Thomas walked two miles five days a week in order to "help out a lady" who lived "in the town," and she was back in time to cook supper. Her mother had once worked for the same white family whose name, Tomasello, resembled the one her daughter, also named Ruth, would assume upon her marriage. Her mother, whose name was Sarah Holmes, talked of her one-time employer with respect, even affection: "They be good people. He owns a hardware store. He owns a couple of houses, besides the one he lives in. His wife, she has her troubles—she has a 'sclerosis,' they call it, of her nervous system [multiple sclerosis], and so she gets wobbly, and she's headed for a wheelchair, the Mister would say sometimes, and shake his head, and he'd pull his handkerchief out and blow on it. We chuckled sometimes, the Mister and me. He'd come home a lot to look on his wife, and we got to talking. He said, when I told him my daughter, Ruth, would be marrying Andrew Thomas—he said her name would be 'kin' to his. That's the time he explained to me that his grandfather came from Italy, and so his name is different from the others, the white folks. I always did know that—I liked the sound of it; there's a ring to it. He said little things can make a big difference—people sometimes will ask him if he goes back to the 'old country' on visits. 'They have an "old country," too,' he said, 'but you'd never know it by how they talk. You'd think they've been here forever and a day.' That's what he told me. I'd never heard a white man talk like that—so honest, and out of his heart!"

That story became part of table talk in the Andrew Thomas household. Years before the civil rights movement came to Mississippi, Andrew Thomas had learned something important from his mother-in-law—had taken a moment's confidence, offered by a prosperous white man to his "cleaning lady," and turned it into a reason for social reflection: "I've often remembered what 'Mamie' told us. She liked it that our name and her boss man's sound alike; but I've told her a hundred times that, like our minister will tell you, the truth comes in lots of disguises, so many of them, and Mr. Tomasello was confessing something then. He was letting Mamie in on a secret—that the white folks have bad blood between them, some of them: they can treat their own the way they treat us, not all the way, not as whole-hog, but they can go sideswiping each other (see what I mean?)—and for us colored, that's news.

"No, sir, I can't say I didn't know that before I heard Mamie tell us what he'd told her. But it's one thing to have your suspicions, and another to hear the evidence come right into your ears. My brother works in the town; he loads and unloads in the Piggly Wiggly [supermarket], and he hears lots of fights going on among the white folks. But that's different—it's human nature to fight, you know that going back to the Bible. There's fighting, and there's fighting! Mr. Tomasello, he told Mamie that he couldn't count on people, his white folks, not one hundred percent, because they've always got this 'idea' about him, that he's not the same as them, not completely [because of his Italian name]. When Mamie first told me that, I laughed it off. I'd think, she's got the biggest imagination I've ever met, and it will run away from her if she don't watch out. I'd say, 'White folks don't go after other white folks—not when they have us colored to kick around!' "

The time came, in late summer of 1964, when that hunch of Mr. Tomasello's came true, so Andrew Thomas would come to realize. Moreover, Andrew Thomas was to some extent responsible for Mr. Tomasello's experience with his neighbors and business colleagues in a

Mississippi town that had heretofore boasted of its "friendly atmosphere," so a Rotary Club description once averred. "The whole thing got going by an accident," Mr. Thomas always insisted. He had gone into town to buy some seed at Mr. Tomasello's store. He'd talked with his mother-in-law's employer for a few minutes and was preparing to leave, when a SNCC "field-worker," there to buy a flashlight, approached him and engaged him in an informal conversation. The field-worker identified himself as such, gave his name, Rob Simpson, and told of his background. Andrew Thomas remembered that initial encounter this way: "He was a colored fellah from up North; he told me his folks hailed from near Memphis, not so far from Mississippi, and they tried it up in Chicago, and they missed their kinfolk down in Tennessee, but it's better up there. He wanted to know if I'd ever been away from here, and I told him no. I asked him about being a field-worker. He told me he was trying to help us out here—so we can have a better life. I wasn't sure what he meant. I thought if he was a field-worker, he was doing what I'm doing. I'm a field-worker, all right! But he said no, it was the vote he's working on—and was I interested?

"I shook my head and told him I had enough to do without taking that on, the vote. I could tell he wanted to persuade me, but he looked at Mr. Tomasello, who was looking at us, and so he asked me if I'd mind if he paid me a visit sometime, and I said no, I'd not mind. When he left, Mr. Tomasello told me he was wondering if my mother-in-law could do some extra work, come the next weekend, and I said yes, I was sure she could. That's why he'd been looking my way. I realized afterwards that 'Chicago Rob,' the way I first thought of him, had made a mistake—he thought Mr. Tomasello was cross because I was talking to a field-worker from one of those civil rights organizations."

Within days "Chicago Rob" had found his way to Andrew Thomas's "place," as he always called his home and the land around it. The two men talked, and Andrew kept telling Rob that he wasn't interested in voting. When Rob asked why, Andrew responded with his own, shrewd social and political analysis: "Things here are pretty well set. You can't vote the folks who own everything out of office, because they don't have any offices to their credit. I mean, they have their offices, but that's where they count their money and make their calls! My aunt, she cleans a law office, and she can tell you a lot!"

But the two young men, for all the differences in their lives, had further talks, got on well. Andrew made clear, however, his political indifference, based on his sense of how things worked in McComb County and elsewhere—rather than his fear of the consequences that an attempt on his part to register, to try to become an eligible voter, would set in motion. Andrew also got into a conversation one day with Mr. Tomasello—a discussion of SNCC and the fieldwork being done by Rob and others: "I was in his store, and Mr. Tomasello and I got to talking. He told me Rob had come by, and he seemed nice, even if he was 'mistaken.' I told him I agreed, it [the voter registration drive] was a mistake. He said you don't come in from a distance away and think you can turn a world upside down, all in one summer. I said yes, sir—but then he asked me if I was just 'yessing' him, and I was about to say 'yes, sir' again, but it came to me that if I did, I'd be admitting to him the wrong thing, so I out and told him what I believed. I tried to be nice, but I said what I told Rob over and over—that you can't vote on a lot of things, the most important things, because they're just *there,* the way it is. That was when Mr. Tomasello turned around; he said, 'Yes, that's true, but there's always a start.'"

Such a comment, a seeming offhand banality, struck fear into Andrew Thomas, who fell silent. Even in retrospect, he was hard put to figure out that moment, or describe it fully: "I heard him say the words, but then I got confused or something. He didn't say more; it was my turn to talk, but I didn't know what words to use—they didn't come to me, not one. I think I looked at him, at his face, and then I looked away fast, because he was looking at me, staring. So I said I had to go, and I did. There might have been some talk before I left—I'm not sure. I was so lost in my thinking. I drove home, and on the way, I got to wondering: has Rob gone and persuaded Mr. Tomasello? I didn't think so, though."

Once home he spoke with his mother-in-law, recited the sequence of events at the hardware store. Mamie wasn't surprised. Indeed, she was only surprised that her son-in-law was surprised—that he hadn't given any thought, apparently, to Mr. Tomasello's relationship to certain other white people in the town: "She gave a big laugh, Mamie, and she told me I'd better 'widen' my eyes and 'alert' my ears, because there's 'lots to' Mr. Tomasello I hadn't been taking in! She said she'd seen him watch the TV, and there'd be reports of those three young men, who'd disappeared [the SNCC members who were killed in Neshoba County, Mississippi, early in the summer of 1964] and he said, 'They're dead, for sure, and it's a damn shame.' That's what he told his wife, and she said she agreed, and she said, 'There are a lot of people who end up doing wrong, because there's no one to show them how to do right.' I think on her deathbed Mamie will remember hearing that—she told me she never heard anything better come from a white person, not in her whole life!"

In fact, Sarah Holmes and Andrew Thomas didn't see eye to eye on that score. "We had ourselves a bit of an argument," the younger of the two recalled as he tried to give a chronicle of what happened to him in the summer of 1964. Always practical, and more attentive to the world than his mother-in-law's estimate of him allowed, he quickly challenged Mrs. Tomasello's comment on moral leadership, its prevalent absence as an explanation for what had occurred in Neshoba County: "I said I wasn't one to know better than the missus [Mrs. Tomasello], and I know she got herself a college degree, but someone can stand up and try to tell people what's right, and they'll get shot down, and that's what happened to those three guys in Neshoba, and it would happen here, it's the same here. People hear what it suits them to hear—that's what I told her, and if they do bad, they've got a reason for it. You know what? They think they're doing good—that's the truth!"

He hadn't convinced his mother-in-law with that earthy take on social behavior as a response to money and power as they, in turn, shape the moral standards of a particular community. She had argued strenuously for the potential influence any one person can exert. To clinch her point, she summoned "the Lord Himself"; she spoke passionately of Jesus, *His* lonely moral vigil and its eventual significance, the sway it came to hold over so many. But Andrew Thomas was not at all won over: "I had to stop myself from laughing! I said, 'Mamie, stop yourself and think.' I told her God isn't likely to show up and start leading people to be good and stop hating their neighbors on account of this or that. He spoke up, Jesus did, you bet, but they killed Him. Now, He's in heaven, with God, His father—but that doesn't make people down here, most of them, behave the way Jesus did. No sir, they go ahead and do what's best for them: that's what they're figuring—what will work out one hundred percent in their favor. Then they'll go to church and tell Almighty God that they love Him."

He stops abruptly at that point in his narrative account of this important moral discussion held weeks earlier with his mother-in-law. She had been shocked by that last comment—she told him that the devil had caused him to say it. He had made the mistake of dismissing her out of hand, had pushed the matter further, declared the devil as a powerful protagonist, still, *within* the various Christian churches, never mind in his thinking. She was aghast, and let him have it: "She told me I was sounding worse than the worst white man! She said it was 'ideas' like I had that had given us all the trouble, forever! I tried to get her to slow down, but she kept coming after me with talk of the devil, and she said she'd pray for me, but I should remember that God hears everything, and He doesn't forget. That's when I came back at her. I said, I wish He'd come down here again and straighten out this sorry, sorry world. I said that's the trouble with church: you pray and pray, and you hear all these good things to think, and good things to do, but then folks walk out, and they're right square in the devil's hands again, and if I'm in the devil's hands for saying it's so, then all right, I'll own up and admit that I could be one more slippery shoe that the devil wears, but let me tell you—I told her—there's no one who doesn't get used by the devil, even that minister who comes and tells us what's right and what's wrong every Sunday. There's lots of them around, ministers, be they white or colored, and I don't notice them leading folks, any of us, out of the land of bad and into the land of good, the way the missus told our Mamie people need leading."

They had reached an impasse, a man and his mother-in-law; they had repeated discussions over a couple of weeks, and those fractious engagements of mind and soul became amplified by Mamie's insistence on sharing with Mrs. Tomasello what she and her son-in-law had talked about—even as Mr. Tomasello soon enough heard from his wife about her conversations ("chats," she called them) with a maid who had become a constant, enabling presence in her life. Indeed, Mrs. Tomasello's very vulnerability made for her moral sensitivity, so her husband once observed as he looked back from the vantage point of 1966 at the complicated relationship between him and his wife and Mamie and Andrew Thomas during that hectic, intense, politically and racially momentous summer of 1964. "You'll note," he told me to keep in mind, "that Sally [Mrs. Tomasello] spent more time with Mamie than anyone else, even me."

He stops to sip a Coke, lowers his head a second or two, resumes: "The two did a lot of talking! If she wasn't sick, and could get around like others, she'd not have dug beneath the surface of things the way she did then (she still does). She was *there* with Mamie, helping her do things, and the two are both talkers. Here in the store, I mostly listen; I've learned to let each customer talk and talk! Back home, those two really hashed things out. Mamie would get all riled up, on account of what young Andrew said to her. She'd tell Sally that her son-in-law was coming up with 'devil talk.' My wife wasn't so sure! Andrew laughed at her thought—that over in Neshoba, and right here (and everywhere) people need to be taught how to behave better. Sally said for years that a good leader, and a leader who fights for the good, finds followers—and that's the story of Jesus' ministry on earth. Mamie is right on Sally's side—but when [Mamie] got angry at Andrew, Sally wasn't upset, not as much as his mother-in-law was with him! Sally told me she thought Andrew had a point—that 'he'd taken the matter further.' You know, people aren't always ready for that 'good leader.' In fact, they're *not* ready for him at all a lot of the time—isn't *that* the Christian story, too? I mean, Jesus came here with all those good things to say, the best of intentions, and look at what people did—the same as in Neshoba. Hey, I'm not saying those SNCC guys were like Jesus. Don't get me wrong! I think they were pushing an agenda, a 'voting rights' agenda, they called it, and they had a right to do it—that's where I parted company with ninety-nine percent of the whites of this state, or maybe ninety-five percent (I could be underestimating some of us!). But those SNCC people weren't the Lord, or His agents or ambassadors—I don't think so. But, you know, there is this truth: that if you come into a community from outside, or if you come *at* a community from the inside (if you start criticizing it or going against the mainstream, you could say), then you're sure as hell headed for a lot of trouble—as we put it here, God's share of it, and doesn't that [expression] fit!"

He stops to reflect upon his own extended stretch of words, which have actually taken him by surprise. It is as if someone else, a provocative moralist or religious historian, has been reminding him concertedly of the implications of Christianity, and has also been commenting on what might be called the sociology of everyday life—the way some people have accommodated themselves and their revolutionary religion to the normative requirements of the status quo. He seems to want to return to the comfort and luxury of an attitude that goes with going along, adjusting one's views to those held by the privileged majority. He is, after all, a member of a town's, a county's, a state's bourgeoisie. He has a substantial sum of money in the bank; he owns a store, his home, and even the homes of others; he has a tidy sum invested in the stock market; he carries a "bigger life insurance policy than most others," because he worries constantly about his wife's illness and what would happen to her were he to "go," given the medical costs of her condition.

Still, he can't quite clear his head of Jesus and His life, of McComb, Mississippi, and the contemporary challenges of *its* life. He moves from Jesus the outsider come to naught (during his lifetime here on Earth, at least) to "all the civil rights trouble" taking place during that summer of 1964, and finally, to his customer Andrew Thomas, who has his own terse way of talking with him, a counterpart conversation, as it were, of what has been happening between his wife, Sally, and Andrew Thomas's mother-in-law, Mamie. He worries that Andrew may "get himself a bundle of trouble" because he's been "listening a little too hard to those SNCC people" and most especially to "Chicago Rob," who has become a friend of Andrew's. Not that Mr. Tomasello thinks the two of them don't have a lot to say to each other that is interesting. He himself confesses that he'd like to be the proverbial fly on the wall in that cabin of Andrew's, "taking in what they say to one another." But soon, he worries, idle but weighty talk might lead to risky, maybe calamitous activity: "It's one thing for someone to come spend a summer here; it's another thing to live here, and have to take the heat for the rest of your life if you do something that stirs people up, so they start trying to get even with you! Those civil rights folks, they fill Andrew's ear with right-sounding talk, and I can understand if he's convinced, but he's a smart one: he's a man of strong will, and he loves his wife and those four kids they have, and he doesn't want to bring the roof down on them. It's not much of a roof they have, anyway!"

He stops abruptly—just as I'm convinced he has a lot of wind in his sails, and will keep going for some time. When he resumes, only a few seconds have passed, but they seem much longer—he has both changed the subject and not at all done so: "Let me tell you, I don't know how they live the way they do. I've taken Mamie home many a time—when Andrew can't come get her—and a lot of the time I'm too busy with my own thoughts about my life to stop and take a hard look at theirs. But there will be times when I *do* notice, and I try to put myself and Sally, and our kids, when they were younger and growing up, into that old shack—that's what it is—that they call their home (and they're proud to [do so], they really are). Those times, I bleed for them; yes sir, I do. Maybe if I was living there, I'd listen real closely to the civil rights folks when they came knocking on my door. But even so, I'd know the danger: every member of that Thomas family would be in much worse trouble if they get tied to the civil rights folks than they are now, living in such a broken-down place. There's trouble, and there's *trouble,* you know!"

Another unexpected break in the narrative run of his words, which have quite a tug to them, a consequence not only of their meaning, but the emotion he conveys, the anxiety and the worry, as he speaks. It is as if he's picturing the worst in order to prove his last statement true: he has lowered his head, maybe because in his mind some shots have been fired by night riders, or a tenant farmer's cabin, Andrew's to be exact, has been torched to the ground—neither rare occurrences all through that summer, at that moment only half over. Finally, he is addressing me again—and I begin to sense an urgently delivered exhortation: "We're soon headed for more trouble here. The civil rights people won't leave until they have some kind of confrontation, and our local police, and the state police, will be waiting for them, and besides, there's the White Citizens Council, and you must know, the Klan. I don't know how it'll happen, or when, but as everyone says, colored and white, 'the day is coming!' I've refused to join the White Citizens Council, and if there was another hardware store in town I'd be out of business. My Sally pleaded with me not to join, and you know what they told me when I didn't want to? It was three years ago, and it was something said that I'll never in my life forget: 'Well there, Mr. *Tomasello* (boy did they linger on my name!), you're not really one of us anyway with a name like yours!' They didn't say anything else; and I didn't pursue the matter. I was angry, but I'll confess, I was scared. I thought of my business—and my wife, and our kids, even if they're up in Oxford [in college at the University of Mississippi]. I was almost ready to reverse myself, sign up with them. But I just couldn't find the words to.

"I sat there shaking with fright and rage, the two feelings in a mix I couldn't separate then, I can't now—and you know, I've told Andrew about that [incident] recently. I thought he should know what I thought: if he's letting himself even *consider* joining up with those civil rights 'types' (as they're called by a lot of my [white] customers), then he should know that even for me, a white man who is way 'up there,' compared to him, it could be scary, plenty scary, just not signing a private piece of paper, never mind walking up those courthouse stairs to try to claim the ballot, what 'they' want Andrew to do, that Rob guy and the others [who have] come here these last few weeks."

Now he seems ready to work himself into a fit of vexation and fury against "them," against "Chicago Rob" and the rest. He takes his glasses off, pulls a handkerchief to wipe them, and I regard that gesture figuratively: he's all steamed up, and his glasses are a clue to that mood, hence his need to make them clear again. But I'm dead wrong. I will shortly learn that he is, rather, trying to achieve for himself a clarity, a lucidity of vision: "Hell, I'm with them, in my heart. My wife, Sally, she's sure with them—'the sooner the colored become American citizens like everyone else, and vote, the better off we'll all be': I've heard that a hundred times this summer! Maybe so—but *we* won't be so 'better off,' I tell her—they [the white customers of his hardware store] will start driving twenty-five miles to buy a rake or a pair of pliers or a hammer, and they'll use the hammers they've got to smash my store's windows, and they'll come here and try to scare us to death. Two can play that picketing game, you know, and the boycotting—and the white people are the majority and have most of the money! I've told Andrew all this—I tried to be tactful, the way I put it in words, but I want him to know, to get the message, otherwise he's headed for the worst trouble. Why, he could just disappear, you know. It's happened before. Or he could be arrested for some trumped-up charge: they'd be waiting for him somewhere, the police, and by the time they'd finished with him, doing their 'questioning'—he'd be lucky to be breathing. He'd be one sorry fellah!

"If you ask me, Andrew isn't going to pay me no mind. I see him as headed for that courthouse, no matter what. He's weighed everything, and he knows the odds of success—zero, I'd say; but he just doesn't seem to be able to control himself—he'll be skeptical about the civil rights people for a few minutes, but they seem to have roped him in, that's my estimate."

Unaccountably, his face shows a smile. He has stopped talking, has directed his eyes toward the street. He shakes his head, returns his attention to the room where we sit, his study in his home. He jokes that he's surrounded by "integrationists." His wife would like to walk up those courthouse stairs with Andrew "and the others." His wife, actually, doubts Andrew will end up taking that big step—he'll worry too much, finally, she estimates, about his family. To try to register to vote, after all, likely means to make a widow of your wife, to make your children fatherless. Andrew has the "gumption" but he's not "rash," not a "fool," not anxious to "take it on the chin—or the belly or the chest." His wife once put it this way, "on the dime"; she asked a rhetorical question: "Does Andrew have the will and the brave soul in him to be a leader of his people—to be their real leader, who stands up, through thick and thin, for what is right and true?"

Mr. Tomasello looks around the room. There are family pictures on the wall—including one of his grandfather who came to America from Turin, in Italy; he landed in New York City and got a job helping a peddler, and soon thereafter, "cleaning up after the customers left" in a series of stores. He worked all night, every night. He scrubbed floors on his hands and knees. He did what would "now," in Mississippi, be called "nigger work." He wasn't one for self-pity. He never voted. He wasn't a citizen. He simply wanted to "get a leg up here," and he did.

Then, "a fluke," an accident or incident that "changed everything." This immigrant from Italy, walking on a New York City street after an arduous night of toil, saw a man get out of a taxi, pay the fare, and begin to walk—but he inadvertently dropped his wallet: it hadn't been put securely in his pocket, and so it fell to the ground, noticed by that immigrant, who spoke up. "That was how he got here," his grandson tells me: a grateful southerner whose wallet had been saved took an interest in the honest Italian immigrant who helped him, and who was more than willing to "take a chance," to "move anywhere," to "try to make a go of it" where this southerner lived.

A pleasant, proud reverie, a story of assimilation and success, comes crashing down, though: "I'm still an odd one, in the eyes of lots of folks here. 'Tomasello, he's a nice guy, an Eye-talian—he'll try to please you all he can': I overheard that once in my own store! I was in the next aisle, out of sight. My own father-in-law had to practice and practice, so as not to call me an Eye-talian. He wasn't all that happy at the start, I'll tell you, to call me his son-in-law! Now my wife is telling me to practice: 'Don't say colored, honey,' she'll tell me. So, I say 'nigrah.' 'No, honey—Negro.' I have trouble using the word, saying it right, so Sally said: 'Think of a knee growing, a knee-grows, then it'll come out all right, and you know that works!' "

He has laughed; but abruptly he is straight-faced, serious—and mordantly self-critical: "I am ashamed of myself, talking this way! My grandfather adjusted to everything in this country except for segregation. He ended up being a shoe repairman—he had his own shop. He bought the building [that housed his present day hardware store], and other buildings. He took care of the buildings, built up equity. That's how I learned to buy property: my dad got into the real estate business, through his dad. My folks always felt sorry for the colored. I remember Daddy paying them more than anyone else in town would dream of— he'd say it often: 'It isn't fair, the way they're treated.' I guess we were enough outsiders, with our background, with the name Tomasello, to sympathize with those on the outside, the colored! It could have been different, though—I'll say that in self-defense. There's my cousin, who's in Greenwood, and he's an outstanding lawyer, the leader of the White Citizens Council there, and he talks segregation all the time—I get sick, listening to him, I feel like reminding him of our family's past, and telling him what I've overheard—not just once! But he'd blow up at me, I know. He can sense where I'm at, though—I keep quiet when he comes out with his hate talk."

He was tempted to keep quiet when he learned of Andrew's intention to go ask for the right to vote. He was also tempted to tell Andrew that he was making a big mistake "to mess around in this protest stuff," as he put it to Andrew when they had occasion to talk. Andrew remembered it well. "We had ourselves a talk like I've never had with anyone, be he colored or white! I told him I was likely going to 'take the step.' He turned whiter than white! He said I should think twice, three times, four times, a hundred times, before I dive into water as deep as that, especially since I can't swim! Well, I told him I'd learn how when I got in the water and I'd have to—besides, us black folks (Rob says we should call ourselves), we're always in water above our heads, and we're always trying to stay afloat, and you can drown any second, being who you are, the colored.

"What about your family? Your wife, your kids? He asked me that several times. I said, 'Mr. Tomasello, I should let you know—my family has no future, the way it is now here. This is their big chance, to feel there's something ahead, waiting for them. As it is, we're treated like things. Maybe someday we can be something.'"

On the other hand, Andrew confessed to apprehension, even alarm.

He believed what he'd told Mr. Tomasello, but he wondered if he himself would ever really "go through it"—he envisioned himself as becoming wobbly, hesitant, and, in the clutch, reluctant. He knew he might well be arrested on the spot, taken to jail—and thereafter hurt beyond repair, if not killed. What was the point, then? Such an acknowledgment on Andrew Thomas's part, surprising to his white listener, elicited an unexpected response—indeed, a stunning reversal on the part of Mr. Tomasello, one that would prove to be a memorable, critical moment in the summer of 1964: "I think I took leave of my senses—I wasn't thinking coolly and rationally. I told Andrew I'd support him in what he did, if he decided to do it. I told him I'd do it for him—and my wife, and for the people of the state. I said, 'Hey, our [last] names are practically the same, and we've been helping each other out for years and years—why, his mother-in-law is my wife's 'best friend,' that's what she says. So I said it's about time we shook hands and agreed we're friends, and we'll stand by each other!'"

Not so easy to accomplish, this asserted desirability of a friendship, a newly balanced manner of getting along. Mr. Thomas kept silent after the handshake. Mr. Tomasello had more to say, but also kept quiet. Then, a remarkable admission from Mr. Thomas, as later relayed by Mr. Tomasello: "He told me he wasn't going to show up the next morning—that he felt he'd be 'walking out on his family,' leaving them for good, and it wasn't right! He was going through agony, I could see. I wanted to give him a hug." Did he? "No, I didn't—because I thought he'd get frightened! All of a sudden, standing there, I realized what it was *really* like for him, what it meant to be a colored man, a Negro in our society. I felt overwhelmed with shame: for what our country had allowed—no, for what it forced on all of us, from the start of our history. There we were, in the second half of the twentieth century, and the segregationist laws were on the books, and in the hearts of us white folks, and a few blocks away, the sheriff and his police were ready to make sure things stayed as they are! I wanted to ask for Andrew's forgiveness, but I knew he'd think I'd done gone loco!"

Instead, the two men had a "practical talk," Mr. Tomasello called it. He did most of the talking. He told Andrew that "whatever he did, whatever he decided to do," he had "friends" in the Tomasellos. He spoke a lot through his wife, through references to her opinions and values, and told a taciturn, somewhat perplexed, definitely astonished Andrew Thomas that he had "admirers" in McComb, two at least, among the town's white population, and that "if worse came to worst" those two would "stand up and be counted." That last phrase stuck hard in the minds of both the one who used it and the one who heard it used. Neither of them at the time quite knew what those words were specifically meant to suggest, imply, convey: maybe they were meant as a gesture of affiliation, connection, rather than as a plan or strategy spelled out. Yet, in retrospect, both of them believed that somehow those words pushed matters along decisively.

Andrew Thomas: "I'm not one for being smart with words, but I do know this—I kept hearing Mr. Tomasello, when he said he and his missus would 'stand up and be counted,' if trouble came my way. I never knew whether I'd go there and face those police, but I thought, it's about time someone stood up and be counted on the colored side and on the white side, and there we are, Mr. Tomasello and me!"

Mr. Tomasello: "I wasn't sure what I intended to indicate when I spoke like that. On the way home, I was asking myself: what *will* you do if you find out they've gone and arrested Andrew—or God forbid, that he's 'missing.' I wouldn't let myself go further—I knew in my bones, though, that those so-called law enforcement people were perfectly capable of taking his life, *murdering* him, and pretending it was some accident. Look what happened in Neshoba County! I got home and I told Sally, and she said *she* knew what I was doing—I was giving young Andrew some encouragement, some moral support. I was telling him he's not alone, and if he dares take on the Klan and the [White Citizens] Council, then so will I. Sally said the two of us were standing together—'You're working for the good, to make it better here,' she kept saying, and 'you're getting your own kind of integration going—it's moral integration you're bringing to Mississippi.' Well, what's that? I wanted to know! 'It's two Americans agreeing they'll stand up and be counted, just like you said, and one is a Negro, and one a white man, and they're both doing what's right, come what may—

that's moral integration.' I guess I saw what she was trying to tell me, but that sounded pretty high and mighty, those two words, and I was a lot more worried and afraid than she realized; or maybe she *did* realize."

On his first try, Andrew Thomas was firmly rebuffed—no way he'd be allowed to vote. But the international furor occasioned by the Neshoba tragedy, the killing of three civil rights activists, gave the Mc-Comb ballot applicants a good deal of protection. "They were un-friendly, that's all," Andrew remembered. Meanwhile, as he left the courthouse and descended its steps, he saw his newly declared "friend" standing on the sidewalk, watching. A smile, a wink, even a public thumbs-up came Andrew's way, and the smile, the wink were cau-tiously returned. "I couldn't return the thumbs-up," he remembered. "I think I would have gotten wobbly knees and fallen down if I'd tried that. Someone would have arrested me, I feared, for being a 'sassy nig-ger'—that's what they'll call you at the drop of a hat! But you know what? I felt like one! I felt like I was on my way to a little of that 'free-dom' those civil rights people keep talking and singing of. Once I'd climbed those stairs, I knew I'd be back, until they finally gave up stalling on us, those folks in the offices there—just to start the ball rolling, that was what I had to do. I told Mr. Tomasello: he and I got this started—I told him he was a big help to me as I tried to figure if I'd dare. He's here 'for the duration,' just like me, he says, and it helps to know a white man who's ready to be counted on your side."

By 1965, a voting rights bill had passed the Congress, and Andrew Thomas was readily (if still reluctantly in spirit) put on the voting list in McComb, Mississippi. As soon as he registered, he drove over to see Mr. Tomasello at his hardware store. The two of them stood and talked in the front of the store, then went back to the office, where they chat-ted over coffee. They called the Tomasello home, shared the news with Sally and Mamie, who excitedly congratulated both of them, as if somehow they'd together discovered and explored a new world: led an expedition that, finally, had gotten somewhere—hit together the moral pay dirt that for so long eluded them and so many others in their town, their state, their region.

2. A TEACHER'S MINICOURSE IN
MORAL LEADERSHIP

In 1960, when school segregation came to New Orleans, all eyes were on the four African-American girls who had entered two formerly all-white elementary schools, and on the subsequent boycott by the parents and children heretofore enrolled in those schools. What would happen to Ruby Bridges, all alone in the William Frantz School, heckled and threatened? What would happen to the white children who once went to school on weekdays and now stood with their parents and shouted at Ruby as *she* went to *their* school—and who afterward, "hung around and horsed around," as a boy described what he and his pals had been doing since "that nigger girl showed up"? I would spend years trying to learn the answers to such questions, and so doing I would have many opportunities to observe the courage that hard-pressed children and their families could mobilize—and the fear and meanness of spirit that could envelop other children, and of course, their parents, brothers, and sisters. As I wrote up that research, I concentrated on all those children, those families—and learned from them much of what happened in their lives. But there were other stories that unfolded in connection with those early, fiercely contested efforts at school desegregation—stories in which the protagonists weren't even directly involved in the two particular schools that were so embattled, and yet who chose to take seriously the moral challenges a racial crisis posed for everyone, for onlookers as well as those who became, suddenly, out-and-out combatants.

When the federal judge J. Skelly Wright chose only two schools in New Orleans as the scenes of desegregation, and only four children as the bearers of that mandated educational future, he was hoping to ease a particular city gradually past its loudly stated outrage. At a meeting of the city's teachers that followed, by a week, the actual onset of integration (such as it was) in the city's school system, I heard a virtual refrain of relief from those not assigned to the Frantz School or the Mc-

Donogh 19 School—the term being "spared" kept being summoned. Another word used, often in conjunction with "spared," referred to the deity—as if a divine intervention had rescued certain people from a tragedy inflicted on others: "Thank God, we've been spared," or "Lord, we sure are grateful we were spared."

It was, actually, just such expressions of relief that first bestirred Elaine Vogel, a fourth-grade teacher in a McDonogh School, but not McDonogh 19, the school besieged by a mob in response to the fact that three six-year-old African-American girls were attending. One of those girls, Tessie Prevost, had been quoted in the New Orleans *Times-Picayune* as calling for divine scrutiny and assistance: "I say to God, in my prayers, please don't let those people push their way into the school and ruin everything here."

Elaine Vogel read that comment of that six-year-old child, and when she did she couldn't help but go back to her days as a religious studies major at Sophie Newcomb College in New Orleans. She had always had a meditative side to her, even as she wondered where it came from. Her father was a banker, her mother an amateur artist; they lived a privileged life in New Orleans's Garden District, and were rather surprised, even concerned, when their only daughter decided that she wanted to teach elementary school children, and do so in the city's public schools. Elaine's brother, Carl, had gone to Tulane, then headed north to business school at Northwestern. Her parents were constantly comparing the two, wondering why their daughter "takes life so seriously." Their worry had become hers: "I'm twenty-seven, and my folks think of me as in trouble, because I'm not married to one of the eligible lawyers or stockbrokers of the city! They thought teaching was 'nice' until they learned that I wasn't going to be at Metairie Country Day [a private, suburban school]—I was hoping to be at a public school here in New Orleans.

"When my mom heard I was going to church every week, and teaching there, too, in Sunday school, she called me and said maybe I was 'turning too serious.' She said I shouldn't carry the whole world on my shoulders! I had to laugh: I've got all this money in a trust fund, and this nice apartment off St. Charles [Street], and a convertible, and all the clothes I'll ever need in a lifetime, and I'm in good health, and I'm not the worst-looking gal in the city of New Orleans, and I like my work with those kids, and I've got some really great friends, but my mom and pop are in a sweat over there on Prytania Street because their Elaine hasn't tied the knot with some young millionaire, and she's spending her time with children who live in 'one of those troubled neighborhoods,' Pop called it—meaning any place in the whole city where folks work hard, hard, hard for a living but aren't rich like they all are where my parents live!

"And now, for God's sake—well, that's it: I'm asking God what *He* wants, what *He* would have us do, to advance *His* purposes, and my folks are throwing up their arms and groaning as if I've lost my mind. The last straw was the other night: Mom had met a 'marvelous doctor' at a party, and she told him what I was doing, and she asked him if I might come and see him. 'Mom,' I said, 'I'm feeling fine. Why should I see a doctor?' She came back at me with this: 'Dear, he specializes in talking with young people.' 'Mom'—I laughed—'are you trying to fix me up with some shrink?' She didn't know what to say—I'd made a joke of the whole thing, when she was trying to be so damn serious! But later, I was fit to be tied! My parents love to go to that Episcopal church every third or fourth Sunday, it's a big social time for them. They don't pay the slightest attention to Jesus, to what He preached, to what Christianity is supposed to be about. 'What a lovely man, a sweet one, that minister is,' I'll hear; or 'The music was *wonderful*.' I'll hear those 'reports,' Mom calls them, of their activities, like going to church, and I wonder what God thinks of, makes of them. I sure know what they think of Him—He's a 'sweet one'! That's why Mom wants me to go talk with that doctor—so I'll stop having all those 'troublesome matters,' she calls them, on my mind."

Even before the city of New Orleans was ordered to make a start at school desegregation, Elaine Vogel was beginning to teach her fifth-grade American history classes in her very own way. She used the standard text, but chose to emphasize parts of it that her colleagues, as she put it, "glided over," even tended to ignore outright: slavery, and its continuation as segregation, most especially. She also asked the children to stop and think about "all the Negro people have done to build up our country, the labor they have given to it." She even worked with those boys and girls on the word "Negro," worked very hard in that regard. Indeed, that effort first made her teaching controversial. She was merely asking children to pronounce a particular word correctly, but in 1959, in Louisiana, in a working-class neighborhood, such instruction had many consequences.

What started as an afterthought of sorts turned into an occasion of argument, strife: "We didn't have mobs like those you're seeing in front of the two schools, but we had parents coming in here to see me, to see the principal, and they were complaining (*were* they!), and a few threatened to take their kids out! I couldn't believe it! The principal called me in, when all this started, and she said: 'Elaine, how did all this get going? What did you do—what did you say to the children?' I told her I was simply trying to be a good history teacher—and English teacher! I was asking them to read a book, and I brought in newspaper clippings and magazine pieces I'd cut out. In all of them the word used is 'Negro.' But when I called on the children to recite, they talked about 'the colored,' and if they were trying hard to do the right thing, they spoke of the 'nigras.' I heard some of them snickering behind my back and during recess—talking of the 'niggers.' I even heard a couple of boys calling me a 'nigger lover'! I sat on it all for a few days. I was tempted to move on—get us past all this touchiness, get us into a subject they'd enjoy, and [one in which] I'd not be inclined to badger them, 'correct' them too much. You see, I'd overlooked the fact that when you start going after the way children use or pronounce certain words, especially a word meant to describe—well, *Negroes*—you're touching on their home life, the way their parents think, their values. I was dumb or naïve—'innocent' would be a nice word, or if you want to be critical, '*foolish.*' That's what the principal thought of me, I could tell right away: I'd been *stupid* to get all this going! You know, it didn't take her long to start in with *me*—as if the problem wasn't the children and their language, or the parents, and their complaints, but my background. 'Elaine,' she said to me, 'you've been protected by your life, and you can speak as you like—but for a lot of people here, it's not so easy.' I wasn't clear on what she meant, other than that I was from a well-to-do family, and the neighborhood where I teach is—I guess you'd call it modest."

Not that those in her own family, or their neighbors, were any more inclined then to favor the word "Negro" than were the children she taught. She wanted to argue, as she did with the principal, in country clubs, in elegant living and dining rooms, in galleries, and yes, at musicales: "Friends of my parents play music beautifully: he's a violinist and she's a cellist. They have friends over; they're part of a quartet, and they play in their 'music room' for a dozen or so guests. First, Bach or Beethoven or Brahms, then great food! You know who cooks it, prepares the tables, serves the fanciest of *cuisine française*? The 'colored,' or 'our good nigras.' I've been to those soirees; I've heard what liquor does to tongues, the crude jokes, the stories out of their lives: 'I was trying to get some gas in a hurry, and they have this real slow nigger, who can't shake a leg to save his soul, and he spills some of the gas on my car after he's filled the tank and I say something to him, but he's too slow to understand me.' I heard that from a woman of 'great refinement'—those are my mother's words about her. If the white man who owns the gas station had waited on her, she'd have found patience for him, and she'd have overlooked a little spilt gas on that fancy Lincoln Continental of hers. She might 'overlook' my teaching her children how to use 'Negro,' pronounce it, but if I started talking about what happened here in Louisiana during Reconstruction, if I started asking her children to start learning about the wrong done to those 'Negroes' in Louisiana, and the way it affects the *doer,* that wrong done—I think she'd come marching into the Newman School or Metairie Country Day [both private schools] to 'register her reservations,' a polite way to say *complain*!"

The Worth of Indirection:
Teaching "Approved Moralists"

In fact, as she well knew, certain teachers in both of those private schools were entirely in sympathy with what she was trying to do, and were even pursuing the same kind of morally energetic historical inquiry. But, as she put it, "in a private school you can find, *sometimes,* nooks and crannies where you're left alone, [whereas] in a public school, when you take on something that's a 'live wire' with people, you've got to be careful, that's what I've been learning." Yet she wanted to keep at her job; she wanted her schoolchildren to continue the kind of learning she was offering them. She began to realize the worth of indirection, of a gradual approach to matters she'd heretofore taken on vigorously, frontally. She let the pronunciation of "Negro" go for a while, confined herself to books and magazine pieces, to established writers and their pronouncements, and she paced herself carefully: a gradual buildup of a point of view buttressed by various "approved moralists" she called them, sages such as Emerson and Thoreau, the remarks of presidents and generals and cabinet officers that, in their sum, emphasized (in her words) a "certain tone"—the fair-minded, egalitarian side of our nation's political and social thought.

Especially interesting was her original and shrewd use of C. Vann Woodward's *Tom Watson: Agrarian Rebel,* a story of the political rise and moral fall of a southern politician—a man who eventually became a U.S. senator, but who in so doing turned away from his early interest in furthering the cause of the poor of both races. Here was a book favored by college professors, now being used in an elementary school—the teacher read certain passages aloud, copied them on the blackboard, asked the students to contemplate what an Arkansas-born white historian of great distinction had to say about a nineteenth-century Georgia leader's career. She used that word "leader" often, and its kin "leadership," but not as a political theorist might, or for that matter, a moral philosopher (though she was tempted in the latter direction). She worked hard to come across to the children as "plain, direct"—she regretted her early "exercise in finger-pointing." She was tempted to ask her class to think of children in other schools, to consider Ruby Bridges and her situation, that of the other three African-American girls and their experience at another McDonogh School, but she held back, even as she had her moments of regret, frustration, self-accusation.

All during that first year of civic turmoil in New Orleans, while those four children struggled for a toehold in the schools abandoned by white families, Elaine Vogel tried to enrich and provoke the moral imagination of her class of twenty-eight ten-year-old boys and girls, whose parents worked in stores and factories and offices, wore blue collars and white collars, and, as she once starkly told me, "worried about the color black as if their lives were in danger of being blackened." She was, naturally, being the "amateur psychologist," so she characterized herself after giving expression to such a characterization of others. But she had come to fathom the depth and complexity of race as a constant and many-sided presence in the lives of those she taught, not to mention those she knew socially or as kinfolk. She read and read books, many by social scientists, some by writers she admired, such as Robert Penn Warren, or Faulkner, and those white southern novelists were helpful to her, indeed—enabling her "to get some distance" on her own melancholy assessment of her beloved city's seemingly endless racial turbulence. More than anyone, however, she relied upon C. Vann Woodward and his "story," as she called the Watson biography: "I showed the children pictures I got from the [Tulane] library of the young Tom Watson and the older man. I read to them what Watson said he believed when he was starting out, and what he said he believed when he was a leader of his state of Georgia, a leader in the United States Senate. I asked the children to take that word 'leader' very seriously, instead of worrying how they pronounce 'Negro'; I worked day after day at getting them to stop and think how one person can mean something important to another person, become a leader. I asked them what they think our leaders should stand for. I have to be careful, because their parents are the chief leaders they know in their lives—and maybe, some others: religious people or Scoutmasters or athletic coaches. But we're studying history, and I try to get them to react personally to the people we come across in our lessons—vote for them, you might say, and explain why [they're doing so]. Of course, there's no magic to this—the kids don't suddenly turn into civic-minded citizens who are respectful of others and want to make their country better through idealistic actions! There are days when I wish I had that tape recorder of yours in my classroom, because what I've heard is so amazing and often discouraging, but always interesting and revealing. You hear a whole range of opinion, that's always the case. But if the children knew they were 'on record,' I suspect they'd not be so candid—and besides, the principal (and their parents!) would be alarmed. Anyway, I don't forget the gist of what goes on, and there are things said that I'll never forget: I can hear them in my head, word for word—those ten-year-olds trying to figure out where the country should be headed, and they with it!"

Needless to say, I wanted to hear all she could recall—whereupon she told me, first of all, about what she called an "amazing" class she'd had only a week earlier. She'd brought in a copy of *Life* magazine, showed the class several pictures in it of our American envoy to the United Nations, Ralph Bunche. She talked about his education (a doctorate from Harvard), and his work as a representative of this nation—someone who had tried to mediate conflicts in various parts of the world. Then she posed this question: if you were Mr. Bunche, what would you try to do—what would you consider to be important enough to take up your time? At no point had she referred to his race—nor did any part of the magazine pages she handed out mention that he was a Negro (the descriptive word that would then, in the late 1950s and early 1960s, have been used).

At first the children were "slow on the draw," as she remembered it. They weren't sure, most of them, what the U.N. was, nor did they have any substantial idea of its responsibilities—though one very bright girl, who loved "current events" and read the New Orleans *Times-Picayune* from cover to cover, went to the library to browse through magazines, and had told the class several times that she dreamed of being a foreign correspondent ("a reporter who keeps traveling"), helped her teacher by talking about the U.N. ("a place where all the governments come and they decide things"). This youngster also got the discussion going by saying that if she were in the job held by Ralph Bunche she'd bring the Russians and the Americans into a room and tell them they *had* to settle things, or they'd not be let out.

The comment prompted a wide-ranging debate. Some children took offense at such an arbitrary confinement—wondered, anyway, whether "anyone could get away with it," meaning Mr. Bunche. Soon enough, these children pointed out, the respective governments would "come to the rescue." Moreover, it didn't seem right to use force this way in order to end the use of force by two governments. A boy put it this way, so Elaine Vogel remembered: "He's a quiet one, so I was surprised when he raised his hand, and tackled the problem in a thoughtful way, as a moral philosopher might, actually: 'Miss Vogel, I'm not sure, but two wrongs don't make a right, that's what my mom and dad say.' I hadn't thought about this like that—I guess I hadn't thought about what it means to lock the door on two parties who are disagreeing. I guess, really, I was thinking about not 'locking the doors' physically, although my student, Beverly, made the point literally—*did* tell us, specifically, that she would lock that door, and she even said she'd hide the key so no one could go find it when she was busy eating and sleeping! (Otherwise, she intended to 'keep guard' outside the conference room.)

"We went on and on. A girl said that 'if you force people to do things, then it won't work in the long run.' They'll *pretend* to agree on something, she guessed, to get free, then they'll go back to their former positions. That really struck a chord in the children—and that's how we got closer to home! Another girl pointed out that 'the government up in Washington' is now forcing 'the colored and the white people' to stay in the same room! She'd found her metaphor! The children got it immediately! Yes, 'they, up in Washington are forcing nigra people and the rest of us,' a boy said, 'to stay in one room,' and then the children mentioned movie houses and restaurants and motels and schools, and they pointed out that 'force is being used, just like in the U.N.' (Beverly's speculative scenario).

"I was stunned. I have to admit it; I admired the way these kids picked up on one child's idea, her dramatic elaboration in class, her story, and connected it to their lives here in New Orleans. In fact, the more the kids talked the more I realized how much they actually knew about the desegregation struggle. Ordinarily, they're mum on the subject—they must worry that it's controversial, or that I'm one of these people who worries about 'fairness' and who can't be trusted with some of the resentments they've heard expressed at home, but in their bones know shouldn't be spoken lightly or casually in a classroom. (I'm speculating here!) But all of a sudden they were running away with themselves: they told one another about their more or less uniform sense of felt jeopardy: 'The way it's always been is being stopped by people who don't even live here,' one boy put it, a bit awkwardly (his sentence structure!), but I'll tell you, everyone got it real fast—except for poor Beverly. She'd started all this, and it didn't take long for her to become the class outcast! She dared disagree! She said we should all remember that the Supreme Court 'speaks the truth,' because it is our highest court. She said that if you disagree with the law, that's your right, but you have to obey it. She said that we were all wrong (her classmates, not me!) in making the analogy between New Orleans and Mr. Bunche and the U.N.—its international disputes, on the one hand, and the civil rights struggle on the other. I can't remember all she said, word for word, but I do remember that she tried hard to distinguish between a rift between two nations and a disagreement between citizens of one country who, all of them, are under the jurisdiction of a national government. I'm dressing up the language, but she sure got her point across."

That intense class started a lot going in Elaine Vogel's mind. She hadn't, for one thing, gotten around to mentioning to the class that Ralph Bunche was a Negro, even though no one in the class regarded him as such, or if some did, the matter was not brought up. She had intended to use the magazine story, with its photographic accompani-

ment, as a means of discussing racial attitudes—but Beverly's sophistication, shared with the class, triggered a lively series of exchanges that
had to do with the local scene rather than the U.N. and its relatively
different responsibilities. She had been surprised by the willingness of
her students to ponder the nature of leadership, albeit indirectly and
anecdotally. She wanted to hear more on that score—but she also
wanted to put to rest her own wish that Ralph Bunche's eminence, his
leadership, be considered, and ultimately done so in connection with his
racial background. Moreover, she was quite anxious to learn, at some
point, in some way, whether anyone in her class had actually taken note
of Dr. Bunche's skin color. (He was a light-skinned African-American
who wore glasses and whose facial features were significantly "white.")
She debated whether to "finish one piece of business" (with respect to
Dr. Bunche) before starting another (a hope on her part to ask the students to tell one another what they would do, were they a senator, say,
or president, or what they would recommend or declare important
were they a minister or a priest, hence moral leaders—there were no
Jewish students in the class). When the class reconvened (for its social
studies session) she was knocked off her feet by Beverly, who raised her
hand, and when called, announced what she knew by asking this of
her teacher: "Miss Vogel, did you know that the man we talked about
yesterday is colored—the man from the United Nations?"

"I didn't even think to say yes," the still-surprised teacher recalled
later that week. She had instead dwelled on Beverly's choice of words
—a real disappointment coming from such a sophisticated and smart
girl, who was so widely read. She sat at her desk "for three or four or
five seconds, a long time under those circumstances," and then blurted
out a dismayed "Beverly!" Silence for another second or two, and then:
"I thought we'd all agreed to use the word 'Negro' when it's called for."
Now a public apology from an articulate, self-confident child, not usually inclined to speak of her missteps or mistakes: "I'm sorry. I should
have known the right word to use, but I forgot." Then, a compelling,
poignant explanation: "My daddy says 'colored' is the right word for
most people here [in Louisiana], and 'Negro' is the word people use if
they're in college and educated, or if they're friends of colored people."

A smile from her teacher, both in that class and afterward, as she contemplated the irony of that statement, never mind its sociological savvy. "I was stymied," she pointed out days later. She had been made aware yet again and concretely that if she was going to ask the children to make a change in the language that they use, she would have to go beyond *yes* and *no,* approval and disapproval: "I can mark a word 'right' or 'wrong,' 'correct' or 'incorrect,' but the word 'colored' or the word 'Negro'—that's different. Beverly sure taught me to stop and think there, and I did: I tried to come up with a way of making us all in that class realize the power of certain words, their meaning. I set aside the words 'colored' and 'Negro.' I got us talking about the history of our country: we were 'colonies' of England for a long time, and then we became the United States of America—a new name to describe us. I pointed out that there were arguments back then—not everyone in the Colonies wanted them called the United States. It occurred to me, as we talked, that many of the 'loyalists,' who sided with the British, were from the upper class—so, as Beverly had pointed out to us, our class background affects our choices in many ways, including the words we use to describe other people, or to describe our country itself. Sure, the analogy doesn't completely hold between what was going on back then and what's happening now, but there *is* a political struggle taking place here in the South, just as there was in the Colonies before they became the States—and my point to the class was that words can count a lot, some of them, and they can tell a lot about what you think is good or bad, what you think of other people.

"The children were surprisingly thoughtful as we talked about the American Revolution. They could see how hard it might have been for some people, as a boy, Tim, said it, 'to give up the king.' His friend Jimmy *couldn't* see that, so they argued out loud before all of us—an example of a difference of opinion, all right! Jimmy said he didn't think the loyalists really cared about the king—only about 'being on top.' Tim said that there were probably some folks 'back then' who weren't 'big-shot types' (he kept using that phrase, and I kept thinking of the young populist, Tom Watson, who we'd been studying!)—but they had learned to 'worship' the king, and they weren't going to give up that attitude so quickly. I was moved by the way he spoke—more simply and directly than I ever could. If I recall correctly [he said]: 'You don't just forget what you believe. If you sort of worship a king, you stick by him, when others are telling you, "Hey, forget it!" ' Then he brought us to our time—very nicely, to suit my purposes! He said that if you live in a neighborhood, and everyone is 'the same,' and then someone tells you to 'forget it,' because some 'new kind of people, really strange and different' are going to move in, then you *could* forget it, and not worry about those newcomers, or you might decide you just won't forget it, and that means trouble, lots of it."

She stopped there, interrupted a narrative account, to register the charged atmosphere in a classroom. The subject was the American Revolution, but somehow the boys' use of the topic had brought the entire class well into the twentieth century. At first their teacher thought *she* was the one who had made a connection between the loyalists of yore and the defiant segregationists of mid-twentieth-century America. But the brief silence, she noted, was "electric"—somehow, in some region of those many young minds, a similar connection had been made. The pause was broken by Beverly, who delivered an observation both banal and yet strangely affecting: "It's hard to change your ideas, but sometimes you do." Immediately, others wanted to explore the implication of that remark—the class had moved from history to psychology. The children wondered out loud why some people could shift their opinions, while others did so with great reluctance or, indeed, wouldn't budge an inch. Their teacher didn't need to encourage the discussion so much as moderate it. She was constantly tempted to refer to the contemporary racial tensions in Louisiana, but she feared that such a maneuver on her part would be self-defeating. There was such a flow to the class—it was, she mused afterward, a real "pow-wow." She had trouble remembering specific comments—all the remarks seemed to "merge," by which she meant this: "I honestly believed they all convinced one another—that you have to change your way of thinking sometimes, but you also have to understand why it is that some people have more trouble doing that than others do. I was so impressed and touched by their sensitivity on both scores—the need to move along in your thinking, but the need to be aware of the reasons some people can't do that easily, or at all."

She kept having reservations about her own behavior during that "extraordinary time of it" they'd all had. Why hadn't she, at an appropriate moment, "steered them" a bit—gotten them to make their exchanges more specifically tied to the everyday struggle then and there taking place in the American South? Why had she resisted what was on the tip of her tongue, an observation about "our changing attitudes toward colored people, Negro people," the very words that crossed her mind but never got spoken? Had she "failed at being a good leader of the class"?

That question wouldn't let go of her—it was asked with obvious reproval. There were other questions, too—all of them, really, versions of the first, and all of them meant to query her moral leadership of a fifth-grade classroom. She strongly believed that integration would be coming soon to the school where she taught, and elsewhere across Louisiana, across the states of the one-time Confederacy, hence the obligation on her part (and, of course, others') to prepare the young for the inevitable and, she strongly believed, the desirable. Yet at the time, segregation was the law throughout Louisiana, and in its neighbors Mississippi and Arkansas. Moreover, the parents of her schoolchildren strongly opposed the early efforts at desegregation then under way, and their sons and daughters, unsurprisingly, echoed in corridors and classrooms and playing fields what they'd heard handed down as "right" and "wrong" at home. How might she, nevertheless, "carve a wedge," she put it, "get a conversation going" with the aim of "opening up some eyes"?

Like her students, she had to contend with "home," with what *her* parents thought, and their friends, and hardest of all, her own brother, two years her senior and an outspoken segregationist. He was a stockbroker, and owned a significant amount of real estate in downtown New Orleans. She had tried to appeal to his self-interest, warned him that riots and public conflict that enveloped the schools would be "bad for business," but he had held firm, spoke of his "principles"—whereupon she was moved to self-doubt: "I don't know what to think or do!

I know in my heart what I think, what I believe, but is my opinion 'correct,' when my own family disagrees with me, and my friends do, and the parents of the children I teach do, and most of the people who teach with me do? Sure there are some who will look both ways, then whisper to you that they think integration will be here soon, and it's 'the right thing.' But even they will cover their bases—tell you it's wrong to impose something on people, when they're overwhelmingly opposed to it, and not only wrong but dangerous, and not only dangerous but un-American. That's why I was so upset when I let that opportunity in my class go—to connect what happened when this country was being established, in the eighteenth century, with what is happening now. But I guess I feel in my heart that I have to pace myself, and wait for the children themselves to see the point, to understand that history isn't only something that happened in the past, but something that is happening right now—and so we're all part of it, we're all participating in it, and so we should stop and think hard about what we believe and want to see happen in our country."

After much soul-searching, Elaine Vogel decided one morning while sitting at her desk in her fifth-grade classroom to work into her teaching of American history "one theme," which she'd try to bring up in various ways. Weeks after she'd begun doing so, she would remember the details of that early-in-the-day spell of rumination, followed by a particular bout of activity: "I was thinking about the teaching ahead of me. We were headed to the Civil War in my history class, and I was remembering how unpopular Lincoln was in my home. He may be the favorite president of most Americans, but among us—it's different. By 'us' I mean conservative southerners. The Negro people down here like him, I'm sure, and southern liberals do; but my dad used to say that Lincoln 'brought on the Civil War,' and he was a 'stubborn man,' and if he'd been a better leader—well, a lot of lives would have been spared. My sixth-grade teacher disagreed with my dad, I could tell—I knew, even back then, not to tell my parents some of what I heard in school, for fear they'd get real upset, and they'd go to the school and demand that the teacher be confronted, and maybe fired, and I'd be the one responsible.

"Anyway, all of that was running through my head on how to teach the kids about Lincoln, and slavery, and the Civil War. I wanted to show them the photographs of Brady [Mathew Brady documented nineteenth-century battle scenes with his camera]. I wanted to read to them from Carl Sandburg—his biography of Lincoln really moved me. I wanted to have lots of discussions about slavery. But we shouldn't do much on the Civil War—that's what I was told: 'It's not an easy subject to teach.' I had a scratch pad in front of me, and I picked up a pencil and I started to doodle. I do that a lot when I'm thinking! I was writing 'battle words,' like Shiloh and Gettysburg and Antietam. I was thinking: wouldn't it be great if I could take the class to those battlefields; and [then] we could talk [while there] about what had happened *and why*. About all those young soldiers, and their *lives*! That's what I'd like to do—not just look at those historical markers, but ask the kids to think about causes and reasons, about how it all got started, and for what reasons: people treating other people as 'property,' calling them 'slaves' without the slightest embarrassment. You know, the Negro people were treated so badly—but the white people treated *themselves* so badly: if you end up being callous to others, you're in bigger trouble than the people you mistreat! But how in the world do you get children to think that way—I was sitting there, wondering!

"I can remember thinking the word 'moral'—after all, the Civil War was a war fought by people who had different ideas about right and wrong. I wrote the word 'moral' down, and then I thought: it is our leaders' job to steer us toward the good, away from the bad, even if it's hard to do, and hard on them to do. So, I wrote the word 'leader' down—I was thinking of Lincoln, Lincoln the leader. I was going to write *that* down, the phrase 'Lincoln the leader,' but then I heard my brother's voice saying, 'Yankee propaganda!' I don't even listen to him when he gets going, and yet I know what he keeps saying: it's all in my head; 'this integration thing,' he calls it, has this strange influence on me in some way! All of a sudden I drew a line from the word 'moral' to the word 'leader'—and I looked, and I thought, and I knew I had something: we would be studying 'moral leaders'—their influence on our history! So I got up; I went to the blackboard; I picked up the chalk and wrote the words 'moral leader,' *printed* the words, actually. Then, before them, I printed the words 'who is a.' When I was finished, I turned around, and what I remember noticing was how quiet, real quiet that classroom was. Those boys and girls were really paying attention!"

Yet for all the silent regard extended that question posed by their teacher, the children were reluctant to try answering it, perhaps because Elaine Vogel had put the matter to them so unconventionally, with no preparation, and, too, as she later realized, with her back to them—as if she were, yes, backing into the matter. Moreover, when no one raised a hand, she didn't say anything to clarify her intention, or to encourage the children before her to speak. She could feel her own indecisiveness, even a bit of apprehension—what would they all have to say, and just as important, what did she herself have to say about a topic not exactly on any teacher's agenda at the school, so she knew.

She "froze"; she felt no words coming to her; she moved on to the "regular order" of the class, began a spelling lesson that had been promised the afternoon before as the first order of business in the morning. As she recited the words, though, and the class wrote them down, she kept going back to the dramatic but anticlimactic moment that had just passed, to the point that she became absent-minded, waited too long between her recitation of the words, forgot her place, and so repeated certain words, rather than moving on to the next ones. Finally, a burst of spontaneity: she went quickly to the blackboard, grabbed an eraser, and wiped away the sentence she had earlier written. Then, she asked the children to spell "moral" and "leader," and heard murmurs of delight: "They laughed, and they clearly enjoyed the connection I made between what had happened a few minutes earlier and what we were doing then and there with that list of words. That's when I said to myself: come on, Elaine, just plunge into the water and try to stay afloat! So when we'd finished our spelling quiz, I said to the class: 'Now that we've all *spelled* those two words, "moral" and "leader," let's try to find out what the two of them, together, actually mean!' "

The class exploded with comments, and she tried days later to remember what she'd heard from the children. She emphasized, as we talked, that she may have "jumbled" the remarks, omitted important ones, misinterpreted what had been spoken—but she was at least certain that the children had "strong ideas" on the subject, and had been more than willing to share them with others, with her as their teacher. She especially remembered what Beverly, one of her favorite students, anyway, had to offer: "'A moral leader is someone who isn't only out for himself. He'll do something that he knows is right to do, even if it'll give him some trouble'—that's the gist of what she said, not exactly word-for-word, but pretty close."

She tried hard to convey not only what took place in that class, but her own various responses to the children: "I was amazed at the level of sophistication—what got going once the kids let loose! I think it was Freddy, just about the quietest one in that class, who took on Beverly, who is so *formidably* articulate and smart. He said that maybe the person who does the right thing, even if it's not so popular—'well, he hopes it'll *get* popular, and then he'll be popular, like he was before he had to make his decision.' I had to intervene there, at that point, because I felt we were slipping into opportunism! But maybe I was being unfair to Freddy! I basically rephrased part of what Freddy said—I used the phrase 'a sense of history': some leaders take the long view of things, and they hope that they'll be proven right, that the right they do will be accepted and praised years later (rather than at the time). Of course, the children quite properly worried about what would happen to the leader who had such a perspective—might he be roundly defeated, and disappear into one of history's many dustbins? No, they didn't quite put it that way, but that's what they found bothersome, you could say: they didn't want to see someone trying to do good end up failing, and never coming back—not being recognized, approved for what he did! Freddy also stopped us short when he asked 'if a woman tries to do what's right'—whether people would believe her more than they'd believe a man. His question took us all by surprise, and stopped us in our tracks, the girls and me as well as the other boys! One of the boys, Andy, I think it was, was contemptuous: women aren't mayors or governors or senators or presidents! Yes, the children nodded. But then one of the girls, Francie, said that 'we' aren't only talking about politicians. She'd read in Sunday school about Joan of Arc, and there were other saints who were women, and besides, she was sure 'some women *had* been politicians,' and besides—well, what about all the women who teach in school (and take care of their children at home)—aren't *they* 'moral leaders'!

"It was then that the class fell silent, as I remember. They were suddenly looking at me, as if I was now an example of a 'moral leader'—so I'd better speak up! I didn't know what to say, though. I thought I should continue the discussion we'd been having—but I also felt they'd done a great job, and they'd almost exhausted the topic. Then I thought I should say something that would get us going again—get *them* going. But I glanced at the clock, and I realized that we'd been at it for fifteen minutes or so—that's a long time in the daily life of a fifth-grade class to stay on one subject! We were supposed to go over an arithmetic assignment, lots of multiplication, and my conscience was telling me we should just stop, and get to our 'numbers.' But I also couldn't help but feel that maybe I should say something myself—that maybe the children were expecting me to give them my 'answer,' my opinion, or maybe even give an example of moral leadership, some story. The best moments in teaching are when you share an anecdote with your class, and you can see it lighting up the minds of the children in front of you, connecting with some memory, some moment, some experience, some concern in their lives."

No matter the depth and extent of her moral introspection as she stood before her class, she found herself unable to "complete things," unable to "come up with comments that would summarize" what she had heard, and most devastating to her, in retrospect, unable to "be a little bit of a 'moral leader' " herself. She knew, in that last regard, why—knew later that same day, in the privacy of her apartment, while taking her late afternoon cup of tea: a time when she regularly revisited her classroom, remembered the pleasant times, the successes, even breakthroughs, but also remembered the failures of imagination, of will, of ingenuity and improvisation. In fact, she was often inclined to turn things upside down, regard what seemed to be a success as a failure, and vice versa. So it went that day—she had been witness to a spirited examination of a substantial, even crucial subject matter, and she had, in turn, knowingly negotiated the class's transition from that lively session to one in which a more dry, more pedestrian obligation (that of working well with multiplication and long division) had been fulfilled—yet, at four-thirty or so, even with the boost that strong tea can supply, she had felt strongly dispirited. She could have said *this;* she might have pointed out *that.* She had a chance to seize a favorable moment, and she had flubbed it, retreated into the safety of a regimen. Why? Worse, she had, thereby, taught the children something—that a teacher could stir them to contemplation on a moral matter (who leads whom, in what way, to what effect), but herself abstain from teaching by example. "I could have brought that 'symposium' we had down from the clouds of speculation to the earth of our city here, New Orleans"—her way of summarizing her self-critical afterthoughts.

The next day she woke up with a resolve, "to regroup": she would manage to find time for a remark or two—a time in which she'd "redeem" herself (the use of that word a measure of the almost religious nature of her self-arraignment the previous afternoon). Just before a "time-out" period, a fifteen-minute spell in which the students were encouraged to do free reading, or catch up on their schoolwork, she asked for the class's attention. Somewhat dramatically she once again approached the blackboard, wrote those two words, "moral leader," on it, this time underlined them, put the chalk down, and launched on her statement, whose content she'd mulled over nonstop after waking early that morning: "I cleared my voice and told the class I wanted to 'pick up from where we left off yesterday.' They were listening carefully, I could see right away. None of that half-dazed look you see when you try to get them to spell 'enough' correctly, and you can see on their faces the word itself: *enough!* I told them I'd been thinking about what we'd all said, and that I wished I'd said 'a little something' myself. Then I told them that maybe I didn't [say anything] because I needed to stop and think. I said it's like that sometimes, I'll bet, with our 'moral leaders': they have to weigh all the choices, and try to predict, in their minds, what will be the outcome, if they go in this direction, or in another direction. Then I said I wanted to talk about 'the here and now.' I said we've got a 'big crisis' right in our city of New Orleans, with the Negro children coming into the schools, to be in classrooms 'with all the other children,' that's how I worded it. I said, 'you know, citizenship is our birthright.' I explained that 'a citizen is a citizen—*that's* what the Supreme Court is trying to tell us!'

"Well, I'm giving a digest, a summary of my 'oration.' I remember translating Cicero's 'orations' when I was in high school, and I think all I needed was to be wearing a toga to qualify as one of those 'senators' Cicero was trying to persuade. I suppose you could argue that *he* was a 'moral leader'! Anyway, it was a beginning for me: I told the children, I got the point across, somehow, that I thought we had to be on the lookout for ways to be moral leaders *ourselves,* not just students who *discussed* moral leaders or moral leadership! I told them that 'history isn't only some subject you study in the fifth grade, or the eighth grade, or when you're a senior in high school, or in college—it's *something happening right before your eyes;* it's what the newspapers are recording, and it's what you're seeing on the TV.' I mean, that's obvious, but I needed to say it and I needed to get specific—to remind those children that a few other children, only three or four years younger than they were (those first graders a bit across the city from them), were 'making history'; and then I added (I said it): 'maybe they will go down in history as moral leaders, who helped our city of New Orleans become a better city.' I quickly added, 'a fairer city.' I could see when I used that word that it struck a bell—but I needed to do more explaining. So I went into another mini-oration on 'fairness,' what it is, what it means, how we've got to work all the time so that people are fair to other people. Of course, even as I spoke, I wondered if some of the kids were thinking I was being fair or unfair in the way I was talking about our school desegregation struggle!"

In fact, even by her account (she was always tempted to find fault with herself) those boys and girls had responded quite favorably to her talk, universally so, she had to admit. She resorted to musical imagery at one moment—she had sung an aria, and the audience had been thoroughly won over. She was sure, however, that there were, substantively speaking, more than a few "naysayers," with "boos" in their hearts, no matter their apparent assent to her "performance." The question now was what, if anything, further to do? She vacillated: one moment she had plans to proceed, to keep bringing up the issue of school desegregation, of Negroes and their position in our nation's history, not to mention that of the South, including Louisiana; but the next moment she felt jumpy, fainthearted, even panicky. She feared she would be called to the principal's office; she would be told she had lost her job; she would become the subject of "those investigations" by one of "those Louisiana politicians" who represented "the segregationist bloc" in the state legislature. More significant, she feared that she'd be called on the carpet by the parents of some of her schoolchildren—that a boy or a girl would tell his or her parents that Miss Vogel was saying things she shouldn't say, that she was causing some of her class anxiety, apprehension, prompting ire and outrage in them. She knew, after all, what most of the parents of the children in her class believed with respect to the rights of Negroes, even as she knew what her own parents and her brother and her various relatives on both sides of her family firmly believed. In her more tremulous times she was ready to call herself a needlessly stubborn, persistent "troublemaker" who had in her a large self-righteous streak. At those moments she posed (maybe, hurled) questions at herself: why was she sticking with "this moral leadership idea"? Why did she feel it necessary to be so forthcoming with the children about her own social concerns, political values, race-connected worries? Why had she been so "emotional" that first time—and thereafter, as well? Three weeks after that "outburst" (one name she gave for her "Ciceronian oration") she was still "plugging" the same tune: "my tolerance song." So doing, had she "taken possession" of the class, denied dissent to it in the interest of a stern disapproval of those who denied expression, freedom to others?

Still, she kept up her self-allotted fifteen or twenty minutes of free-for-all—"serious palaver," she called it. She taught the children that latter word, its meaning and spelling both. She kept using that word, a slightly offhand, even pejorative one, with reference to what she, at other moments, called their "morning gabs," that phrase casual but not critical. She gave voice, on certain days, to opinions and attitudes other than her own, a running dialogue, as it were, if not a recitation of arguments as she had heard them, and now, was trying to articulate them. It didn't take long for the children to join her, and to follow suit: they, also, learned to argue with themselves, to put in spoken language not only what they had come to (been taught to) believe, but what they felt to be "the other side." That was the phrase they all used when they "switched," tried to guess how "others," holding ideas different from (adverse to) their own, would have their say. For Miss Vogel, anxious to conceptualize, occasionally, for the class, this was a "debate within ourselves" as well as a chance to speak openly about one's beliefs.

For a school year, then—the same one in which mobs took occasional control of certain New Orleans streets and four Negro girls dared enter two once all-white elementary schools—slightly older children in another elementary school in that old, cosmopolitan port city tried to figure out what was happening. The time spent, the topic, became known to some of the children as "palaver about plenty of things." No one lost sight of that phrase "moral leader," or "moral leadership." Some described Elaine Vogel as anxious to teach about "Negroes, and all that's been done wrong to them," and others, less specifically, as "talking about what's going on in Louisiana." Once Beverly, always the master at verbal enunciation and negotiation and reconciliation, proposed "learning what's wrong in Louisiana"—and hastened to remind all her listeners that such a description could be "anyone's," that is, applied as that phrase fits the mind of the person in question. Such a spaciousness of thinking, such an ambiguity and subtlety of conceptualization, struck everyone, and especially the teacher, as appropriate, desirable. They all *were* learning precisely that—what others thought was wrong, what *they* thought was wrong; and, too, what might be, what would be, very much worth happening. Elaine Vogel's minicourse in "moral leadership" had, in its realization and furtherance, become itself an act of collective moral leadership, a witness to it: dozens of worries and ideals and frustrations and fears and excuses given air, and not rarely, a moment of agreement—that, for instance, "there's change ahead for us, whether *you* like it or not," as Beverly and others put it, and that being the case, "you need to be a step ahead of trouble, if you can." The latter was tendered by Beverly as the essence of her definition of the "moral leader": "the person who is looking ahead, to prevent trouble, even if it causes you a lot of trouble when you do try to look ahead and spare everyone getting into hot, hot water," to which a teacher said "Amen," and with her all factions in this fifth-grade seminar on ethical reflection as it pertains to one's authority as a citizen or government official.

3. DONITA GAINES AND RALPH McGILL: WRITERS AS MORAL LEADERS

In 1961 Jane and I moved from New Orleans to Atlanta. High school desegregation had begun there, and the office of the Student Nonviolent Coordinating Committee was located there. We felt it was more important for us, then, to commute from Atlanta to New Orleans than the other way around. The ten high-schoolers who desegregated Henry Grady High, Northside High, Murphy High, and Brown High told us a lot about what leadership meant—there were no riots to confront, but plenty of resentment, rancor, whispered threats in hallways, on steps, in the streets. "Atlanta is a city of law and order," its mayor, William Hartsfield, had proclaimed, and so it was—yet when Lawrence Jefferson (one of two African-American students who entered Henry Grady High in 1961) walked from class to class he heard insults, found spitballs sent his way, and had no friends coming to his side. Many times he told me he wanted to "pull out," end the constant tension he experienced; but he knew the practical and symbolic significance of his effort, and so he quietly persisted. His was a calm stoicism, occasionally interrupted by bouts of moodiness. On those occasions he mocked his white classmates—their haughtiness or callousness: "The more uppity they get, the more pathetic they are! They all talk about going to church on Sunday—I wonder what God thinks of the way they act in school, Monday through Friday!" Every once in a while he told God what *he* thought of some of his classmates—but he also told God (and his folks and his sister and his childhood friends) that "no way" he'd let them get the better of him.

Not so with Donita Gaines—she was one of two of her race to enter previously all-white Brown High School in 1961, and rather soon she found the behavior of her fellow students "a terrible drain." She was especially upset by the snide looks and comments of certain "cracker girls," she called them, with the undisguised, retaliatory anger in her voice meant to accompany the words she used. After three months of day-to-day isolation, loneliness, and countless moments of alarm (offhand warnings of danger that would come upon her) she decided to call it quits. Her father, a postal worker, tried hard to dissuade her, but she had had enough. I heard from her a searing indictment of young parochialism, smugness, insensitivity (not to mention racism), and finally, I heard from her this self-rebuke: "Maybe if I was stronger, I could just hold out. But I'm not meant for this! Some people are, I know. I admire them. But not me—I told the [NAACP] lawyer, I made a mistake [agreeing to be one of the pioneers in school desegregation]—I'm not a leader. I like my privacy. If you're going to be a leader, and do what's not been done before, you're going to be on display, all the time. That's not for me. Everyone tells me I'm 'doing good'—they mean I'm adjusting to all the trouble I go through at school; and they tell me I'm 'doing good' because I'm 'leading our people.' But I have nightmares all the time: it's the same thing—I wake up and I can remember that I was in a building, and there were a lot of people, and they were making fun of me, calling me 'coon-girlie' [she had heard such comments at school], and so I see an elevator door open, and I rush in, and the door closes, and I'm alone, and the elevator is going down, but it's very fast, and I'm afraid it's gone out of control, and it'll crash, and I'm looking at the switches and buttons to see if there's anyway to stop it—and that's when I wake up, and it takes me a few seconds to realize that I'm in my bed, at home, and not in that horrible place in my dream."

She needed no help from anyone about the meaning of that dream—its implications for her were obvious and portentously telling. One morning she balked, announced to her stepmother and father that she wanted "a day off." Was she sick? No, not sick—but rather, sick and tired. Encouragement by her parents meant little to her. Indeed, she became morose as they tried to boost her spirits. Finally, they relented, reversed themselves, told her to take a day, even two days off—such a respite would be good for her. She did take those two days off, and when they were over, she wanted two more—and by then it was clear, too, that she had no desire to return to Brown High School, ever.

In no time, the newspapers and television stations had caught wind of what was happening, that one of the two students at Brown High, one of the handful of African-American students whose assertion of their constitutional rights was (to quote Atlanta's mayor again) "changing the face of Georgia and the South," had for some reason decided to quit, give up a fight that seemingly, by then, had been securely won.

It was then that my name first came to the attention of newspaper and television reporters. They had flocked to the Gaines residence and tried with all their might to learn Donita's reasons for pulling out of the desegregation struggle. The family fought hard for its privacy, kept saying the same thing, that it was "best" for Donita that she return to her "old school." The firmer the resistance to self-disclosure on the part of Donita and her folks, the more persistently inquisitive the journalists became. Eventually Donita's father mentioned that she was seeing a psychiatrist. She most certainly had been "seeing" one: Jane and I regularly visited her home (twice a week), as we did the homes of other African-American youths attending those four Atlanta schools, and as we did the homes of some white students in their classes: we were in the midst of a research project that, in Atlanta, was sponsored by the Southern Regional Council, a group of "white and Negro citizens" interested in furthering "interracial understanding and progress." The council maintained close connection with journalists from all over the country, and especially, of course, the South. With Donita's decision a front-page story in the Atlanta papers, and elsewhere across Georgia and its neighboring states, Jane and I soon enough had our own problem with the press: what to say—both in connection with Donita and with respect to the overall work we had heretofore been doing in welcome privacy.

I refused to talk with anyone until I had spoken at great length with Donita and her parents. I asked Donita whether I should meet with the reporters, and if so, what I should say. Her response was as interesting a comment as I'd heard in the months I'd known her: "You've got to say something. I've learned that! When all of this got going none of us realized we weren't just going to be high-school kids anymore. We've been on a stage. We've been up there, for folks to come and look at; that's the purpose: to show the whole world how it's changed, here in Atlanta. The Negro people are standing up for their rights, and the whites are saying 'Okay, okay, we'll let you come be with us, but we won't welcome you, mind you, and we don't want you near us, not as our equals, only looking after us, picking up after us.' 'Sure,' they're telling us, 'if you keep getting the government up in Washington after us, we'll give a little ground, but we'll make you pay for it, each one of you.'

"I've heard them talk like that—no exaggerating! 'We'll make the goddamn niggers pay for this integration, boy will we!' That's what I heard, in the *women's* room, not the men's room! They have filthy mouths, those honey-blond ones!" Abruptly, a pause, then an apology, followed by a recommendation: "I'm sorry. I shouldn't talk like that! That's what happens to you—that's why I want *out*! When you start thinking and talking bad, real bad—like the people looking down on you and out to get you—then you know well, 'full well' my daddy says, that you're in deep, deep trouble. It's then that you need to figure things out. Are you ready to stick through it, or are you down to the bottom of the barrel, your strength all gone from you? For me, the answer is clear: I've given all I have, and it's not enough! To be honest, really honest—it's hard to be honest—I'm not as idealistic as I should be. If I was idealistic, *really* idealistic, I'd stick with this battle. That's what our minister calls it, a battle. But I'm not a civil rights person. My daddy isn't, either; nor anyone in our family. We sort of got caught in all this! They asked Daddy—they said he had a good federal government job, so no one could 'get' him, he was safe; and they promised, they said it would be all right, and I'd get a scholarship to college, for sure, and it would be a big feather in my cap. 'You'll be a hero,' they said. 'You'll be a leader, doing good, doing the best, the top of the best, for your people,' they [the NAACP folks] said. They said they'd get me a dress, or two or three, if I needed more. I didn't really need new dresses, but a lady came over, and she said she wanted to do something for all of us, the 'pioneers,' and couldn't she just buy me a dress, and I said sure, all right, and Daddy said it would be helping *her,* because she was one of the first colored, the first *Negroes* to get to vote in this city, and now there's another war to be fought, she says, more battles, and I'm one of the 'generals'! I didn't know any girl, any woman, has ever been a 'general'—but that was fine with me. I mean, I knew I wasn't what she was building me up to be—some boss, someone at the head of the class. They said in church we kids doing the school integration are 'moral examples.' I looked at Daddy and smiled. If we was at home, I'd have had me a belly laugh over that one—maybe for some of us, maybe, but not for me, it isn't meant for me!"

I wasn't sure why she so insistently excluded herself from the morally elevated company to which others believed she belonged. She replied that she knew herself well—that was why. I asked her, again, whether I ought respond to the numerous requests coming my way with respect to her and her reported withdrawal from Brown High School, her supposed (and proposed) return to an "all-Negro institution." Her instructions were clear, forceful, relatively terse: "You can tell them the truth. You can say Donita thought she'd better leave that school, because it was all too much—she felt she'd be happier where she was than where she is now. That's what I've decided—that I *could* stick it out, but I don't want to, and that I think they made a mistake when they picked me: I like the company of people, my friends. I'm not the person to bite my tongue and be alone and be a leader. I'm not the person to be out front. I can't 'lead' those white kids—to be better, to behave themselves as Jesus would want them to, so I'll go to a place where I can try to 'lead' myself—to find what's good and what's right in life."

In fact I said very little to the reporters—other than to indicate the obvious: Donita Gaines had felt uncomfortable where she had been going to school, and so she concluded, after much reflection, that she ought to "bow out," a phrase she used several times with her parents, so they told me, but not during our conversations. Amidst heavy press coverage, including editorial comment from *The Atlanta Constitution,* the city's major newspaper, Donita did, indeed, "bow out"—and refused any interviews or opportunities to make statements on the telephone, or through intermediaries. Her father said that she had made her decision for "personal reasons," and that was that. Meanwhile, a number of reporters were trying to learn whether this attractive, intelligent young lady had been "driven" from her new school by an unfavorable set of circumstances. Interviews with students at the school told little—and Donita's one African-American fellow student, Madeleine Nix, was steadfastly unforthcoming. At the same time, student activists in the civil rights movement (in SNCC and CORE and Dr. King's SCLC) began asking publicly whether there wasn't something inherently and outrageously wrong in sending one or two black (then the word) students into what James Forman, the head of SNCC, called "a sea of unwelcoming whites." It was then, against such a background, that I received in the same week a telephone call from Ralph McGill, editor of *The Atlanta Constitution* (his front-page-left column ran seven days a week in the paper) and a letter from Lillian Smith, the distinguished writer, whose novel *Strange Fruit* and nonfiction book *Killers of the Dream* had been an extraordinary and personally dangerous witness of sorts for a white southern lady: in both volumes she probes the psychology of racist hate unflinchingly—and she did so (in the 1940s) when segregation ruled without any real social, cultural, or political challenge in the universities, never mind the newspapers, radio, the state legislature, and yes, even the federal government.

It turned out that Ralph McGill wanted to know more about Donita Gaines and her experience with desegregation than his reporters had been able to learn. He was close to various members of the Southern Regional Council, and through them had learned of the work Jane and I were doing, even as we were quoted in several published stories as saying that Donita did not have a "psychiatric breakdown" and was not afflicted with any "medical condition." One morning I received a call from him: would I be willing to come over to the newspaper, discuss what he called "this latest turn" in the unfolding and quite tense effort at desegregation? Yes, for sure—and two days later I was in his office. He was then in his sixties, had seen a lot happen; he was called "Mr. McGill" by everyone in Atlanta, he was a big eminence for that city's privileged people; indeed, for many he was "Mr. Atlanta," though for many others a "nigger-lover," a "commie," the swearwords that poured out of the mouths of frightened, confused, enraged, and vulnerable people (some of whom, by then, I had come to know in the course of my research). We talked about his daily column, his attempt, thereby, to "educate" his readers. He kept coming back to that word, even told me that when he sat down at his typewriter he often closed his eyes and imagined a classroom, with young people sitting before him. Then, he asked himself: "What is the lesson of the day—what should I try to say, and how should I say it so that I'll be given the respectful attention of those thousands and thousands of readers?" He pursued that line of thinking in other ways: "You don't hector a classroom"—I still remember that comment because the word "hector" was occasionally used by my dad but no one else I knew. Mr. McGill explained one truism with another: "Pacing matters"—and I began to realize, as he talked, that he had been trying for years to change the moral and racial climate in Atlanta through his columns, always coming back to the subject, yet doing so in a way that didn't exhaust the patience of his readers. Another of his truisms: "You don't overdo your stay"—and he let me know that he quite consciously controlled the frequency of his references to racial tensions so that he'd continue to have some "credibility" with his readers.

Writers and Readers, Leaders and Followers

With that word he saw on my face a frown that I didn't know I'd shown. Then he got me consciously annoyed when he asked me where I'd grown up, how long I'd been "down South." He also asked me how old I was and where I'd gone to school. I recall thinking that this encounter was not going well at all—I remember, too, thinking of some white southerners I'd come to meet in SNCC meetings; Bob Zellner, for instance, who came from Alabama, and didn't ever, to my ear, get called Mr. Zellner, and never "paced" his expressed disapproval of segregation in all its forms, no matter the consequences for him (repeated arrests, jailings). I was getting ready to leave—a spell of silence had fallen on this newspaper office. Then a shift in Mr. McGill's manner and talk, both. He got up, went to a filing cabinet, opened it, rummaged through obviously packed stacks of folders, pulled out some, brought them back to his desk, examined them, then started sharing their contents with me. Here were letters of approval and disapproval, messages of gratitude and contempt, expressions of loyalty and outright hate, promises of remembrance ("I will never forget what you wrote . . .") and threats of confrontation, even murder ("You just wait until . . ."). I was struck by how familiar he was with these many letters, how they still commanded his reflective interest. I was also struck by the way he used the letters: they affected him deeply, and he took them very seriously. He told me that he tried to answer every letter sent him, those of approval and those of disagreement or condemnation—and that as he wrote he thought of those who had written to him: a writer very much aware of his readers, a writer handing them along, addressing them, giving voice to their concerns. The only exception were letters written by obviously disturbed people, whose writing is incoherent: "I'm no psychiatrist, but over the years I've learned to make a diagnosis of 'insanity' or 'psychosis.' I get letters that are impossible to understand—those I throw out." Not too long out of my psychiatric residency then, I took special note of what he said. I'd worked with schizophrenic patients but hadn't read any of their letters—hadn't, actually, realized that the incoherence, the jumbled thinking that I heard in those clinical encounters could also be shared with strangers on paper.

The matter of "craziness," in fact, very much interested Mr. McGill. He spoke at length not about the craziness of particular "mental patients," but that of society—"those times," he put it, "when people are encouraged to get out of control," to do "wild or wicked things" that are "very destructive." He brought up Adolf Hitler—it was only fifteen or so years after Hitler's suicide in his Berlin bunker in 1945. What did I think of him, psychiatrically? He was an evil monster, a mass murderer—that was what I thought of him; and I made clear my distaste for the psychiatric classification of public figures like Hitler and Stalin, whom I wanted to regard morally. Yes, Mr. McGill saw my point, but he *did* think those two were "sick" in the "ordinary, commonsense" version of sickness: one a rabid, agitated hater, the other a "paranoid manipulator" who trusted no one and played everyone against the other. Moreover, he reminded me, both of them were "leaders, heads of state, dictators who ruled millions"—so, what to make of *that*? I pointed out, unremarkably, that they were *evil* leaders—and he said yes, but he thought that each of them "reflected" the psychology of "plenty of their followers." At that point I took strong issue—said I thought the word "manipulate" should be substituted for "reflect." No, he wasn't at all sure that would do—there's a lot of "real craziness" out there, and certain leaders, he felt, "give voice to it." He handed over to me, again, a batch of letters that were comprehensible, or full of intensely felt hate or envy or both, and he said that his mail, constantly heavy with such stuff, was surely a mere "drop in the bucket": there are "ten or twenty," he ventured, "potential letters" at least, of a similar nature for every one he received. I wasn't in the mood, it seemed, to go along. I pointed out that even if his statistics were correct, that hardly made for a majority of Georgia's population. Letter writers aren't to be equated with everyone—they aren't Emerson's "representative" citizens. He disagreed— he'd been "in the business" long enough to know what the high volume of mail he received meant with respect to public opinion: "I'll open up but two or three letters, only two or three, and I can sense what's out there."

We were obviously talking about the relationship between various kinds of leaders and their followers, be they voters, readers, students, or in the case of young Hitler and young Stalin, party members. McGill, the veteran journalist, saw the leader as someone who "picked up on" (his phrase) "what was out there" (another phrase he kept using), even as he regarded himself as a teacher who had a sense, again, "of what was out there," and was trying through words to "address" it, another word he favored. I wasn't sure what that last word entailed: how did he address the wide spectrum of readers whose eyes happened upon his words every day? After all, by now most of them had likely concluded who he was, what his values and beliefs were. By his own description, "a large number," alas, tossed him aside, scorned his social and racial views. He was enraging them, inflaming them, not reaching or teaching them. As for others, he himself had said to me at one point that he worried about "preaching to the converted," another truism that clearly crossed his mind rather often: "[To do so is] a great temptation, and the better-known you are, the greater the risk [of that taking place]."

Still, there were "plenty of people," he insisted, who were "uncertain"; and he pushed the psychological matter hard, asserted a complexity, an inconsistency, a contradiction, even, in the minds, the values and ideals, of "thousands" of his readers, whom he described as "ordinary folks," as "torn" by their "mixed feelings" and therefore as much in need of "whatever help they can get in sorting things out." In that regard, he reminded me, a newspaper editorialist or columnist can be a "therapist"; the same holds, naturally, for politicians. Then one more truism: "People look to others for help in knowing what they should do with all the ideas that cross their minds." Why, he himself did so— before he wrote certain columns, he picked up the phone, dialed certain people whose reactions and opinions mattered a lot to him. They, too, he claimed, "stood for others"—he mentioned, in example, businessmen, educators, clergymen, professional people, working people, and of course, various public officials, not to mention other journalists: "If I'm not sure where I'm hoping to end up on a subject, that's when I'll put out lots of calls for help—I'll sound them out."

I sat there thinking how morally dangerous such an approach could end up being—a fishnet ethics. He must have seen the smugness in my face. He patiently began to explain to a thirty-two-year-old physician with no experience, then, of journalism or politics, how a city is run—the way the mayor and the business owners and the newspaper officials (the editors, the publishers) "stay in touch." Of course they do, I now know. But in his office, I was learning a good deal about leader-

ship as it gets exerted (and I was learning a good deal about my own ignorance, too). He enjoyed explaining all of that to me—I now realized
that he recognized right off my naïveté, understood that I was, actually,
a stand-in for many of his readers. After about fifteen minutes of such
explication, and a few questions about Donita that he had forgotten to
put to me, he suggested that we meet again, this time for lunch, at a
place called the Capital City Club. "You'll need a coat and tie, and
slightly more formal pants," he told me, looking at my khakis and open
shirt.

We had several of those lunches, and Mr. McGill also allowed me to
tape two of our talks in his office (where, well-fed, indeed, we repaired
after the glamour of those times at "the Club"). I'd never been in such
a place, and told him so. He laughed, made me feel comfortable by letting me know that he'd never been in a psychiatric hospital, or "in the
homes of the kind of Negro folks you're visiting here in this city." He
saw that once I saw that club, saw and heard him saying hello to various
big shots—got from him an informal résumé, of a kind—I didn't need
any formal lectures on upper-class urban sociology, on wealth and influence and how they bear not only on business and politics (and yes,
university life) but on the very people I was getting to know, the poor
people of a great city who were African-American and the only somewhat less vulnerable working-class white people with whom Donita
Gaines had recently gone to school. In one of our postprandial conversations, he told me this—gave me information that was no secret, of
course, but never quite put forward, I believed, quite the way he did
then: "What you saw in New Orleans [during the school desegregation
crisis of 1960] with your own eyes—the mobs that turned that city upside down for a while—we saw up here [in Atlanta] on our television
sets, and read about in the papers. By 'we' I mean our business and political leaders. The mayor called me up and said, 'A sure way to ruin a
city!' He added, 'We're trying to make Atlanta a business hub, and
street riots will tear down everything we've done—stop us in our
tracks!' 'Yes, sir,' was my answer!

"It didn't take us long to get going on a plan to avoid what had happened in Little Rock and New Orleans. We talked with the leaders of

the city—the heads of the banks and the stores and the companies and the universities and the church people (they're very important) and the professional groups: I knew all those folks, but it was a real education, first touching base with them, and then pulling them together—but in a quiet way. We didn't want to seem to be running things—people don't want orders coming down to them from some 'group' up there on top of some skyscraper building! We had public relations people advising us and we had 'lines' out to the governor, the state people, and to 'the Feds.' I was in constant touch with Robert Kennedy and the people around him, the attorney general. The Kennedy administration really wanted this thing [school desegregation] to *work,* work without violence, and that makes a difference: when there are clear signals coming from political leaders up there, telling you what they want and what they'll do to achieve what they want—well, it makes a *big* difference. We came up with that slogan, 'A City Too Busy to Hate,' and that said it all—the message was there, plain and simple: you'll hold on to your job, or you'll get a job or you'll get a better job than you have, if you just let this go through without creating an uproar. Hey, it's the law of the land; you live in America, and the law rules here, so let it be and count your blessings—that you're making a living and things are going good in the economy, so you'll keep making a living. That was the message, rock-bottom."

I wondered aloud whether there was any disagreement voiced during the various meetings he described with "groups of important people." No, not really—though some did express "moral reservations" about a "pitch" that was so blatantly economic, when in fact the "real issue" was "right versus wrong." One minister, Frank Ross, who was the rector of All Saints Church on Peachtree Street at the edge of the downtown area, doubted "people would be fooled." He was eloquent in his conviction that the "intelligence of the ordinary person" was being "insulted" by what he regarded as a "campaign aimed at the stomach," when it's "the head and the heart that are the issue here." Mr. McGill, himself an Episcopal layman (he attended St. Philip's Church, farther up Peachtree Street in a well-to-do suburban area) admitted to being touched by that remonstrance—yet he was "a practical man," he declared in his office that day, as indeed he had declared to himself after some deliberation: "Frank was reminding us that there's a moral side to all this, and Lord, I agreed then and I still do. But that's the bottom-line question we were trying to answer: how do you lead a troubled and divided city so that you avoid violence and a deterioration of the social order? How do you help change to take place—social and racial change? How do you lead people—so that you're doing good for them, for all of us as a city, and you're also just plain doing good? Those aren't questions you answer by looking them up in some textbook! I'm not even sure you find the answers, the *specific* answers to them in the Bible—general principles, yes, but in the here and now of this daily life, you've got to improvise and plan and think ahead and calculate and see if you can be pragmatic while still keeping your eye on what you're trying to do and where you're trying to go."

There he stopped, lowered his head, and stared at the floor for a second or two. When his eyes were back at a horizontal level, a smile crossed his face, and he extended his right arm as if he were surveying a countryside, or maybe preparing a listening audience for a pronouncement—and then these words: "I don't believe that 'might makes right,' or that jobs are the only thing. Hell, I've lived long enough to see Hitler give the German people plenty of jobs—and a bellyful of hate. I've told the ministers and the teachers, both white and Negro: let's just get us all through this crisis and avoid violence, and then the kids [in the desegregated schools] will learn to get on together, and before you know, we'll have this behind us, and the city will prosper and the races will have a bit more understanding of one another, because there will be some growing contact. That's about it—what we've been hoping to get done. Sure, it's 'incremental change,' that's what this sociology professor at Emory called it. I asked him what other kind of change he had in mind—in mind for us. That's when one of the ministers answered for him: 'A change of our thinking, our assumptions, a change of heart.' Sure, who's against that? Well, to tell you the truth, *lots* of people! That's the big problem, the way people hold on tight to what they believe—you're lucky if you can nudge them away, and sometimes the only way, or the best way, is to remind them of what they *want,* and remind them that you can't have everything, and you have to make your accommodations in this life. That's what leadership is often about—reminding people of 'the facts of life,' and trying to make sure you strike the best deal for the most people.

"That's being ethical, I'd say—an ethical kind of leadership: let's get on with being an expanding, prosperous city, and stop this mean, bad-mouthing behavior between the races!"

Now he was staring right at me, his eyes fixed on mine. I blinked, and for a second I became the one looking at the floor. I said nothing. I thought I should nod—that's what he wanted—but I couldn't. I half agreed with what I'd heard, was convinced of its shrewd truth, but it also sounded too neat and pat and self-serving—and I felt in my head the presence of some of those civil rights workers I'd been getting to know, not to mention the children in New Orleans and Atlanta, who were, often enough, hearing plenty of hate, no matter how "busy" (that slogan!) they kept trying to be. I recall looking at my tape recorder, thinking of other kinds of eloquence that had come its way (from those young people), and wishing, then and there, by some piece of magic, that those voices would start speaking, loud and clear, so the two of us in that place of power would be stopped in our tracks, moved to think anew, prodded to explore different aspects of the moral and social terrain Mr. McGill had just surveyed with obvious sincerity, no small amount of intensity, and for sure, plain old savvy and plenty of practicality.

4. LILLIAN SMITH, AN "UNREALISTIC VISIONARY": THE DIFFERENCE BETWEEN "PRETEND LEADERSHIP" AND "REAL MORAL LEADERSHIP"

Up on a mountain in north Georgia, in Clayton, where Lillian Smith, the novelist and social essayist, lived amidst the high, lonely beauty of the pines, and views that carried the eyes across dozens of miles, the word "practicality" was not greeted with outbursts of applause. Jane and I first went to see Miss Lill—as so many of her friends called her, and as she tried, unsuccessfully, to get us to address her—at both her written then spoken invitation. On the phone she suggested we initially pay her a weekend visit, and she was right: it took some time, as she had predicted in a long letter to Jane and me, for us, a generation and more her junior, and Yankees born and bred, to make certain connections, even to understand certain assumptions that informed her life, as against the kind we two had lived. She was a great storyteller, of course—and an inventive, industrious cook. By Sunday afternoon we had "clicked"—and then, more phone conversations, correspondence, return visits. We read all she'd ever published, the novels and the essays—with much in them on the subject of race; and besides, we learned of the price she paid for her unflinching stand, as far back as the 1930s, with respect to the desirability, the necessity of thoroughgoing (as opposed to nominal) integration. Her novel *Strange Fruit* carries the matter as far as it can go: a story of miscegenation— banned, incidentally, in Boston in 1947, when it was published. Her house was once burned down by the Klan. She was called "every name in the book—and then some." Her life was constantly threatened. But most painful of all for her, as she looked back at her then fast-disappearing life (she had cancer and would die in 1966), was the treatment she got at the hands of a host of southern "liberals and intellectuals."

Miss Lill could be icily ironic, if not sardonic, as she recalled the way "moderates" constantly tried to gauge "how far they could go" in championing this or that piece of legislation meant to further racial "progress." She was especially mindful of certain landmark moments—for instance, the anti-lynching efforts of the 1930s and 1940s, or the struggle to extend voting rights to African-Americans. Not that either of those long-fought battles had been decisively won even in the early 1960s, when we met, talked, and exchanged letters. But her memory was detailed, at times unforgiving, and, for Jane and me, startling in its factual command, its moral energy, its occasional moral ferocity: "The Negro people of our South have carried many burdens these past centuries but none as pointless (if 'educational' for anyone interested) as the so-called moderates, who have always prided themselves (and gauged themselves!) as one to two millimeters ahead of the pack in their sublime and hugely generous 'tolerance for our fine colored citizens.' Please excuse me if I shock you two with some of the ugly, stock phrases of the past, the self-congratulatory drivel that passed for 'progress,' no less, just a few years ago, and *now,* too."

She was a great talker. Sentences poured from her, well-wrought ones, vehemently or tenderly expressed. She moved effortlessly from the prophetic to the pastoral, from the abstract (usually psychological in nature) to the concrete. She had been a close friend of the New York psychoanalyst Lawrence Kubie, and she summoned easily and a touch proudly at times a learned psychodynamic vocabulary (in 1963, in Atlanta, a measure of her intellectual boldness). I had no great admiration for that way of putting things; I'd also learned it, and was trying to hold on to its wisdom but set aside the reflexic, incantory use of it that could so readily deteriorate into a reductionist jargon. But Miss Lill, with her vigorously demonstrative manner of narrative presentation, her astute eye for the telling moment, her mastery of social detail and, too, historical backdrop, was psychologically inviting—she had Jane and me attentively awake with her various interpretations, explanations, and pronouncements. We yearned, at times, for humor—but listen, here was one hell of a courageous southern lady whose talent and energy had been expended for decades on behalf of individuals and causes that other, more "respectable" people had shunned outright or only warily approached as worthwhile.

As we talked about the children I was getting to know in New Orleans and Atlanta, and their schoolteachers, Miss Lill asked pointed questions. She was enormously helpful in her conjectures about Donita Gaines, Donita's reasons for wanting to "retire from the ring, stop fighting it all," to return to an "all-black world." Miss Lill would probe psychoanalytically, go back to her youth as "a white southern lady," refer to her "suppositions," and then (once or twice) take note of the evident gratitude on Jane's face or mine—not so much to point something out as to keep an explicit record of where we all were conversationally. At one juncture, *The Atlanta Constitution* came up—a remark by Jane about its influence, across the color line, on the families we were visiting. Miss Lill nodded and launched into a discursive, spoken essay on journalism in the pretelevision era, and its "nervous accommodation" to "monied interests," a phrase she used repeatedly as she relayed instance after instance—all the way back to the segregationsit Tom Watson's political career (just as Elaine Vogel had handed over Watson's southern political life so regularly and unforgettably to her students).

At one point, I lauded Ralph McGill's columns, their clearheaded decency, their sustained civility and goodness of heart. She froze for a second. Now it was me who noted her "psychology"—and who was becoming plain worried that I had said the wrong thing. She gathered herself together, managed a feint chord of agreement ("I can see how you'd feel that way"), even went further by acknowledging "McGill's essential intent" as a spokesman for "law and order," for "pieties," she called them, such as "good human relations," "a peaceful approach to racial problems," "progress for all people of both races."

Yet eventually she launched an across-the-board critique of the very journalism she'd just praised, and specifically evoked that phrase "moral leadership," which I'd sometimes heard in a New Orleans classroom: "For years I've heard the same argument—it's dinning in my ears: you can only push so far so fast; you have to be sensitive to the 'limits of possibility'; you have to couch your message in language that won't threaten people too much; slow progress is the best kind, because it really lasts; only a change in the hearts of people will solve this racial problem—and on and on. Who can really disagree with all of that? I'll say it: I can—I feel I must! I've lived long enough to see what *pretended leadership* doesn't do and *real moral leadership* can accomplish— and I have to say, there's a big difference there! Until a moral leader arrives and 'breaks the mold,' every rationalization and excuse, every 'high-octane gas talk' (people around here call it) seems plausible; seems absolutely correct. That's the trouble with those newspaper editorialists—they sit there and *gauge,* and *measure,* and *calibrate,* even though they know full well, *damn* well, what's the right decision—but they're always hemming and hawing, trying to get it *just* right: that means (get it, say it) so that all their 'constituencies' clap and clap, and especially the businesspeople, who buy those pages of advertisements, and, of course, the owners, the publishers, who are themselves first and foremost businessmen.

"I don't mean to launch a tirade at businessmen—or at newspaper people. I guess I'm just tired of letting their rationales be regarded as 'the truth,' or what will *work,* what is *practical.* That's what everyone thinks—until someone comes along, like those SNCC young people you're studying, or Dr. King, and says, 'Hey, no, this just won't do no longer! Enough is enough!' Then, you'll notice, everyone goes scurrying to catch up, to adjust their talk to this new 'reality.' You want to hear something? I was told by a friend of mine who is also a friend of Ralph McGill's that he said, 'Thank God for Lillian Smith!' You know why? I could make him seem like a moderate! That's what I mean—this craze for 'the mean'! The issue isn't what's right, but who's where on some 'spectrum'—it's like the blind leading the blind, that kind of leadership, the leadership of clever, self-serving calculation!

"Oh, I'm getting on my high horse and preaching (or ranting!). But it's so sad to read his columns and know that he's got a ruler, a rich boss, sitting right there beside that typewriter of his, and he's measuring, measuring away, and he's watching his every word, so he can cover *this* base and *that* base, and come out 'all right' with the people who 'matter.' Then all of a sudden, out of nowhere (that's always how it is, how it happens!) someone stands up and says something or does something—to say can be to do!—and then someone says yes, I'm with you, and someone else [goes along], and you know what? The whole climate changes, the whole 'reality' that those 'realists' hold so sacred is blown away, and they go rushing around to 'catch up'—they readjust their slide rules to calibrate this new shape of things! A few folks up until now dismissed as peripheral are suddenly at the very center of things—and that's what's called the making of history, or the process of change!"

Unrealistic Visionaries

"Thank God for the people who help us all go that way—who take the big chance, who aren't 'utilitarian' and 'pragmatic,' but are 'unrealistic visionaries.' Once, when he was trying to be complimentary, Mr. McGill called me that [last description]—of course, with the word 'unrealistic' he was taking a big swipe at some of us who have tried to say what we believe is right. And you want to know something? Our foes, the segregationists, they know what's going on—they don't miss themselves a trick! I got into a jab with one of them in the post office a year or so ago; he said, 'Miss Lill, at least we know the truth of where you're at—a lot of people, they're dodging around, and trying to dance to whatever tune will make them the most dough and get them an invite to the big house on the hill!' I've never forgotten that; I didn't have that tape recorder of yours around. I didn't need it! I can hear his every word in my head. I don't want to forget it. I wish Mr. McGill could hear what that fellow said when he started with his 'Miss Lill.' "

She is, finally, tired. She looks longingly at an ample couch across the room, and at her desk, with its inviting stack of papers, books. She sags a bit in her chair, reaches for a nutcracker amidst a bowl of walnuts, contemplates them, starts her cracking—though she doesn't eat the "meat" she's obtained through her concerted, noisy exertions. She smiles at what she is doing, gives us a knowing, psychoanalytically informed wink—the satisfaction of getting to the heart of the matter, and yes, the irony of this affirmation of herself as a "Georgia cracker," a term of derision thrown at working people who don't hold "advanced views."

She had, earlier on, launched into a populist critique of those who claim for themselves "advanced views" but who are, when push comes to shove, "moral cowards," so she called them. She was tired of "Emory cocktail parties" or "Buckhead [an upper class neighborhood north of Atlanta] smart salons." She preferred a blunt exchange, such as she described taking place in the post office. She'll "take every time" someone who's "open and clean" with that he or she believes, to someone who "watches every word," "sniffs the direction of the wind before saying a word." The "end" was near, she knew—and she was, "these days," remembering her remarks of decades ago, called "wild" and "loony" and "way out" and "miles away from the mainstream," and now, very much "accepted," "conventional." She hopes, on her "final morning," she'll be able to smile at that turn of events—"right at this time," though, she is still feeling "the emotion of disgust," a strong word, she admits. But then, the matters she just mentioned (the way people privately and publicly come to regard other people, and for which reasons) are "big moral shadows that stalk us throughout our life," so she says she has never wanted to forget: "The price we can pay for the acceptance, the approval we try so hard to obtain from others—the cost of yearning every minute, every day, to please."

No wonder she became, for so many, one of the "big moral shadows" she mentioned, her life a huge lesson to her readers and others who knew of her—that moral leadership is best exerted in deeds, that it can be undermined by asserted platitudes and pretenses that have no real connection to a person's experiences or daily manner of being. At times Jane and I felt her to be cranky and difficult, all too demanding, even overbearing in her mix of righteousness—her psychology perhaps a reminder of the vocational hazards that can accompany a vigorously affirmed moral leadership. Yet her poignant, provocative, and pointed comments—about what a moralist or a moral leader can accomplish for listeners and readers (of which she had many during a long writing and lecturing life) inhabited our minds for long spells.

V

Eliciting the Assent of the Follower:

Emerson's *Representative Men*

For Ralph Waldo Emerson, the leader is one who elicits the assent of the follower. Emerson said in his own way what Robert Kennedy and Dorothy Day knew to say—each of them had read *Representative Men,* and each echoed that book's emphasis on the relationship between individuals (their ideas, actions) and those who meet them as followers, readers who absorb words eagerly and take them to heart, or soldiers who also heed words, called military orders—and, not least, politicians, who attend what voters have to say and then oblige with their own responsive comments, on the stump or while preparing to vote as legislators.

In the precise middle of the nineteenth century, Emerson became excited, even at times entranced, by the military and political successes of Napoleon, and also by the work of certain writers, who in different ways had become triumphant—intellectual commanders, in their own lifetimes and thereafter. For example, Plato's philosophical authority was never decisively challenged, nor was Shakespeare, with his continuing prominence. Emerson called those three leaders "representative men."

Other people, less daunting but promising with respect to a future that would hold them high, also held Emerson spellbound; their writing and thinking had established them as reflective eminences: Goethe, and Montaigne, with his refined, shrewdly doubting observations on our human inclinations. Yet Montaigne's skeptical appraisals and Swedenborg's spiritual mysticism only tempted Emerson, the religious-minded sage of Concord, so far.

Unlike Montaigne, Emerson wasn't always looking for salt to shake, eagerly or with regret; and unlike Swedenborg, whose embrace of the Lord, soaring and passionately inviting, had enthralled thousands, Emerson kept a careful distance from the enthusiasms of prayer—he was forever reminding himself that what we declare believably true is not necessarily to be confused with a spirituality whose message and meaning can readily elude us in this contingent life, with its inevitable confinements and restrictions of factual knowledge, whoever we are, wherever and whenever we live. Emerson the writer has Montaigne looking askance at Swedenborg, but also renders a rational doubter's awe of religious ecstasy as it can seize our cognitive humanity.

In a sense, Emerson's cautious embrace of Napoleon, and arguably of Swedenborg, was a reckless one for an inveterate dissenter suspicious of ideas and people granted immunity from close, critical consideration. Indeed the word "genius," bestowed on the likes of a Napoléon, say, and others, surely alarmed Thoreau, Emerson's naturalist friend, who had his own reasons to worry about those granted high regard, in Concord or elsewhere. But Emerson wanted to find geniuses, and leaders, too, he called them, in the arts, on the battlefield, and in politics. He wanted to comprehend human singularity, to hail certain special guides, individuals whose lasting achievements and whose affirmations of the moral or literary imagination still hold us readers in grateful sway. If those individuals Emerson wrote about are "representative," they are connected to others, and stand for them: here was an American for whom democracy, as it works in a republic, meant so very much. It is as if we are told to imagine, through an encompassing adjective, that a group of special men have been sent to a most significant or exemplary congress, where each of them stands for others, for followers—though without their votes, a power in itself, since no election to that congress is going to be possible.

For Emerson, again, the leader is one who obtains the consent of the follower; the one who has *that* genius—through words on paper or through deeds. The geniuses given attention in *Representative Men* are leaders who have had the willing consent of followers, for whom they speak, on behalf of whom they act—whom they "represent." Inevitably, of course, Emerson joins the company of those followers—like them, he votes for certain individuals, sends them symbolically to Washington, to a pantheon of the chosen, the admired, the followed. But to follow is not only to stay in line, to read with enjoyment, but to attend with a conviction and devotion that draw upon our moral needs, our hunger for a self-approval that the conscience prompts, hence the search for something to believe, someone to admire wholeheartedly.

Not that Emerson wanted to analyze either the leader or the follower. Freud's *Group Psychology and the Analysis of the Ego* would be published over a half century later. Yet Emerson, a shrewdly self-aware, even confessional narrator, a New Englander who was writing before the first psychoanalyst was born in distant Vienna, understood quite well the way we connect with others, the bonds we establish, and why—our past experiences as they shape the years of our later life. In his own self-regarding way, Emerson grasped the emotional entanglement that takes place when a reader absorbs a writer's words or a philosopher's ideas, or when a soldier says a personal yes to a general's orders. Emerson also knew that he himself was a writer, a philosopher, and not without his own substantial power in America, where he was granted so much regard. Indeed, what we read today as *Representative Men* consists of essays Emerson spoke in crowded halls, delivered to large audiences. Still, a voice in him worried, looked to the future—he knew he wrote during one of history's moments, so why not be nervous because of his own emergence as a leader, or at the selection of Napoleon as company for Plato! Why not worry at that latter choice—Plato's analytic sensibility applauded, whereas the powerfully affecting dramatist Aeschylus, for example, is not mentioned!

Plato's *Statesman,* in another Concordian mind and heart, could have been set aside for Aeschylus, who gave us, in the mighty verse of the chorus to *The Suppliants,* the highest of theater—art wedded to religion, philosophy, and as a matter of fact, the natural world tied forever to the sanctuaries of the worshipped: "City and Earth and shining Water,/ And God's deep-honored underground/ Who hold the tombs,/ And Zeus, third, Savior!" A chorus in the Greek theater of Aeschylus (as opposed to the seminar rooms Plato led) was made of avidly singing followers, thrilled to be affirming a leader's exclamations of inwardness, of visionary expectation—a moral leadership proclaimed to an audience, embraced with a voice and the body's evident display of passions shared, all with the sanction of art and of conventional theatergoing.

No wonder that in his rough journals, in his polished texts, the sometimes brooding, saddened Emerson, ever aware of his own limitations of intellect—of sensibility, he would call it—wrote of his reservations about his choices and confessed his doubts with respect to those he'd elevated highly, though he had, indeed, called attention to their flaws. "Every hero becomes a bore at last," he reminded others, indirectly remonstrating those he had selected for high approval—including his friend across the Atlantic, Thomas Carlyle, who doted on heroes, and wanted more of that line of secular idolatry in the "new world" from its then foremost introspective writer, who had already become a hero but in his private thoughts knew to be nervously edgy about possible missteps of stated respect, if not adulation. Might *this* hero, in his own inimitable, admirable manner of self-awareness and self-criticism, become a bore to himself? But he might be spared that destiny, he must have hoped. He was, after all, a leader given to utter realism, to a candid awareness of his situation, a leader with a moral outlook, a person ever ready to behold close to home as well as far way—and close to home Emerson's mind ventured, after the compilation of those "representative men," close to himself, of course, but close to others within sight: "Many afterthoughts, as usual, with my printing, come just a little too late; and my new book seems to lose all value from their omission. Plainly one is the justice that should have been done to the unexpressed greatness of the common farmer and laborer." He immediately thereafter gets specific, and more than a touch cynical: "A hundred times I have felt the superiority of George, and Edmund, and Barrows [those ordinary farmers, laborers just mentioned], and yet I continue the parrot echoes of the names of literary notabilities and mediocrities, which, bring them (if they dared) into presence of those Concord and Plymouth Norsemen, would be as uncomfortable and ridiculous as mice before cats."

Here is the well-known American exceptionalism at work: an honorable egalitarianism does allow the elevation of leaders, in the arts or in public life, but they ought be accompanied by their equals—and the one who has singled out those leaders has to stop and give careful thought to what has pulled him down a path of such generous appreciation, at the quite possible expense of all those others who go unmentioned. This "seesaw," Emerson knew to tell himself and others, must be employed—one notion of leadership expanded to include other notions, so that the leader statesman or playwright or poet (or essayist!) himself becomes a follower, not only of citizens who vote, or of those who read (or join armies), but of the men of the soil or of the factory, whom Emerson takes care to notice and place in a high position, indeed—their daily work, its very own obvious contribution to society, also worthy of our unstinting praise.

A great writer or thinker, exploring greatness among writers, thinkers, and among a man of military and political action such as Napoleon, turns toward a larger, a more inclusive definition of greatness, and does so with introspective energy, even anxiety—Emerson's moral leadership addressing that of others, and addressing us, too, who come in succeeding generations, and have our own ways of struggling to recognize for ourselves, for the society or culture to which we belong, what it is that truly counts (the moral matter) as we think of leadership (its various substantive aspects).

Emerson did the above belatedly, in worried retrospective. His book's title, its political, historical, and national imagery, tells of his penetrating awareness, his vivid social and psychological realization that we send forth ourselves when we subscribe to others, so it is best that one who glimpses the world, nourishes dreams or aspirations for it, keep in mind how that immediate world works, who does what for whom—the moral leadership, for example, of Concord's farmers and workers, several of whom he singles out for mention: individuals whose daily endeavors have meant much to him, impressed him, earned his admiration, prompted in him gratefulness, appreciation, no small amount of awe. With that slant, a prominent intellectual leader was asserting a moral followership on his part, even as he scanned history's horizons for moral leadership. He meant to tell the rest of us that leadership is enabled by (represents) the led, whose yearnings can stir those ahead of them in rank, fame, power, and heralded achievement, can stir them to thought, to moral reflection, to actions that owe their completion to what others have wanted or made clear as desirable to them, hence *their* actions, the reader's or soldier's or voter's gesture of consent, applause—steps taken into battle, or declared satisfaction with words written, speeches made. Thus it goes for all of us, in Emerson's metaphor: the democracy of a shared moral inwardness, of a leader and follower become neighbors, kin, or, as it is put more broadly, fellow citizens, members jointly of a country, and of the world to which they both belong, its time, its possibilities, and its difficulties.

VI

Dorothy Day and Peter Maurin
in Tandem: The Moral Leader
of a Moral Leader

Dorothy Day, one of the cofounders of the Catholic Worker Movement, was a moral leader whose leadership was based on prayer and faith leading to action—and on a felt reliance upon the leadership given *to her* by her colleague Peter Maurin. She spent time working with and on behalf of the poor, and she and Peter Maurin initiated a newspaper, *The Catholic Worker,* still very much with us, still selling, as the slogan goes, at "a penny a copy"; and they inspired others to start "hospitality houses"—soup kitchens—across the nation, and in foreign countries; a Catholicism of concern for the vulnerable and needy.

Miss Day was also a writer of conscience who knew how to take care of herself in the inevitable polemics that were sparked by her social and religious efforts. Early in her career, she had been an independent-minded, scrappy journalist, no stranger to radical politics and its consequences (she was jailed, for instance, as a picketing suffragette). She had also written fiction. Indeed, to mention the moral leadership of a woman who is now being considered by many within and outside the Catholic Church as a desirable candidate for sainthood is to risk the tautological.

Like Robert Kennedy, she understood the necessity of learning how to get along and work with people to achieve visionary goals—the combining of moral ideals and effective action into leadership.

Day was a vigorous social activist who wanted to be of help to the poor and hungry in an America that was very much unresponsive to such people. She started soup kitchens in the 1920s and 1930s, when they were often unknown, and she took her followers into new worlds of human need, desperation, and injury. The hospitality houses she established with Peter Maurin, a fellow leader of what became a social movement, were portents of what we now call centers of community service or welfare assistance: places where jobless men and women, ill and hungry, were fed, clothed, and steered toward whatever housing and work was available. No wonder she was praised by one pope after another as a spiritual and social leader, a writer and reformer and thinker worthy of admiration and veneration. Yet she herself saw her inspiration as coming from Maurin, a moral "needler"—the leader of someone others saw as the moral leader—and from God through the "notions" she received during prayer.

The Usefulness of a "Needler": A Leader by Proxy

In the 1970s, I interviewed Day with my tape recorder nearby. I wanted to talk about *her,* the ideas and values she espoused, her achievements, the lessons she had offered all who read her words or knew of her political and charitable deeds. To be sure, anyone who had worked in one of Day's soup kitchens and read her newspaper or her autobiography, *The Long Loneliness,* knew of Peter Maurin, his spiritual engagement with her: she was a young, cosmopolitan woman, well-read and a friend of writers and artists and intellectuals; he was of French peasant background, considerably her elder, a working man and a wanderer who talked of Christ's life and teachings. But many of us who regarded ourselves as savvy about her political as well as spiritual and social movement knew to pay mere lip service to Day's constant mentions of

Maurin. *She* was the leader, the bright, articulate, insistent, tireless person whose moral voice and vision had stirred thousands across the world—through the printed word, and through those soup kitchens.

She was aware of that distinction made over the years, between her highly visible leadership and the "legend" (some call it) of Peter Maurin's companion role in getting *The Catholic Worker* going, shaping its mix of spiritual advocacy and concrete connection to human vulnerability. But Maurin was no legend for her; he was the one responsible for all this.

In fact, she was trying to tell me about moral leadership, her leadership as someone else elicited it, drew it out of her, and she would have no part of my indifference to Maurin; she relentlessly put the kibosh on every effort I made to return us to her important ideas, for which (through an indirect egoism) I was waiting. Eventually, she had a long say on the "needler"—on how a person can be a leader by proxy: "The world notices some people, and it doesn't know much about others. I've had writers come talk with me—they want to know how I did this, and when I did that, what I think about one or another subject, and I tell them we've got to settle this business of pronouns before we go any further. I tell them about Peter, and what he did for us—*to* us. I tell them that they should stop all the time putting me first, forgetting Peter. He was the one who got us all going, kept us all going here, when we started as a community—he was very much a leader, you know. But I'm not being heard—so I try to get us into the details: that's where the truth lies, every novelist knows!

"I'll volunteer this: if Peter hadn't driven us all [to get on with things] you'd not be sitting there, worrying over that machine—whether it works or not. He had a sharp eye for what needed to be done, and he figured out, all the time, who would be the right person to do this, and who would do *that* the best. He knew his own limits, so he bore down on others. It took me a long while to realize that he knew exactly what he was doing when he wouldn't stay out of your hair, when he wouldn't drop the subject, until finally, to get him off my back more than anything else, I went along and did whatever it was that he'd say 'wanted doing.' "

Now, as I read those words, I think of mothers, fathers, teachers, older brothers—moral needlers of others, we can all be.

What "Wanted Doing"

"How I remember those two words!" Day said. " 'Wanted doing.' There's more to them (I began to realize only years after Peter died) than any of us ever realized as we heard the expression used over and over. Now I can be the literary critic; I can examine his language, the way he chose to put things. I can observe the 'passive voice.' I can realize that he was, in two words, making a huge statement to us about what we believed, and also it was a way of getting around us. I mean: he was telling us that we are about something larger than ourselves, that there were things that 'wanted doing'—that God wanted them done, or if you weren't a believer (many who have worked with us have not been Catholics, have called themselves agnostics) then they needed to be done on the face of it. But don't forget this was a leader at work; he knew in his bones how to get done what 'wanted doing'!"

In a sense, she was letting me know she had learned a lesson about leadership from someone who in two words could sometimes move mountains of pride, of self-absorption, or maybe of divergent interests that took various individuals away from the "doing" that he and they could agree was "wanted." Whatever the reasons that *had* kept those tasks or obligations undone, Maurin developed a way of alerting others to a need, and then "needling" people with respect to that need. The refrain was constant, but Peter had various ways of insuring that the doing would, in fact, get done. Again and again I'd hear about those ways, even as I couldn't help but note Day's own success as a student of his—as herself a needler, because she was no stranger to the moral gestures and psychological approaches she described so devotedly as being in her friend and colleague.

"Peter was always telling me he learned one thing from so-and-so, and something else from someone else," she once let me know—about a half an hour after she told me how lucky she was that she stumbled into Peter, who taught her so very much; and then she mentioned others who had been "strong" when she was "weak," or who had supplied her with a necessary long-range perspective when she had been in grave danger of being shortsighted. She was sincerely grateful to Peter, who was, she insisted, the one who got so much going in her head, in her soul. Indeed, once she went so far as to say that if I really wanted to know about the Catholic Worker Movement, I'd "need to understand what Peter brought to it." I tried hard to get beyond such self-effacement, to learn about her accomplishments. I first met Day in the 1950s, while I was going to medical school and did volunteer work in one of the Catholic Worker hospitality houses. She could be aloof, moody, and intimidating. In the 1970s I talked with her in order to write a history of the newspaper *The Catholic Worker.*

She had memories of her early years as the coeditor of that newspaper, as one of its major contributors, and, of course, as the energetic organizer of a soup kitchen, a place where some homeless people could have a temporary stay. She, too, had memories of herself: "I never planned it this way—that I'd be called the leader of anything. There was a long time when I had trouble leading my own life, never mind having a thought or two about how others should lead theirs! I get letters, still, from people who say all these wonderful compliments—that they're 'inspired'; and I have to smile to myself, because for me the book [*The Long Loneliness*] is a confessional, much of it. I know how distant I could be—off in my own world! I learned how to 'make confession' when I became a Catholic. Many of my friends back then, in the late 1920s and early 1930s, were 'confessing' to psychoanalysts; I was going to priests! They'd tell me that they didn't see their analysts, they sat behind the couch; and I'd say, the same with us at the church—the priests are also out of sight when you go to tell them what you've been doing, and ask for forgiveness. Of course, they'd tell me I should forget the forgiveness stuff: I needed to go see a psychoanalyst to *understand* myself—that was 'the bottom line.' I wasn't against understanding. Who would be? But I'd try to help them understand what the Church had come to mean to me. I'd say that understanding is a step toward forgiveness, that if we can find reasons to forgive ourselves, then we can be in better shape to take on the world—but I'm afraid their assumptions and mine had become quite different. To tell you the truth, I think these days [the 1970s], it's changed: priests are more interested in psychology, and psychoanalysts 'understand' the limits of pure understanding that isn't accompanied by some human gesture. But I've gotten us off the subject here."

In a way she had, though I was impressed by what she had said, and that phrase, "human gesture," has echoed in my mind over the years as I have listened to some of my colleagues and myself: the temptation to try to be cleverly abstract, to put one's confidence in the cognitive side of mental life—those clarifications and interpretations of emotionality that we offer our patients in the name of psychiatric and psychoanalytic healing.

Dorothy Day brought us back to a discussion of the vicissitudes she experienced as a leader of a social, political, and religious movement— she did so by addressing an interesting aspect of medical as well as psychiatric practice, and indeed, of social science as it aspires toward the "objectivity" of the natural sciences: "I used to listen to my friends talk of their experiences in analysis—that was the phrase they started using, 'in analysis.' They learned X 'in analysis,' and they learned Y, and then, I'd notice, it would be 'my analyst says'—about everything: it was as if they'd surrendered themselves to someone else, and they had to keep telling the world what that someone else thought about everything. I know, I've read about 'transference,' about ways patients react to their doctors, turn them into parents, gods! I once said to one of my old friends: you've turned yourself over, lock, stock, and barrel to this other person and you don't even know who he is, *really*—what he believes in and how *he* behaves. He's busy 'working things out' with you, but who *is* he, and since everything is so 'subtle,' you keep on saying, what kind of subtle messages are you learning from him?

"I was worrying about the erosion of her values and principles. She'd been a fighter, a labor organizer; and now she was spending her time in libraries studying sociology and psychology, and she was telling everyone that the best thing we can do is figure out things, figure out how the mind works and how our society functions. I thought to myself, yes, no one can argue with that, really, but she doesn't see what's happening to her: there's a big shift taking place in her moral life—she's absorbing the beliefs of her doctor, and putting aside her own, past beliefs, and her actions, and she's *unconscious* of that (God forbid!), and maybe her doctor is, too! He's giving her more *direction* than either of them fully realizes, that was my thought. But I'll tell you, the Church helped me there—I'd learned by then to be on guard against the sin of pride: I could feel the smugness in my heart, and to be honest, I think it showed in my eyes, and maybe a thin smile that would come over my face! I remember catching myself. I talked to myself: 'Dorothy, if she's being "taken in" by someone unwittingly, then how about you and the people who work with you?' Peter Maurin had always warned me that if you're going to teach people, you'd better be clear about what you want to come of it, because a teacher is a leader, and if a teacher doesn't know that, there's trouble to pay!"

She had gotten at the whole matter of a "value-free" psychoanalysis, proclaimed for so long as both desirable and possible (as in Heinz Hartmann's *Psychoanalysis and Moral Values*). But she had also managed to bring up the subject of moral leadership as it takes place not in politics or religion or in our educational institutions but in our clinical offices, where doctors see patients for "troubles" and end up becoming more than healers, or maybe, healers in the larger sense, that is, guides who prompt, persuade, suggest, direct, even inspire.

Similarly with her and her work: we were, after all, discussing her experience as a leader, her realization that the major issue for her was no longer what words to put on paper (though she would always be a writer) but what words to say to others around her, and to what purpose, and with what effect. Nor were words all that mattered, as she gradually discovered—again, with the help of her cofounder: "Sometimes I'd try hard to get it right, what I'd tell the people in the office [of *The Catholic Worker*], or on the soup line, but it wouldn't work, what I'd said. Peter would remind me later that it's not only what you say, but *how you say it*. You know, that's pure common sense; it's 'folk wisdom'—and yet how many of us really remember that!

"That's why I keep mentioning Peter—he taught me a lot about how to get along with others. I get so tired of being told that I was the one who got the newspaper going and I was the one who turned our idea of feeding the hungry into a reality. I keep telling people that it was Peter who got this going in me and in others—but then I'll be told that he 'energized' me, and that's that! He was a leader, a moral leader, looking for some people who would link arms with him. Notice I didn't say he was a leader looking for followers! I've read many accounts of our struggles here [at St. Joseph's House] and in other places [hospitality houses], and Lord, so often the visitors mean well; they want to write favorable stories, but they miss something. They're always trying to figure out who's the head, who started this, or they've decided before they come here that they know the answers already, and all they need to do is fill in a few blanks by asking me some questions. When I try to steer them away from me, when I talk about Peter, and what he meant to us, or when I try to get them to interview others, they're made uncomfortable, or they get impatient. (I'm an old journalist and I know all the signs!)

"I wrote a note to myself once, after a long interview with a reporter; I said when people come here and ask questions, I think they usually reveal more about themselves—their view of this world—than they end up learning about us, because I notice that when I tell them what I regard to be God's truth about our life at the *Worker,* they right away want to understand it through their values rather than learn about ours. That's why I'm always being asked about my 'leadership role,' and my 'reason for deciding to start the Catholic Worker Movement.' I'll try to be polite, and I'll try not to be angry and dismissive. But it can be very frustrating and hard—for them as well as me.

"Once, a while back, I totally lost control! I became mischievous. I teased the man. He asked me the usual questions (what, why, how); and he wanted to know my 'style as a leader,' how I 'work with others.' I told him I'd never thought about it; I told him we never really thought too far in the future—we weren't planners. We just went with our hearts and we prayed and prayed for direction from God and His son. I could see the disbelief all over his face. The idea of prayer as a means of making decisions—he must have thought that we're naïve, or foolish and superstitious, or maybe that we had our clever strategies and schemes, even though we were pretending that we were throwing ourselves at the mercy of Jesus! Yes, that's what I told him, that we were throwing ourselves at the Lord's mercy, and his face radiated mistrust and suspicion! So I tried to be nicer—to help him. I became very serious—I'd *been* serious but I really *looked* serious now. I told him about Peter Maurin, who he was. I told him how he spoke, and how he could waken up your spiritual side. I told him about that phrase 'wanted doing'—I thought it would help him write his story: it's a way of understanding how we think and talk, and he said he wanted to get to 'fundamentals.'

"You know, that was the hardest, rather than the easiest [for the reporter]. I suddenly realized that he thought I was being a tease! He thought I was pretending to be a dreamy, mystical person who didn't know what she was doing, really, but who had stumbled into something (by chance, maybe)—when all the while I knew exactly what I was trying to do. I didn't know what to say beyond what I'd said already. I kept repeating that. I was trying my best to live the way Jesus told us we should try to live, and I was failing sometimes, but my 'goal' (he kept using that word: what are your goals?) was to keep trying, the best I could.

"We'd reached an impasse. He was getting fidgety, crossing and uncrossing his legs, and looking at his list of questions over and over. He told me once more that he was sent there to do a piece on me—how I functioned as a 'convert,' a woman, doing what I was doing. What's my style as a leader? That was his big question. His editor had asked that, and he was trying to get the answer—and I wasn't giving him much to go on! I told him, finally, that the problem was this: leadership isn't only something in you, in a person—your personality; leadership depends on where you are as much as who you are, and it depends on the company you're keeping. That's why I was trying to get him to spend more time with our folks here, including our guests (the needy people being served lunch, for example) instead of asking me all these personal questions about my 'motives' and my 'authority,' and my 'style of management.' Every time he did that I came back at him with a plea that he realize how much of our actions depend on the people we're here to learn from: we take our cues from them. But he'd have no part of that—and I don't mean to be sly or smug when I say that. The truth is, he reminded me of myself—and not just me as I was when I was a young reporter, but me as I was when I was talking with him, and as I'll always be! I guess that I was *also* someone a bit different then, when I was talking with him, because of what had happened to me [her conversion], and where I was living [in a tenement building at the edge of New York City's Bowery], and because of all that, I had a different idea of what that word 'leadership' means than he did, or his editor—or I myself, my old self that's still a part of me!"

For me, at the time, to hear such remarks was to step in the shoes of that reporter. I conjured him up in my mind, his appearance, the frustrated look on his face as he conversed with her, because, like him, I had trouble accepting Dorothy Day's version of her leadership. She struck me as having a strong personality—self-possessed, even her quiet spells a force to be reckoned with; and, not least, politically shrewd. Indeed, I'd heard her talk of her complex relationships with various church officials who worried that her outspokenly radical social vision (and her unqualified pacifism) would be interpreted by many as explicitly sanctioned by the Church. I'd also heard her discuss national politics—this was no naïf! She could read between the lines of *The New York Times,* and garner from a perusal of various stories "all the news" that *wasn't* "fit to print." She could even make penetratingly astute comments about various politicians—of a kind they themselves, out of their daily experiences, knew to make. Indeed, at such seemingly offhand moments I felt I was in the presence of one of those politicians: a person who was thoroughly in touch with realpolitik, who had in her mind a Rolodex of sorts whose phone numbers would put her in touch with, well, power. She knew influential writers and academics, and she knew who they knew. She knew, finally, the importance of a printed story, be it in a newspaper or a magazine. She had, after all, herself been a longtime reporter, and she had worked hard, in her secular activist years, to change laws, to provoke authority in order to shift the nature of its asserted domain.

In other conversations with her I'd heard that side of her asserted without embarrassment or shame—in fact, I had the impression that for her a lack of political savvy in a reformer or activist had to be regarded as not only a pragmatic flaw but a moral failure. Once she'd even, by not so subtle implication, spelled out that line of reasoning: "If you're going to try and change things, you'd better have your wits about you. One thing you can be sure of—those who are your opponents know exactly what's at stake. If you don't know that—if you assume their innocence or naïveté and (I hate to say it) their good intentions, then what you don't know will be your undoing, and you can take down others with you, so you're carrying a lot of responsibility on your shoulders."

What I remember most about those words was their resemblance to remarks made by Robert Kennedy as he tried to tell us doctors about the tough reality of politics. I also remember a visual moment: her blue eyes, directed right at mine, a slight glint to them. Though the words make her sound more than slightly canny, she looked to me like a tough old fighter who had waged many a struggle, known not a few prison stays, had long ago found out what makes for success, what increases the odds of failure, when it comes to taking on "principalities and powers," a phrase she naturally knew well, and was not rarely inclined to use.

How, then, to reconcile this secular, shrewd mind, this forceful presence, with her avowals of virtual ingenuousness, inexperience, and innocence? She was a perplexed, newly converted Catholic young mother, husbandless and vulnerable and unsure of herself, who unaccountably became the lucky spiritual confidante of a man, Maurin, whom so many others regarded as a well-intentioned wanderer, far from adept at dealing with either people or the requirements of daily living, but whom she honored as the one who envisioned the need for a particular social and intellectual movement within the Catholic Church, and more than anyone else, herself included, helped turn such a dream into an effective organizational reality.

A Loner Learning to Lead—To Get Along with People

She knew what was her own downside—the melancholy that could work its way into her thoughts and her way of getting along with others. Moreover, she had always been an introspective loner, for all her ability to be appealing, lively in company—and that side of herself, she knew, imperiled her involvement in the community of Catholic Worker Movement people who lived and labored together.

When I asked her to describe Peter Maurin to me, it was as if she was addressing that aspect of herself by indirection. She emphasized his unassailable hopefulness, which she attributed to a kind of faith that was not hers to take for granted. She spoke of his selflessness, his eagerness to reach and teach others. I had my (psychoanalytic) doubts about anyone's selflessness, and she made clear she understood what I suppose could be called, ironically, the narcissism of selflessness, the way one can attract attention to oneself, gain satisfaction for oneself, through an insistent, apparently sacrificial interest in others.

She even went further, addressing what might be called the psychology of sainthood, and called Maurin "saintly"; she told me that such people are "extravagant" in their generosity—a reckless ambitiousness, of sorts, I thought she was implying, though she was unwilling to put the matter quite that way. I tried to amplify, spoke of the "enterprise," the "push," that even a saint would possess. "I think some of our saints have thrown caution to the winds," she replied, and gave this as their reason: "They are called by God to behave as they do, and the rest of us can't figure out His reasons, or theirs."

Protecting Against the Darker Sides of Altruism

Maurin was her spiritual *leader,* so she firmly believed. Finally, I began to realize the nature of his role in her life as a moral leader: he lacked some of the qualities or traits that in herself she least liked. No matter what others had every right and reason to think of her, she herself had quite another sense of what she had done! She had an eye, that is, for the darker side of her altruism.

Some of that candid self-criticism had been publicly acknowledged in her autobiography. I heard even more expansive references to her bouts of "arrogance," her moments of disregard for the worries or apprehensions of others. At the time I thought such self-confrontations excessive, themselves an aspect of her pride; though, Lord knows, an expressed repentance as a defensive maneuver against moments of self-importance or self-absorption has to be compared to other more familiar aspects of what George Eliot called our "unreflecting egoism," a phrase used in *Middlemarch,* which Day had read and read—a smugness and a self-satisfaction, for example, that all too often go unchecked in the secular world. She was quite clear, actually, about what life had been like for her before the confessional booth became a much-sought place of a self-examination: "I'm afraid many of us who were fighting the good fight on behalf of social justice had no sense of humor about ourselves, no ear for our own self-righteousness. We could be scolds! Pity anyone who didn't share our tastes or values! I remember with great pain what we thought of others, said of them—those not belonging to 'us.' "

She extolled confession as a saving necessity for herself—and then she was remembering Peter Maurin this way: "He had less vanity than anyone I ever met! Yes, we all do have vanity, I know. But he was too scattered and helter-skelter in his ways to be vain. Vanity requires a concentration of effort—a commitment to something that makes you pleased but tempts you to go too far, to become all too pleased! Peter would be here and there, he'd be all over the place; it was as if he was an errand boy for the Lord, and not himself, someone trying to fulfill his own agenda! I once heard someone say about Peter, 'He's not really of this world, but he's not otherworldly, either, and so he sure gets a lot going without being in the way.' "

She was getting us close to the heart of the matter: a certain kind of moral leadership of a moral agent for her—Peter's psychological qualities enabled him to become a much-needed lay-confessor or spiritual guide, but also a person who enabled Day's idealism to be implemented in daily life through her various involvements with others. Without him, she was convinced, the Catholic Worker Movement would not have been realized. "I've always been a private person, and yet here I am, living in a community—no great privacy here! From the very start I had all these ideas, but I didn't know how to put them into action. I knew how to picket or protest, or write articles; but I didn't know how to take personal and daily responsibility for what I'd done on the streets or written—I mean, live it all out. I always wanted my own place; I wanted to be alone at times—even when I was in love with someone! A place where I could go and read and write, stare out of the window, look at a tree, the squirrels running all over it, look at birds perched or playing, flying—that was my idea of happiness. True, there are other kinds of happiness—but I guess what I'm trying to say is that I'm not a 'social animal,' and yet I've ended up living closely with others, and if I became a 'leader' (as so many people call me)—then it's been a strange psychological evolution!

"That's where Peter is the key; he was the one who turned my head around! I'd be out there hawking our paper, or protesting something, and then I'd want to go off and be by myself, or be with Tamar [her daughter] and no one else—but there Peter would be, reminding me of what had to be done, giving me his pep talks. I'd be grouchy, and he'd be mentioning those Bible stories and telling me, 'Dorothy, this is our big chance, right now—*here!*' No wonder I quote Catherine of Siena at the start of *The Long Loneliness* ['All the way to heaven is heaven']. I can hear Peter saying to me that there is *here* and there is *heaven,* and our job is to bring the two as close together as possible.

"Now, you know, I could come up with that idea—borrow it from Catherine, and put it into the vernacular of this time and place; but to go further and make those words actually mean something *real* (to live out what I'd written or spoken)—that was 'something else again,' as our young people put it.

"There's where Peter turned me around: he taught me how to get on with people—not at a cocktail party, I knew how to do that, and not at a rally or a conference, I was an old veteran, but in my life. We started with a soup kitchen, and in no time we had a community of us, living together. It wasn't 'us' versus 'them,' a few with 'ideas' and 'ideals' and the hungry poor 'we' worked to feed; it was a mix of people—some who had no place to stay, and 'us,' who were searching, you could say, for *our* place to stay!

"Can you imagine how difficult that transition was for me—and for my daughter? There were times when I wanted to flee for my life: I'm not just using an expression—I wanted *out*! I'd be rude or irritable or short-tempered. I'd go to my room and look at myself in the mirror and see a phony, or someone in deep trouble: I'd be saying one thing but doing another—I'd be nowhere near living up to what I told others I believed! Thank the Lord for being there to hear me, and thank the Lord for Peter, because he was there, too—he'd reassure me, or he'd tell me that we had no time to worry about our mistakes, or try to second-guess ourselves, because there was *this* to do, and *that*. He'd say things I just couldn't get out of my mind—that we were living for Jesus, so we can't be bothered by ourselves. He meant by that the petty worries we all have: I didn't say the right thing, or I made a big mistake when I did X or Y or Z! 'Dorothy,' he'd whisper, 'let's try to forget ourselves and help others do likewise.'

"Easier said than done! But it wasn't long before his words were in my head—in a big way! I'd quote him, of course. But more important, I'd think of what I'd learned from him while I was talking with our people [her coworkers], or with our guests [who came to be fed], or with my old friends. They [the people she'd known in her 'secular days', as she called them] thought that I was 'different' because I was a 'convert'—I was 'spouting church talk,' I'd be told. But the truth is I was learning how to be polite with people and considerate of them, and firm sometimes when firmness was needed, but firm in a way that didn't result in hurt feelings. I was learning to be an administrator— not an opinionated writer or journalist or party-goer! They thought I'd become 'prayerful,' but I think 'polite' was more like it: I was praying, all right—for the patience and tact to be able to be one of the people in charge. I hated to be called a founder of our paper, or the leader of our 'movement' (I didn't like that word 'movement' one bit). But I was the someone who had to make decisions: people did come to me, looking for direction, and it was Peter who made me aware of the fact that I had to be aware of what a leader is, who a leader is, what kind of person you become when you're being held up by people, and they're looking to you for 'nods and nays,' Peter would put it."

She had much more to say about her increasingly astute ability to work reasonably well in an "organization." She remembered, actually, when she was first told about her "organizational role," her "leadership style"—by a Catholic sociology graduate student, who immediately incurred her wrath, until she realized how accurately he had taken the measure of things. She did indeed know how to smile on some occasions, appear worried on others. She knew how to ask others to do one task or another in a quiet, unassuming way, sometimes with an apology for doing so. She knew how to call "time out"—to suggest the need for collective prayers. She knew how to be self-effacing—when, in truth, she was very much trying to get her point across. I'd see that happen— she would speak softly, to the point that she was almost mumbling; and as a consequence, the one(s) addressed would draw nearer, pay more attention to what she was saying. She sometimes prefaced her suggestions or requests with impersonal phrases that clearly were the progeny, as it were, of Maurin's legendary "wanted doing." For example, she'd say "I'm told that" something "requires action," or "It's been said that we ought to think about how [or when] we get to" do a particular job.

When I asked her about those "passive-voice constructions" she looked at me as if I "wanted" some praying for—I'd used a pretentious way of talking that was, maybe, too clever by half. Yet I thought I saw a look of self-recognition in her eyes, and she did give it right back to me, so to speak, with this terse reminder of where I was: "Here we're trying to be the Lord's servants—He uses us all the time; that's our faith." God the leader, the hidden one who is also the source of energy and inspiration for her and those with whom she worked! God the active voice, and us trying hard (hope against hope) to be instruments of His, *that* kind of "passivity"! I have no doubt of the utter sincerity that informed her stated conviction. But I also observed firsthand the way such an article of faith freed her to be a vigorously active person; and as I heard her talk and talk of the past, I eventually realized that she had, indeed, learned how to be a convincing moral leader with the help of someone with whom she worked in tandem, and whom she regarded as a master teacher—or rather, an emissary of *the* master of all of us.

A Moral Routine

Time after time during our conversations, she wanted to give Peter Maurin credit for helping her understand what it means to be in charge—what it requires and what it costs. "Peter kept reminding me that even in the voluntary action undertaken by a group of people, some look up to others, and if you try to ignore that—well, it's foolish. 'Better tell yourself, every once in a while, where you're going, Dorothy,' he'd say, and at first I didn't pay much attention. He was emphasizing that I needed to look at what I was doing through the eyes of others—think of their lives while I was thinking of my plans, projects, programs, proposals! You can overdo that, and get nowhere: lots of times you have to plow on, and hope and pray others will join you; but every so often you ought to call a halt to yourself and ask yourself the big questions, and Peter made sure I did that."

Obviously, I wanted to know how her friend did so—how this somewhat disorganized, passionate man who had wandered the world as a laborer and itinerant preacher of Christ's message had managed to whip her into meditative shape, to get her to pay close heed to the longer haul while she was so fully involved in "a moment to moment hurly-burly life," as she once described the early years of her Catholic Worker efforts. "I always had work to do, and besides, I reminded him I was not a complete stranger to looking inside myself, to questioning myself." Still, Maurin pressed her for a more specific contemplative acknowledgment on both of their parts—a moral routine, a considered moral self-examination.

Of what kind? She had, finally, asked him that question. He wanted to institutionalize a kind of shared and formal conversation on their part with respect to moral leadership—to do so in a humble, streetwise way that contrasts instructively with the endowed institutes, and their curricula and seminars that are the vehicle for various ethics programs in our universities. "Time for a walk," he'd tell her, with a serious look. She knew then that he had "business on his mind." She knew then that he wanted to "look down the road," and also "look back," examine what had happened, see if they'd not fallen short in certain important respects. So the two often set out, kept moving, gabbed and gabbed, wore out the leather. Sometimes they lost all sense of time and place— not in self-absorption, but quite the opposite: a forthright discussion of "ideals and practicalities," as she described it, quickly letting me know of a borrowed phrase: Peter had often used those words to get them going, to give their moral agenda a brief delineation of sorts.

Dilemmas of Leadership: "Serpents and Doves"

She remembered many dilemmas of leadership—*the tension between high purposes and their daily, attempted realization.* The refrain "serpents and doves" (the polarity of shrewd calculation against innocence) echoed in her ears as she went about her chores and thought of new directions. She had always been a dreamer and an idealist, if not a moralist, but now she had to be constantly pragmatic. How to get food for a soup kitchen? How to pay the bills for a place where she and others lived and worked? How to keep a newspaper going—attend the costs and, as well, the attitudes and concerns of those who worked on it? How to present one's views to others in that larger world of the press, the universities, the Church as an institution with its own cultural and political life? When to say what to whom, and why? She could be ever so candid with herself, and sometimes quite forthcoming with certain others; but she could also be terse, tight-lipped—and she knew to worry on both counts, because she had learned that some would take her words, her confidences, and use them for their own purposes, and others would respond to her silences with the noise of irritation or with an unexpressed, longer-lasting resentment.

All the while she had to carry on a conversation with herself, remind herself of this, tell herself that, pat herself on the back for one thing, remonstrate with herself for something else. Now she wasn't creating characters in her head for a fiction, or taking note of real-life people for a piece of nonfiction, but living and working with men and women, who played off against one another in ways she knew how to describe as a writer but in this new life had to encourage or discourage. Not rarely she was too fast on the draw—she spotted trouble right away, maybe even saw it around some corner, but didn't have the patience, the psychological or practical know-how, that would have kept her annoyance or bitterness or disapproval under wraps so that a natural rhythm of talk, of human engagement, would gradually iron out a particular emotional wrinkle.

In one of the last talks I had with her, in 1974 in New York City, as I was trying to learn of her life, her beliefs, her sense of what she had accomplished, and what she had hoped to do but hadn't, she was frank to speak of what it means to be held up high by others, even as one lives with plenty of self-doubt, not to mention an ounce or two of self-accusation. She was also ready to reflect upon what moral leadership requires of one and, of course, what it means to those who seek it, and find it, in others. Gradually, through "the college of hard knocks," she had acquired an education: some knowledge about how to work with others, and a sense of how to inspire them, while at the same time developing a capacity to be inspired by them—affirmed by their willingness to be attentive.

"For the longest time," she remembered, "the word 'leader' never entered my mind. We all had a 'leader'; He was Jesus. That is what I'd say to myself, but to be honest, I'd have to admit that I wasn't being so honest with myself. I knew there are cardinals and bishops and priests, and of course the pope, so it's not only Jesus, it's His designates, I guess you could call them, here on earth: they're our leaders. The same holds for all of us who aren't in the Church's hierarchy. We have our commitments, and we find people who represent them for us: they're 'stand-in' folks for us; they represent what we believe, in a different way a priest or a bishop does for our secular life. I mean, I know a lawyer who admired Learned Hand, the federal judge—he'd go to court to hear the judge, and he had no reason, as a lawyer, to [do so]. He told me he needed to 'check in' with Judge Hand—needed to get a 'boost' from him. I asked my friend why, and he told me that he needed to have someone to look up to, a believable moral figure, and Judge Hand was it for him. His trips to the judge's courtroom were a pilgrimage, I realized.

Learned Hand in Dorothy Day's Mind, and in Life

"Sometimes I'd catch myself thinking of Judge Hand! I'd wonder what he was really like. I'd wonder whether he lived up to his reputation. I'd wonder who *he* admired—and if he ever sought someone out, the way my lawyer friend did. I'd wonder what Judge Hand would think if he knew of that lawyer, sitting there in the courtroom, looking at him, looking up to him. I wondered whether the judge would be embarrassed or worried or pleased—maybe all three! I wondered if he'd be spurred to be a better judge that day, to pay closer attention to what was going on in his courtroom, because of that 'audience of one'—to speak more thoughtfully, even to be eloquent! Judges 'perform,' after all—so do we all, I've come to understand."

Here she stopped for a moment, took a sip of tea, looked away, her eyes half closed and registering obvious psychological withdrawal from the immediate setting. Soon enough, she was apologizing for the lull in her expressed train of thought—and pointing out the reason: she was certainly not an eminent and silver-tongued jurist whose erudition and penetrating brilliance, whose very name, summoned in others regard and deference, homage and adulation. But she knew what it was to be sought out, held in high esteem, even venerated—and she shuddered, in retrospect, at her own unawareness that such was her moral relationship to certain individuals. She returned to Judge Hand, to that word "perform"; she circled around it warily. She wondered aloud whether she had made a mistake in saying that she was "performing"—

the word had a connotation of the superficial. Moreover, if she had been a performer in the course of her duties, she'd "mostly" been "unaware" of what she'd been doing.

She had, in fact, learned that Judge Hand was himself a lover of Shakespeare, and also an amateur performer—anxious to take roles in small, informal plays, put on at home by family members or friends. A grandson of the judge's, Robert Jordan, was an actor, and she had met him—and was thereby told of Learned Hand's "attractive personality." Her memory of what she heard lit her up as she spoke: "He could be mischievous, his grandson said—he had a great sense of humor, and he loved reading poetry, and, of course, he went back to Shakespeare again and again, 'the well of wisdom,' Mr. Jordan said, speaking of both the playwright and the federal judge! I think I've admired Learned Hand for his principled decency, but also for his wisdom; he knew how to share it, everyone tells me, in his decisions, his writing—and he was not an arrogant man, for all his brilliance. That's a big achievement in life, to rise to the top and not become all full of yourself! His grandson said he was 'never stuffy or pretentious.' I still remember those words! There's the biggest achievement, to be learned (to be Learned Hand!) and to be a 'genial, kindly man,' and I recall those words well, too [of Hand's grandson]. There's the ultimate, I thought—to impress people and not be impressed with yourself! There's a moral triumph—to avoid confusing yourself with a pedestal, when you're on one, and with people!"

After a few minutes of what she herself called "stalling," she said, "I think if you're a leader to people, you'll know it in your bones, if you don't already know it in your head—and maybe then you must try hard to be modest, the way Judge Hand was. I think people like me can be in danger—we need to learn from the judge, and not get carried away with ourselves, lose ourselves in the admiring eyes of others.

"I confessed once to a priest the sin of pride: people were asking me what to do, telling me I should tell them what to do, as if I was—as if I'm their priest. But the priest didn't seem bothered one bit. I've been to confession hundreds of times, but I can still remember what I heard that time: the priest said, 'Of course, people will find other people to look up to, and be priestly in their lives.' That word 'priestly' really stuck in my thoughts: I guess I was reassured; I'd been given permission to think out loud (to myself!) that I wasn't some fraud, misleading people into believing I had an official position in the Church!

"I was constantly worrying that I'd say something 'misleading.' I'm surprised someone didn't tell me I was a worrywart on that account! I can eavesdrop right now on some of our [*Catholic Worker* editorial] meetings—I was always saying, 'Let's not be misleading!' 'Dorothy,' Peter once exclaimed, 'you're being misleading when you keep warning us about being misleading!' He was always like that—he'd pick up on what you'd say, and turn the coin over! But he didn't succeed with me, not then: I kept expressing my real fear that we'd take people down the garden path. I suppose that was my way of admitting that I was 'the camp director,' as we used to say when I was a girl—the one 'in charge.' You see, *Christ* was 'in charge': that was our faith, *is*. But Peter well knew that he and I were also functioning as leaders, even if we kept insisting (to ourselves as much as to others) that everyone was 'equal,' and a member in good standing of the 'community.' "

"In my thinking, I was the same loner, and if I had friends and lots of people near me, here at the *Worker,* I was still alone in my thinking of myself (except for Tamar, of course). I'd learned how to be a mother—and remember, a mother is a leader, too! But I hadn't in my mind become a mother to our den!

"I recall Peter giving me one of his private sermons. 'You know, Dorothy'—he always started that way—'every opportunity is a risk, so we've got to make sure all this works. You're the one who has to take the lead a lot, and we'll all be with you!'

"I recall telling a friend from my old Greenwich Village life that I was 'in an organization now'—a big contrast with our anarchist days, and I had to worry about paying bills, and I had to mediate when people didn't get along, and I had to decide what to say about *this* or *that*: 'You're our spokesman,' they'd all say! Well, my friend told me I should go study political science, and learn about 'leadership.' Lord, *that* got me going! I dropped out of college, and now they were sending me back to college! Plato, Machiavelli, Max Weber—I said yes, yes, I'll buy them and read them. I'd heard them mentioned for years by people at cocktail parties or during those intense arguments in the Village—talk about struggles for 'leadership'! Everyone seemed to know how to quote from them or how to appear to know what they'd proposed in their books, and those of us who'd never read a word from any of those books had learned to nod and seem right in there, pitching! Once I told Mike Gold [a writer friend and political activist] that I hadn't read a word of Marx, I think it was, or maybe it was Freud, but I'd absorbed their ideas reading about them, or listening to people talk about them. He told me to stick with Dickens and Dostoyevsky, my great loves! But it was different, once I was 'responsible for others'— that's what Peter kept telling me, and I didn't like those three words. They made me feel inadequate and nervous and very frightened. For a few weeks there I was reading [college] catalogues, trying to find courses that would help me be better at my job. If I was supposed to take 'responsibility for others,' I wanted to know how wise people in the past said you should do it. That friend who talked of my 'leadership role' said there are 'techniques,' and I almost believed her! To be honest, I think I was saved by my inadequacies—I'd have gone uptown to Morningside Heights [Columbia] or nearer here, to NYU [New York University], if I wasn't so overwhelmed trying to beg for the food we cooked [in her soup kitchen] and keeping up with our schedule for the paper. There was never enough time even as it was—I thought that if I left a couple of afternoons or evenings, it would put a big burden on others, and things wouldn't be working as well as before: I'd be studying 'leadership,' but I would be flunking it at the same time!"

Still, she had found time, all along, to notice what *wasn't* working especially well, or was turning out disastrously. She spoke of "keeping a notebook" in her memory, storing up "incidents," which she'd contemplate as she was trying to fall asleep, or when she woke up, suddenly, trembling with anxiety, or in a state of full awareness otherwise denied her by the headlong rush of a busy life. In the light of morning she tried to retain thoughts, oughts and naughts, that had grabbed her so tellingly during the preceding darkness, but to no avail. There was her daughter, Tamar, to attend; there were all those vulnerable souls, called "guests," jobless and ever so needy, to feed and clothe, to help find shelter or get medical care; there was newspaper copy to read and edit. Again and again she and her compatriots stopped to pray, to consider a certain passage from, say, Matthew or Luke or Mark—but then, the approaching deadline of the noon meal for the long line of hungry ones or the schedule for sending newspaper copy to the printer would demand all eyes and ears. "We forgot intention in favor of action sometimes," she lamented; but she qualified that melancholy assessment with these words: "On the other hand, I guess we hoped in our hearts that our ideals were being expressed in the way we behaved with one another, and with the people we served."

She was frank to admit that such was not always the case. Looking back to the 1930s and 1940s and 1950s, she could all too clearly recall failures of omission and commission—times when sharp words and hard feelings made her and others feel at a loss. Often on those occasions she thought back to Peter Maurin's various exhortations of her, his pestering of her through a conviction that she was a "leader," and ought assert herself as such, "a leader of principle and of principles." Nor did Dorothy Day ever really deny to herself the reasons for such an assertion on the part of her close associate and friend. She knew what she'd got going, and she also knew that the very fact that Maurin kept asking her to do things, kept suggesting things for her to do, kept wondering when she'd do things, spoke to her ultimate leadership even with respect to him, never mind all those others who worked with the two of them and regarded themselves as followers—thought themselves staff members on the paper, coworkers in the soup kitchen or on the breadline, fellow picketers or hawkers selling *The Catholic Worker*, daily, rather than *The Daily Worker*: a Christian communitarianism taking on a secular communism. But she also knew something else, knew it in the way troubled people know their troubles, sinners their sins: in her bones or gut rather than in the frontal lobes of her brain. Repeatedly she remarked upon the particular pleasure a hectic life at the *Worker* gave to her: no time at all to be stopped in her tracks by an abrupt surge of self-recognition that in the past could wear her down, even torment her. "I would hear in my voice a warning sign—I'd notice the tone before the words," she remembered; and then a quite local-ized consciousness: "I'd always think of my right forefinger, that it was itching to start wagging!"

The Danger of Self-righteousness

Righteousness becoming self-righteousness was, for her, a danger, a reason for self-arraignment, if not outright despair. She was exhilarated when she had managed to get a deeply or urgently felt point across without stooping to impatience or haughtiness. Sometimes she had tried preventative action, had almost consciously clothed her high-and-mighty side in the garb of deference. She'd asked for opinions, recom-mendations, and suggestions, even as she was not unable to notice that those so beseeched were themselves only too eager to hear *her* thoughts, and yes, follow her lead. Perhaps at times they fell silent be-cause they saw the truth in her eyes, the fierce determination that both informed her ideas and prompted her attempts to elicit theirs; but often, she fully realized, those men and women genuinely looked up to her, understood what she believed, and themselves believed what she did. In their own way they knew to ask: *who* is without sin? In their own way they knew that pride can affirm itself in a scrupulosity of self-examination that goes (egoistically) berserk, that detaches such self-observation from common sense.

In a wonderfully tactful ode of sorts to Dorothy Day, her longtime friend Frank Donovan, who worked steadfastly at her side in the Catholic Worker Movement community, made these comments on her moral leadership, its strengths and its vulnerabilities: "You've got to re-member that Dorothy was shy—the way some very strong-willed people are! I remember her coming into the room, and when she really wanted to get something done she'd walk tall and straight, but when she had her doubts, when she wasn't sure, she'd be a little stooped, and it was then that she'd want us to have our say, and she'd even apologize for not asking us sooner. I'm not saying that she wasn't genuinely in-terested in what we could contribute. She really did pay attention to us.

I could see on her face her *own* worries. But she had a second or third sense to her—she knew when to call the troops in and have a go-around! I can hear her saying that—'It's time for a go-around!' "

A Leader in Action

Frank Donovan was headed for important psychological and intellectual territory, but not the kind easy to explore with confidence and precision. He was describing a leader very much in action—when she was of two minds, she instinctively bent her ear more readily, addressed her qualms through a hearing of other sentiment. He rejected calculation on her part, favored an alternative: a moral intuition that triggered conversational inquiry—a leader deliberately linking herself to those who, reciprocally, rely upon her judgment, her sense of what matters as much as what to do. To call upon Donovan once more: "I never saw Dorothy more devoutly, even passionately Catholic than when she was trying to do something that was hard, or something that made her concerned, because she saw several sides of the issue. You could see her going through the wringer, putting herself through [it]; she tried being careful and weighing every consideration possible on her own, or she tried getting us to do that with her—but at a certain point (we all knew it had come when she'd start looking for her Bible, or if she already had it in her hands, she'd hold it tighter, or look at it for a second, maybe) there was a shift in her, on her face or in her voice. She'd stop analyzing and start praying—and then [after prayers] she'd say that if we end up failing, we'd at least have tried, and *that* would be a great success."

Moral Success: A Leader's Voyage Within

He was referring, of course, to *moral success*—a leader whose mind balanced the things of this world with the ethical mandates handed down by a church in the name of God. That was why, after she'd taken counsel with others, as described by Frank Donovan, she always asked them to pray with her—and this was no fleeting bow to piety. Rather, she became, by her own oft-mentioned description, "lost in prayer." Occasionally she immersed herself so intently in such a mix of supplication and self-directed ethical inquiry that she woke up, so to speak, seeing others quietly, politely awaiting her return: a leader's voyage within, and subsequently, a signal or two meant to indicate what had been discovered.

Frank, one last time: "We knew when to wait on Dorothy, and we knew when she'd made up her mind—and we knew she'd only gradually know, herself, what she'd concluded, so we didn't try to push things. It was as if all of us, Dorothy included, were slowly going to find our way, moment by moment and step by step. If all this sounds mysterious, or maybe mystical, then I'm afraid that's as close to it as I can come—the way we came together and made decisions, and then got ourselves organized to act on them."

To that last observation, Dorothy would add, *did* add, what Peter had sometimes virtually whispered, sometimes exclaimed: "God's ways aren't ours—but we have to find our ways to do His bidding".

When she put that aphorism before me she was trying to sort out, for my benefit, her approach to *choice,* to *decision-making,* to *leadership.* I was bringing up those words, but she dealt with what they are meant to signify concretely, intuitively; she had a narrative and introspective reply to my conceptual inquiry. She often spoke of her "split personality," her many experiences as a social and political activist that preceded her conversion to Catholicism—but thereafter, her life as one who went to church every morning, and sometimes in the afternoon or evening. Back then, churches were open all the time in Manhattan, and she would seek them out, one after the other. She had her favorites, and she went to them for aesthetic pleasure as well as spiritual uplift. When her mind had to contend with problems in the Catholic Worker Movement community (clashes of personality or opinion, disagreements with respect to what ought be done, when, and how), she listened impassively and, to some, inscrutably. She often seemed to hold her own counsel, at least for a while. But invariably she took the matter to prayer in church as well as in the privacy of her spare and small

room. Peter had encouraged her to talk openly to God, and she did
so—most forthrightly when she had the whole church to herself, so
she could speak out loud without bothering or alarming others.

"It Wells Up in Me—A Notion"

Her occasional comments about those times at church tell a lot, I think,
about a kind of moral leadership as it could "well up" (a phrase she
used repeatedly) in a mind's life, first, then be affirmed in connection
with other lives: "Before I became a Catholic I'd planned protests,
'street action,' we called it, with my friends. We argued and argued
about 'approaches.' I don't look back with regret—they were fine
people, their hearts in the right places and their minds awake and
aware! But what we were doing—*that* was what we believed in; and so
we were almost completely centered on techniques and strategies and
tactics! Yes, we did have our broader values or ideals but they were in
the back of our minds—or maybe I should just speak for myself, and
say that's how it was for me! Today, I have a different perspective of
why I'm on this earth and what I should do, and that's why I encourage
all of us to make God a part of what we do, bring God into the midst of
our 'decision-making,' as you called it, bring Him right here, as much
as we can. It would be absurd if we didn't, after all—this is 'action offered to God': what Peter kept saying when people asked him what
we're doing here!

"That is why I'm always mindful of prayer when we talk and plan
and hope and dream and worry—when we try to think of ways to do
our work better, to reach more people, to prove our beliefs worthwhile
by living them out as fully as we can. Of course we disagree, but we
have to keep remembering who we are and why we're here. 'That's
your job,' Peter once told me, and he's right, I guess, though I'd like to
think it's a job we all have: to keep our moral wits about us! So, I listen,
and I go to church, and I remember what I've heard, and I think of
Jesus, and how He lived His life, and what He told the people He met,
and the ones who became His followers, and I sit there, and then it

wells up in me, that's as close as I can get to saying what happens, it wells up in me—you could call it a 'notion' of what should happen.

"I like that word, 'notion'—to me it means something modest and personal, not a big idea that someone thought up that explains every-thing. God has given us that, the big idea, and it's up to us to respond to God in our different ways, with our notions. There have been times that I've not known what to think—and then I pray, and I tell God what I think the issues are that are before us, and I sit there, and I hope He'll help me out. Sitting there on a bench, looking up, I'll feel some answer coming to me, a notion of what we should do welling up. Then I go tell my friends what's happened."

Not that she didn't have more to do thereafter. Those "friends" had, still, their various positions or sides to uphold, their out-and-out argu-ments to make. Once she'd figured out the particular direction to pur-sue, she became more talkative, more confident, really, of what she had to say, and so more willing to use words to spell out a point of view. This contrast between an earlier relative silence and a later entrance of sorts into the conversation at hand (sometimes, more tensely, a joining of the fray) did not, of course, go unnoticed by her colleagues. By no means did they necessarily buckle under, right away or even eventually. Nor did she prevail every time. She was one of many, she insisted; and that, for her, was the biggest accomplishment of all—to have gone from Peter and her, in tandem, musing and hoping, all the way to that newspaper and those hospitality houses, in which the men and women labored and lived in "a community of souls," as Peter and she both put it. But no one doubted her singular importance or failed to recognize her moral earnestness as it found its way to expression; and everyone knew how that happened—her trips to church, her burdened and con-cerned and sometimes vexed stay there, her efforts to find her ethical way there, her return with words that seemed just a bit amplified by that sitting in a pew, that recitation of religious commonplaces, and that outpouring of a mind's remembered points of view as they have been previously uttered and are now assembled in a narrative of a kind that is presented mutely or quite audibly to another, who is the Other—God. Once she'd left those churches, ended those encounters, she was very much on her own; soon enough her friends would receive the news she felt she had received; *her* news, mind you, as she had presented it to the Lord. The hope, on her part, was that those friends would do likewise, and they did: lots of prayers that preceded various arguments and outcomes—the devil wrestled constantly and, needless to say, only with partial success. But to know of the devil (our potentially harmful egoistic assertiveness, as *it* "wells up"), to take, as a consequence, explicit reflective steps, a kind of anticipatory action aimed at blunting an inevitable psychological moral threat, is an achievement all its own: the Almighty Other embraced, and thereby, in the Lord's name, a life lived in tandem with Peter Maurin, and with all those others (colleagues or followers in moral want, even as the street's people were in physical want) to whom she and he came to mean so much in all manner of ways.

VII

Danilo Dolci, Community Organizer
and Writer: The Leader as Loner

Danilo Dolci was a social observer and writer who gave his literary and intellectual gifts to the cause of others—merged his mind's inward life with his political will, his activist's desire to change the world. He became a determined leader of poor people seemingly helpless before the might of established power—and he took on that power on his own, at considerable risk to himself, facing countless death threats from Sicily's Mafia.

In 1967, on the way from his home in Sicily to a lecture tour in South America, Dolci stopped briefly in Chicago, New York, and Washington, where for several days I had a chance to see him and talk with him—I followed him to those cities and others, heard him address audiences, respond to questions put by listeners. Weeks later, I found it hard either to define or shake off the mood he created. He could be labeled easily enough—a reformer, an advocate of downtrodden Sicilians, an exponent of nonviolence on an island with a long tradition of murderous revenge, an Italian social essayist whose vivid and detailed accounts of poverty in his nation's villages and farmlands have impressed themselves on the whole world, and finally, a moral leader who offered hope not only to Partinico or Palermo, but to the great majority of the world's men and women, the rural, impoverished people of Africa and Latin America, not to mention, in the 1970s and 1980s, our own South, our Southwest, and our Appalachia. Yet his presence did not remind me of those "facts," or of all the others I had crammed into my mind before his arrival. If there is a legend about him, one of the first things he did was to dispel it—by bringing to his listeners the lives of *others*. (We heard what it is like for someone who is not a *turista* to live under that warm Italian sun and near those lovely Mediterranean waters.)

In many respects Dolci was like Oscar Lewis, the anthropologist who gave us accessible stories of life in Latin America and elsewhere; it is possible to call them both writers, men of strong moral sensibility who were at the same time able to say what they felt in a convincing and even a lyrical fashion. They were leaders, Lewis as a social scientist, Dolci in the world of politics as a community organizer. Each of them was much more; and I suspect the enormous value of their technical and scientific work is cleverly dismissed by some of those who eagerly acknowledge the "poetry" of Lewis's *La Vida* or Dolci's *The Outlaws of Partinico*. They shared a methodology, a manner of working that emphasized giving direct voice to those described later in articles, books, and they shared an approach to data, a style of putting to vivid word what has been seen again and again. Moreover, they both took risks, one in Sicily's well-known, violent, Mafia-dominated climate, the other in the American academic world, not without *its* cabals and expressions of anger and retaliatory scorn. If they still reach, touch, and persuade people, perhaps they were gifted and effective authors but also men who were on the right track, who lived close to what is real and important without feeling any need to disguise or blunt their findings.

Young Dolci and His Need for Action

Dolci was not born close to the human misery he observed every day. He was born near Trieste, the son of a devoutly Catholic, Slovenian mother and a skeptical, moody Italian father who worked for the Italian State Railways, the vast and cumbersome bureaucracy whose improvement at the hands of the fascists made Mussolini's stock rise so high among the punctual bourgeoisie of the West. Like Oscar Lewis, who wanted to be an opera singer and sang in his leisure time, Dolci acquired an early interest in music, particularly the organ music of Bach. He also became a passionate and committed reader, to the point that his family began to worry about his health and his apparent desire to gain rather than use knowledge.

When he was seventeen, Dolci met up with Sicily; his father had been moved there, to become stationmaster in the village of Trappeto. He visited his father but did not stay with him; there was a college education to pursue in Milan, and then a career in architecture. By 1948, at twenty-four, he had finished school, become a teacher at Milan Polytechnic Institute, and written two monographs, "The Science of Construction" and "The Theory of Reinforced Concrete." He was young and he seemed to be everything that people have in mind when they use words like "eligible" and "promising."

Later in his life he would look back wryly, sardonically, through the imaginary eyes of one of today's psychiatrists, ever ready with normative labels—and so doing, he unnerved me as I listened: "I'm sure some of my teachers thought I was peculiar or strange, and now they'd know to call me 'disturbed.' I wasn't 'normal' enough to overlook the widespread hunger and disease that plagued my country, a Christian democracy. I didn't have the 'psychological resources' to carve out my own destiny without worrying too much (neurotically) about others. My emotions seemed to be getting the better of my common sense—and my parents were desperately worried. All that tuition, all that education, all that proven ability seemed in jeopardy. And for what? Their son could not give them an encouraging answer—the truth was I suddenly realized that I was about to become fossilized. I was about to bury myself in a materialistic society which glorified intellect to the point where it killed feelings, those very feelings which could become actions. And I felt the *need* of action. I suddenly realized that reinforced concrete and drawing boards weren't enough. A home, a car, and all the rest—they weren't enough. Better to be penniless and in shirtsleeves and a nobody, merely alive in the midst of life . . ."

He wasn't sent away to have his head examined (and straightened out) or to get things out of his system; he took matters into his own hands and found his way to Sicily, to Nomadelphia, a Catholic community for destitute orphans run by a tempestuous, strong-minded cleric called Don Zeno, "the mad priest." For some reason Don Zeno could not keep his mouth shut. He disliked the fascists, said so, and was jailed for speaking his mind. He not only wanted to pray for the poor, he wanted to give them food and medicine, and he wanted the rich to do so also, to follow Christ's example. Some "mad" people can be insistently literal-minded! They ignore the evasions and duplicities that the rest of us learn to take for granted. Don Zeno took the Bible seriously—Matthew and Mark and Luke and John and the Acts of the Apostles and the Letters of Paul. Not every Christian falls into that kind of trap.

Dolci rather quickly showed that he was as mad, as vulnerable and earnest and generous, as the priest. He worked as his secretary. He started a small orchestra. He did menial work. He looked after the most forsaken and distrustful children, waifs whose one great fortune in life had been the circumstances that led them to Nomadelphia. Slowly, the fearful children took to Dolci, however guarded they tried to be. He was irresistible, with his music and long walks and lectures and natural friendliness and torn pants and sweaters.

In 1951, he published *Voices in the City of God,* a collection of poems that ordinary life in Nomadelphia had stimulated, poems of people close to the land, trying with all their might to make do against high odds. That same year he had to go into the Army, where he refused to be an officer—he did not want to oversee others in acts of military force often aimed at their own countrymen, unwilling for one or another reason to tow the line of a Mafia-controlled society. While he was away, Don Zeno came under intense attack from Rome—from cardinals and "liberal" politicians who found his relentless interest in poor, homeless children a thorny, embarrassing nuisance.

Italy was then strengthening herself, building herself up to resist the godless Red hordes who threatened civilization from their European steppes. Any kind of effort to reach the "hardcore" poor would be missing the awful point. There is always time for a nation to change things a little bit, make things a little better; but first the *enemy* must be defeated—and if he has become an "inside" enemy, all the more reason to drop everything and pursue him, even if he and his supporters command the loyalty of millions, who are tired of being dropped generation after generation for one urgent reason or another.

So Don Zeno's community was hounded out of existence, and in 1952, Dolci left for Trappeto to work on his own as an outspoken advocate of the poor. It would not take him long to make Rome consider Don Zeno's ideas an attractive alternative to Dolci's, who became a community organizer. The priest wanted to nourish abandoned Catholic children; his young follower had even wilder ideas, and would be far more able to survive the various pressures that rise—from nowhere it seems—when the poor press their case too hard and demand not occasional charity and a promise of heaven, but bread and work as a right.

From February 1952 to his death in 1997, Dolci spent time in Sicily and took on a succession of powers and principalities on behalf of the poor. His labor, his studies, his achievements, and inevitably his failures—which only seemed to inspire in him more effort—eventually filled a biography (*Fire Under the Ashes* by James McNeish) and a series of books that he himself has written. He worked in the smallest villages and in the cities, among farmers or fishermen and among the unemployed who live in dense urban slums. He married a peasant woman whose husband died of wounds inflicted by the armed bandits that Sicilians know so well. She brought Dolci five children from her first marriage and they had five more. For a long while they lived where they worked, and thus shared the daily circumstances that Dolci relentlessly and scrupulously described and tried to change.

Every one of Dolci's books (some have been translated into English) tells the truth he could not shirk putting into strong, intense language—and into a number of graphs, statistics, and photographs as well. In *Act Quickly (and Effectively) Because People Are Dying* (1954) he began to develop a characteristic narrative form—a mixture of moral outrage, attention to specific complaints and problems of individuals, and a more inclusive portrayal of what could be done, were those in power willing. *The Outlaws of Partinico* (1955) shows a student becoming a craftsman. The pages contain an introductory report, a series of questions and answers, and a section called "Inside Some of the Houses of Partinico." Dolci starts out as follows:

> Anyone who comes from Palermo, either by the coast road or over the mountains, his heart bursting with the beauty of the gulf, and takes the road to the Segesta and Erivce across the town, will find Partinico standing in what would seem a privileged position, in the center of an area of intensely cultivated land, between the fiefs and the sea.
>
> If he wanders further on into the backstreets, picking his way among the heaps of refuse which grow in size each day and trying to avoid the slops which may be thrown without warning from the houses, he will come upon wild and dirty children, cripples and signs of mourning in great abundance.

Then come essays on "How They Live," and "How They Are Governed," and "What Are the Possible Solutions?," in which statistics live side by side with social criticism and sharp, detailed documentary observation of customs and habits. At the end Dolci stands aside and lets others talk: "When we come by some bread, it's only luck. We're in the hands of Providence. You should come in the winter, when the sleet blows in on us, and then you'd see what the house is like."

He stayed, and he also looked into other areas of Sicily. Everywhere it was the same: merciless and feudal exploitation that goes under the name of "law and order"; an ornate and effectively distracting kind of mysticism; widespread illiteracy; and for hundreds of thousands, the unconditional and unrelieved fate of hunger, disease, and idleness. Men become bandits to eat. Priests have to risk all sorts of punishments if they make any open alliance with the workers. Lawyers, doctors, and teachers write off suffering as inevitable, injustice as part of life—and make sure *their* lives remain protected and comfortable. Above just about everyone stands the incredibly persistent and adaptive Mafia, whose emissaries work in Rome as well as Sicily, and cross the Atlantic constantly for the United States.

All this Dolci challenged, slowly at first, but eventually head-on. Article Four of the Italian constitution states "the right of all citizens to work" and recognizes the government's responsibility to insure "the conditions necessary to render this right effective." Dolci took the law at its word and organized a fast and a "strike in reverse." If men have no work, yet live in squalid huts without sanitation and clean water or even decent roads nearby, then let the government see its citizens take matters into their own hands by working for nothing, by doing what cried to be done. No one can very well refuse men the right to obey a law that is explicitly declared in the constitution—or so Dolci and his followers ironically suggested. They started to work on an old dirt road that badly needed repair, and were soon arrested. The government was embarrassed and publicly so because reporters were on hand to record the event; as was Dolci, of course—a prisoner who would later describe the whole, grotesque scene of events in a book titled *Article Four of the Constitution on Trial* (1958).

Years afterward Dolci showed no signs of slowing down. His articles, pamphlets, and books continued to come forth, one after another. *Inquiry in Palermo* (1956) turned out to be his masterpiece. Some threescore men and women speak out of the depths of their grim, heartbreaking, and stubborn lives. Their stories are unforgettable. As individuals they defy those who want them all to be one way or the other: thoroughly beaten or ready for any chance to protest; only noble and proud or only tired and brutal; full of every possible wisdom or so ignorant and exhausted that their level of existence has to be called "subhuman" by those who specialize in assigning people to their proper places. Dolci calls them "witnesses"—men who work, like a fisherman, an organ-grinder, a goatherd, or a shoemaker, and their luckless neighbors who can find nothing to do, and speak like this:

"I've been unemployed for three years. I used to work in the fruit trade; I packed oranges, lemons and mandarins in wooden cases, which I stacked on my shoulders and carted away. I can't rest. I've forgotten what it's like to live in peace. I can't even enjoy my children's company any longer. I do nothing all day long but sit or stand about like an idiot, wishing I had something to eat."

Waste, cries Dolci; lives are wasted, and land and water and timber. In 1964, his book *Waste* spelled it all out: energy spent by desperately poor people—in murder and violence, or in futile, pointless exertions of one sort or another; landslides or soil erosion; water ignored or allowed to go its own way rather than being brought under the control of dams and canals; diseases that exhaust and prematurely kill people—and animals and crops and even trees.

Dolci always asked questions of himself and of the people whose fate he so actively and continually shared. "Men and women, how should they be? What should be changed in the life of this area? How?" The answers came, too—in *A New World in the Making* (1965) and his *Chi Gioca Solo* (1966), taken from the aphorism *"Chi gioca solo non perde mai,"* or "Who plays a lone hand never loses." Again and again Dolci and his coworkers learned how divided, isolated, and suspicious poor people become. Not only in Sicily, of course, do the poor sometimes "play a lone hand." Wherever they live, Dolci insisted, from the first years of life they learn how useless it is to ask for what is needed, how impossible it is to get the action that is needed.

Yet someone has to say no, that it is not hopeless and that things can be done by organizing, by striking, by fasting, by pressing fact upon fact upon the newspapers, the intellectual community, the nation, and indeed the world. Dolci conveyed that message to thousands of his countrymen, and word of his deeds spread around the world. As I listened to him, in the late 1960s, I was struck by his earnest, calm, and matter-of-fact manner. He was grave but not dour, stubborn but not rigid. He was a devoted listener as well as speaker. He would not think of defeat: "We cannot afford the luxury of losing." There was nothing flashy or rhetorical or dramatic about his presentation, yet he firmly established his presence at once.

He was a man who deserved knowing. In the America of the 1960s and early 1970s, which he visited, others were taking up the same struggle he had waged. Middle-class youths or professional men worked in slums as teachers, or "community organizers," or planners, or whatever, so he noticed. Their work was not easy, and the resistance they encountered was not always as gross or explicit as the kind Dolci had to face. In a sense, though, the dangers were the same. The helper can become a new oppressor—the victim becomes a pawn in a brutal, ideological plan or program. The concrete needs of the poor are brushed aside, and instead abstract goals are formulated, always in the name of some future that is on the drawing boards. The self-appointed leaders know what is best, and use their knowledge (a form of capital if ever there was one) to frighten and cajole those who wish to "help." Doctrines are pitted against doctrines, and in the name of "progress" one hears angry, arrogant charges and countercharges.

To have resisted that direction may well be Dolci's greatest triumph. In other countries, friends and supporters have flocked to him and organized to help him do his work, his organizing, though no great support came to him from Americans—and a Nobel prize never went to this patient, nonviolent man who used the kind of guile Christ sanctioned when He called upon the imagery of serpents and doves in characterizing the way men must act, as "sheep in the midst of wolves." Grace is not one of those "reliable" things than can be measured or even defined, but its power persists, even in this century—among unknown men all over, and in a few persons like Danilo Dolci, whom many of us are fortunate enough to know about and thus share.

During the days I was lucky to be in the same room with Danilo Dolci, and walk beside him on American streets, to hear him struggling for expression, to narrate a story, to recite the particulars of Sicilian poverty, and indeed, of hunger and social or economic vulnerability anywhere, I marveled at his energy, his vigor of step and attack—a man then in his fifties who was constantly suggesting directions for us to pursue with our legs or our tongues. "It is best," he once said, "to keep on the move," and then a personal statement in which a social observer and longtime interviewer with the skills of an Oscar Lewis, a Studs Terkel, made clear his reasons, both personal and moral: "I am a 'community organizer,' some of you in America would call me. I have spent years in Sicily, in Italy, trying to learn what I can do with others, in their company, for their cause. I talk with people, one person after another. I try to learn from them. They are my teachers: I am their student. My ears help me hear of their lives, and with my mouth I try to tell them what I'm trying to know. A person who interviews another person, who is called, over time, an 'interviewer,' is someone on the move, by necessity: one seeks out others, at their convenience, and leaves with their stories, their memories, their experiences put into statements, their troubles or worries, or their wishes—what they would like life to bring them, to their families and friends, their neighbors. To interview people [as in his *Sicilian Lives,* translated and published in English in 1981] you must keep looking, keep in movement, until you find someone you like, admire, someone whose thoughts, ideas, you'd like to hand over to others: you, the interviewer have met a person whose life will reach and teach many others, you hope, through your interest in putting questions before the person, and getting the answers down. Those answers are, I insist, a sacred treasure: life as it has been lived offered to you, listening with pen or pencil or paper, with a tape recorder machine—the gift of stories that tell of daily struggles, of labor spent, of trials, of losses, of victories, all part of someone's time spent here on this earth."

A big stop, at that point, as he mulls over what he has said and tries to pull it together for himself, for his fellow walker, with whom he has been talking (about how he goes about talking with others, earning their time, patience, cooperation, their willingness to engage with him in a shared effort of conversation, introspection). Then, a sustained bout of reflection, often delivered in forthright spells of personal revelation, ethical contemplation: "I have tried to shake the hands of some of my countrymen, in Sicily, in Italy, whenever I am sitting and hearing individuals speak of what it means for them to try to make a living, to work in the fields, coaxing the land to be friendly, or in a factory. I keep saying that I talk with others, but if they teach me a lot, I try to be the one who brings others to them; that is an interviewer's good fortune, his responsibility, to do his best to tell accurately of a life met, and do that with all the intuition you can find in yourself—it's this quality in you that brings you closer and closer to others, so that you really do get some sense of who they are, what they are getting out of life, for what 'reasons of the heart.' "

A Leader Becomes a Fighter

He talks of Sicily, his many years at work there among the poor, the hurt, the "imperiled," he called them at one point: "I tried to do my best to know the society, from top to bottom. I began to realize how easy it is to fall under the influence of certain 'principalities and powers,' as the Bible warns us. In your country it is common knowledge, the Mafia and all its influence in my nation, but I wonder how many people know what is, every day, a big influence on their thinking, on how they act, what they do (and why)—even without the Mafia, as in any way a part of their world, their living. The Mafia serves a purpose, I began to realize long ago when I was young: it is *there,* it stands for evil and malice and greed and murder, for selfishness as it gets organized, but it also helps people to feel more in control of their lives, and far more privileged than they are, in fact. They can say 'I'm so glad I'm not living under the shadow of the Mafia!' But there are other shadows, less visible and less recognized. The longer and harder I tried to work with the poor, with labor union officials, the longer and harder I tried every way I could figure out so that the hungry would have a meal every day, and poor people would feel free to say what they believed to be true, free to build up their lives, and feel respect for themselves, find work in which they felt useful and get a fair wage for themselves, and not become waste, lowered that way, ignored and treated with contempt [as he describes in *Waste*]—oh, the more I gradually did come to a vision, you could call it: to be a fighter for what you believe is right, to be a leader by working all your might to stand up for it, for what you think is right, to link your own fate to the fate of others who are treated badly in a country, that means you must be on your own. That is what I meant when I used that saying, that phrase, for my book *The Man Who Plays Alone* [published in America in 1968]—I meant that book to tell others that if you want to stand up to the Mafia, and to other institutions it has subdued, made its instruments of power (in politics, in the professions, in business, even in the churches) then you must be willing to stand apart, before you stand up, and you must hope to win others over, or hope they will accept your words, your advice and counsel, so that eventually there is the solidarity of the poor, or the 'underdog,' no matter how dangerous it is for each and every one of us. If you want to lead others, you must stay clear of certain others—the Mafia and *their* underdogs! A leader who is alone, if he's willing to become a fighter, with all the dangers [that come from doing so], he can give others some courage to stand their ground, be alone!

"No," he continued, in response to some questions I posed, "I am not writing out a prescription for anyone, even including myself. Some of us who work in towns or villages or cities—'organizers,' we're called—do our jobs from within ourselves, you could say: we discover what will work in Sicily, or in London or New York City or elsewhere. We try to make known as speakers or writers what we have learned—from the mouths of others who tell us of their life, and from ourselves, living near them, and trying the best we can, the best we know, to be their brothers and sisters. If you are presuming to speak for others, to be their student [learning from them as an interviewer] then you better well know what you hold high and dear and where you'll draw the line—not go back here, and not fear going ahead there! When I hear it said that I'm leading a fight, I right away say to myself: do you know why you're getting into this fight, and what you believe will come of it, or hope might come of it? That is to say, are you free in your mind, never mind your body, of those who want to stifle your thinking, your conscience, your ability to dream on behalf of others, not only yourself? Have you really faced down not only the gangsters, the Mafioso ones, but your own frightened soul, that comes up with quick excuses, and that will do you in, finish you off, make you putty in the hands of the Mafia people, yes, yes, but also putty in the hands of those who hold *their* hands, officials in the government, and I regret to say so, in the church, too. [He had famously taken on Cardinal Ernesto Ruffini—a bulwark of the Catholic Church as it not rarely in this century got connected, unapologetically, in Italy and Spain, to fascist ideology.] That is why we have to make the life of Jesus, His teachings and His actions, our very own, not the property of badly compromised priests and pastors and politicians. A Mafia man I got to know told me once, 'Dolci, we can always beat you because we can count on lots of people who find it easy to go with us and welcome us, our money, and our influence. Your only hope is that those of you, those whose cause is yours also—that all of you know what you're willing to risk losing, even your life, and what you're *not* willing to risk losing, your honor! That's a tough road to walk, a high price to pay for choosing that road.' "

He said that, looked away, lowered his head, and nodded, as if he needed to keep his own alert, vulnerable company. He mused, for a minute or so, smiled wanly, toughened things out with a defiant but wry smile: so it has gone! So you must pay if you want to resist what you detest, uphold what you believe "true." He kept on using that last word, talked of "the true" as it can be found in lives across the world. I heard echoes of his *A New World in the Making,* and I began to appreciate what a social reformer, a community leader, a writer whose message is controversial and offends the powerful—the dangerously powerful who wield guns, intimidate even the police, the judiciary—what it all meant for him to "make" the "new world" he labored so hard to build, no matter the Mafia in Sicily, but no matter, also, the opposition that he has envisioned nonstop elsewhere on the planet: he the constant advisor to, the hero of, others who have followed his example, or seen in him spiritual kin. Indeed, sitting with Dolci, I recalled in that regard Dorothy Day telling some of us that if she ever got to Italy, she'd want to see "not bishops, even the bishop of Rome, but Danilo Dolci," whom she so hauntingly called "one of Christ's children among us."

She was referring, naturally, to Dolci's essential goodness, decency, his brave willfulness that did not flinch before the most brazen of murderous foes. Here was Dolci, in real life, in America, as we sat and spoke, putting into language what had earned Dorothy Day's reverence and respect and, too, had earned him, in his native Italy, plenty of threats and warnings of disaster and death: "I have tried, as much as possible, to do the Lord's bidding, to remember Jesus, His life, and keep His teaching close to me, in the hope that I live up to it, at least some of the time. If you ask others to come be with you, to follow you, look up to you as their teacher or leader, to share your life, then you had better be prepared to prove yourself in their eyes, to live up to what you ask them to stand up for, uphold. Your words are only as good as your actions—you had better know that, because others will say yes, that is true, or they will say no, there is an inconsistency there, and if so, if that is the truth they figure out, then you are blind, and only following yourself, and it's best that others part company with you, rather than share with you, walk in your footsteps!" With that, a silence that lasts. He stands, as if to make clear a disinterest in further talk. He points to the street—he wants to get something to drink, and he wants to walk and walk on the sidewalk, a habit that (he has already told me) takes him out of himself, happily into the lives of others, no matter his distance from all save those with whom he engages on those various streets. As we move along he turns suddenly, surprisingly, to shoptalk: "You walk into a neighborhood, and soon you see new faces—a big relief from the familiar ones in the important places!" A proud loner, I think—quick to make the best of his occasional loneliness, his stubborn apartness, turning both of them into a blessing, a joy.

VIII

Handing Each Other Along:
Moral Leadership in Everyday Life

W ho have been the leaders in your life—the people you really respected, the folks who stood for something?" A colonel, a surgeon in the Air Force, was asking a group of us young physicians. "Think of an example, an instance."

The same man who asked that question also made the point that we young doctors were "part of a hierarchy of leadership"—and "the whole thing is kept going by everyone's consent."

All the time, in the course of our ordinary lives, we ourselves experience leadership and exert it, but in either case we engage affirmatively with it. As husbands, wives, parents, members of a larger family, as residents in a particular neighborhood, as individuals who belong to a particular workforce, we lead or have our say in who or what we follow, we indicate our approval, disapproval, insistence upon what we think to be right or wrong; we may go further, try to persuade one or another person that what we believe to be correct, or entirely out of order, ought to be taken to heart. Religious figures can lead us morally, with their pronouncements, as can presidents, political officeholders from their bully pulpits, or judges at their benches.

In homes, parents assert values, temporary guiding gods of a sort to their occasionally awestruck, eagerly curious children, asking them to follow suit, morally. In schools, teachers make clear one or another ethical point of view, and strive to enlist the responsive agreement of students; in neighborhoods, various men and women (sometimes children, as well) try to uphold ideas, ideals, wrap their wishes in received pieties, win from listeners agreement, a moral consent that will matter and take the form of compliance, of action pursued. Generals, governors, and bishops demonstrate leadership, their words and deeds declared in the name of the moral, the spiritual, the militarily useful, the socially necessary. But so do we, all of us, the ones who go to church or to synagogue, belong to a nation as citizens, to the Army, Navy, Air Force, as officers or recruits.

In the last regard, I recall my own moral upbringing, so to speak, including in the military, my initial experience as a captain under the old doctors' draft that had each of us young physicians giving two years of our lives to the United States military. I recall that colonel who challenged us to *act* like leaders.

I'd experienced moral leadership first at the hands of my mother and father, my grandfather and aunt, certain schoolteachers, and later, professors, but I'd never before heard the word "leadership" used in direct connection with *me*.

I was by then a twenty-eight-year-old pediatrician become an Air Force officer. An older surgeon higher up, a colonel, let several of us know what we needed to be about—and did so in a way we couldn't forget. "You're doctors," he said, "but you're also wearing those captain's bars. You'll be saluted all the time and you're here to *earn* those salutes. Make sure you're ready to be saluted, ready to put on the line what's made you a paid officer, a captain, in the United States Air Force."

We'd heard him, but we also *saw* him—he was standing straight, his shoulders firmly set, his hair scrubbed, neatly parted, his uniform spotless and well-tailored, his shoes polished and shining—a contrast, indeed, with the manner of being, the self-representation and self-presentation we'd only recently enjoyed in our busy hospital lives as residents, overworked and tired and entitled, so we assumed, to certain moments of casual sloppiness, a badge of our hectic, demanding life and of our importance. Back in those hospitals, patients saluted us with polite, frightened attention—and overlooked our relaxed, rumpled attire in the urgent hope that we'd fulfill their anxious expectations and lead them, through our knowledge and skill, from the slough of medical despond to the higher, safer realm of health.

But this "Air Force doc," he called himself, "a regular," wanted us to understand what had happened to us when we put on those uniforms. He wanted us to understand how we'd need to act, think—how we'd lead by how we wore our clothes, acted with others who were ill but needed something more from us than we may have realized—needed us to be leaders. I remember his didactic tone, the tenor of his address, its strikingly memorable onset: "You're military men now, that's the first thing you have to remember."

That statement of the obvious, as he saw it, and of its importance, got nowhere with us at first. Some of us responded with lowered eyes, or turned away from the confident, commanding speaker with glances toward others—looks meant to register boredom, even defiance: he may be a *temporary* boss, but we'll soon enough be pursuing our lives elsewhere. But the colonel, our older fellow physician, saw more of that than any of us realized—and surprised us mightily by his remarks. "You all want out of here," he told us, but then made a strongly earnest request, couched as a plea for a favor—he with his warrior brass not exactly handing out an order or two: "I'm asking you to give yourselves a break, and join us here—it's your Air Force, so make it your own when you're on duty! There are lots of folks here who need you to be their doctors. They also need you to act like captains! You're *leaders* now— that's what will be expected of you by your men!"

At that last comment we were embarrassed, annoyed, even perplexed. *Our* "men"—we didn't like that assertion of authority, its bestowal on us at the expense, so we thought, of others. I remember wondering, right away, why anyone would imagine me to be a leader, no matter the rank insignia I happened to wear. I wrote the word "leader" down on a piece of paper I had in my hand as the colonel spoke, and I put down a question mark, a half inch or so nearby—as if I didn't know what the speaker I'd just heard was trying to let us know. No one had called any of us "leaders" before, as the colonel well knew when he gave voice to our confusion, our skepticism, when he told us we were going to be leaders, our doubts notwithstanding—all of which he proceeded to address. He did so by reminding us that we were in an "organization," that it "stood for something," that we had best learn how to give orders as well as how to take them. Further, he insisted on that "hierarchy of leadership"—on how "the whole thing," we ought understand, "is kept going by everyone's consent."

Lest we continue to disbelieve—he must have seen it on our faces— he hurried us into a sermon of sorts, referred to the "big moral mission of defense" that is "the responsibility of the Air Force."

More empty, self-serving rhetoric, we seemed to say with our glazed eyes, but he had gotten to us, and we became affected by his stories of war, injury, suffering, death, of terrible pain and tears—amidst battles fought, lost for a while, then, at great human cost, won decisively. So that we would not miss the point (how stirred we were by his story-telling remembrances) he switched tracks on us, approached our lives directly, a decided contrast to the recital of personal experiences we had been offered. His brief question, forcefully and repeatedly put, hit us hard—and with it a notable silence in the room that marked the end of the low-level noise we had been registering through the movement of our shoes on the floor, our bodies on our chairs, our arms on the desk upholding them: "Who have been the leaders in your life—the people you really respected, the folks who stood for something?" A colonel, a surgeon in the Air Force kept urging a group of us young physicians to respond concretely: "Think of an example, an instance."

There we were, the officers he'd been addressing, young men, all of us, who had been going to classes forever, and who thereafter had in-habited hospital wards days and nights for what had also seemed like an eternity, but who were taken aback by a question that actually had got-ten to the heart of the matter: the decades of experiences in seminar rooms and bedsides that had turned us into willing, eager students, ap-prentices—all the time, under such circumstances, in the company of teachers paying us heed, telling things to us, testing us, urging us to know one or another body of knowledge, and to try to understand the condition of one or another "body" (the abstract way, through language, that gave us distance from our fellow human beings, called "patients," whom our medical school teachers had kept insisting that we ought understand fully). Now we were summoned to the memory of all that, lead right to it, no matter our skeptical, even cynical indifference.

I well recall at that moment thinking of a medical school teacher who kept urging us to "know the patients inside out." Like the colonel, that teacher was also a surgeon, and he had, in fact, often gotten to us—the arrogant intrusiveness, the unyielding presumptuousness he more than conveyed with such an assertion of a vernacular expression. Still, he worked very hard (and with knowing brilliance) to make things better for the host of men and women upon whom he operated, and whom he saw constantly during their hospital stay; and he worked hard, ever so conscientiously with us, we began to realize after we'd first heard that remark just mentioned: he wanted to show us everything he knew to do, and wanted us, in turn, to show him what we had learned to do, and yes, the "insides and outs" of our patients. We were relentlessly at his side during a so-called rotation: a time of learning, literally, at his surgical hands, and a time of following, literally, as we walked from bed to bed, but also, as we watched him closely, heard attentively his every word, and in general took our cues from him, kept in mind his manner of being, doing, made ourselves in language and deed more and more like him.

No wonder that vigorously able, competent, and composed surgeon and teacher had years later, in a southern Air Force base, returned to my mind as the "leader" he had been for so many of us. Not that he was known to us that way, as some physicians who taught us had been regarded—their dramatic lectures, their evident command of themselves, of language, made us notice them, think of them as individuals to emulate. They made us laugh as well as pay grateful attention; they won us over to their prepared remarks, their informal manner of talking, the clothes they wore, the way of putting things they favored, the gestures that became, in our minds, desirable. In contrast, this surgeon had not impressed us quickly, had not entranced us with the remarkable élan some of his colleagues possessed, but had bore down on us, as it were, made us realize how much we had to learn from him, even made us have second thoughts about him—his constrained, officious side giving way, in our minds, to an awareness of his great skills in the operating room, his almost wondrous ability to figure out, right away, what ailed his patients, and why. So we, anxious to do likewise, looked up to him. In time, with him, we learned how to follow suggestions and recommendations with enough assurance to earn his notice and approval—and so it went: eager and scared young people taking someone in psychologically, intellectually, empirically, taking after him in his habits, even some of his habits of speech, which we'd initially found distasteful.

As I tried to oblige that colonel, senior to me as a teacher had once been, I wondered only so long why I'd recalled that medical school instructor. The word "leader" had made a dent in my thoughts. I was, actually, falling in line with a leader, with the colonel, doing his bidding, even enjoying what it meant to follow his suggestion, take his words seriously. So with all of us as we left that colonel's presence, shared our memories of men and women who now were not only former teachers or neighbors or kin, but leaders, even as the man standing before us moments earlier in his own way had become a person of some forceful persuasion for our minds, someone whose spoken question had enlisted in each of us a willing and searching compliance—hence all the individuals we were remembering, to ourselves and out loud as we talked to each other, described distant times in schools, colleges, graduate meeting places, hospital rooms.

Newly members of an organization, we were accommodating to its requirements, nodding favorably as a designated leader, resplendent in both his military and medical authority, made an inquiry and asked for our interest. Moreover, that authority was also asserted in the name of the desirable, the practical, and finally the moral. We had "better" learn how things work in the Air Force; if we did so, our "tenure" would be more "fulfilling," for ourselves and for our patients—and above all we had best keep our "mission" at the center of our daily introspective activity, "in the forefront of your life," we were told. I recall us all wondering how we were to accomplish that talk, to the point that the looks on our faces must have conveyed our uncertainty, our bewildered doubt, maybe—hence a long moral statement by the colonel, in which he spoke of our "responsibilities as citizens," our obligation to assist in "the defense of freedom." The resort to such unsurprising pieties got the speaker nowhere, he surely sensed—yet he refused to let go of us. Instead, he vigorously pursued once more the matter of leadership, of our memories as they provided experiences of it—and then the request that we have a return try at taking up leadership as a "topic" in a forthcoming seminar, the place and time to be posted.

Memories of Moral Leaders

Soon enough, we were all returning to our earlier lives, separately and under the aegis of a "continuing conference," a hyped-up way of saying that we were all being asked to ruminate about something, talk of past memorable moments. I began visiting in my mind certain moral leaders—as a few of us came to call them—I'd met. We were replying to a teacher's request by making reference to the teachers who had preceded him in former classrooms, ones hitherto abandoned to the fog of forgetfulness that commonly gets called the past, or an earlier life. That class was coming alive, casting light for each of us on what had happened to us—a consequence of a leader's seeming afterthought, his reaction to our quite apparent indifference to tenets, values he much cherished. He had moved us all from the rhetoric of military rank, its perquisites and duties, to shared, personal recollections that became (in, of all places, a military hospital) a collective exposition of personal moral lessons as they had been acquired by the handful of young men we were: each in our late twenties, across the table from the colonel, who was in his early fifties and very much in control of things, letting us wander through our recollections of moral leadership as others had provided it to us—enough so that we were able to concentrate on that "theme," as our instructor had called it, through consistent resort to our private lives, hardly the usual mode of discussion in that rounds room of the base hospital where we were sitting, and where we usually assembled to talk about our patients, their problems and prospects.

Years later, out of the military, we would go back to that class, speak of it when we met at medical conferences, consider it a moment of mighty concentration—all of us called to stop and think about how we'd become the individuals we then were, possessed of ideas about the valuable or the objectionable, possessed of ideals as to what truly mattered, what was of no consequence whatsoever, or thoroughly beyond the pale. We each gave an account of ourselves, and afterward realized that such a requested self-scrutiny had given us a great deal of distance from our lives as they had been shaped not only by our parents or our educational experiences, or friendships, but by certain pivotal exertions on the part of others, their moral leadership described by us: an "instance," as our teacher had put it, in which a person showed himself or herself to stand for something, even to be determined to stand up to others, stand against them.

That Class with the Colonel

When I think of "that class with the colonel," as we sometimes dubbed it years later, I go back to a story told us by a fellow officer-recruit, who grew up in a suburb of Memphis. His father was also a doctor, his mother a nurse. He kept on telling us that they were "average" people, though he also acknowledged to us his "luck," the special circumstances a relatively privileged life provided. Yet one experience stood out as he went back to his earlier life.

He had gone with his mother to the library in the Tennessee town where they lived so comfortably, only to become a witness to a brief but tense incident. His mother was holding his hand, preparing to take him into the children's room of the library, when she abruptly stopped in her tracks, and tightened her grip on him. She listened as the librarian was telling a dark-skinned mother, also there with her son, that there was no admission, for them, that day of the week. His mother had intervened, objected to the librarian's refusal of this mother and son who suddenly had become, by virtue of their skin, unwelcome inhabitants from a foreign land, even though they lived in the same town, and occupied the servants quarters in one of its estates. The result was a dramatic step taken: "My mom asked the colored lady if she could go get some books for her, and take them out on her card. She asked the colored lady if she'd *trust* us to be of help, and she squeezed my hand, as if she was reminding me that I was part of the 'us' she'd just mentioned."

He spoke those words twice, himself moved by them, even as we attended him closely, the colonel included—who suggested we all hold that related incident in our minds. Here was moral leadership in action, he averred—here was a child being shown how to behave, being provided with a parent's beliefs put into action, being literally taken by the hand and figuratively inspired through a mother's unselfconscious yet firm resolve.

I supply now my own narrative version of that colonel's teacherly determination to prod our reflection. Within hours, some of what he said that day, or even some of what we ourselves had said in the class, would be, for sure, lost to us, definitively maybe, or forever, but not that story told by one of us, and not the spoken notice of it, reaction to it, by a gruff, demanding veteran of Air Force service who was anxious to make sure that what we'd heard "hit home"—his informal, intuitive way of pointing out, with no psychological or educational fanfare, that something remarkably important had just been given us, something that would take up residence in the contemplative sector of our thinking life. Home, he knew, is where we first get "hit" morally, first learn from others about the much approved, the outright renounced. To summon military imagery in recognition of a moral moment both stunning and surprising to all of us in that Air Force classroom, we learn as children how to fall in rank morally—and we learn as parents how to give orders morally to the sons and daughters whom nature entrusts to us.

After that library incident was conveyed to us, the speaker who had chosen to share it put some present-day thoughts on the table for us to consider—his way of letting us know that what his mother did, in an instant of spontaneous connection to two strangers, had become for him charged with continuing authority, significance. I can still hear my captain colleague, like me newly arrived for a spell of a couple of years, going gratefully along with the colonel who, in the quick ordering of us around, had often earned our mock caricature. "Yes, sir," our captain classmate had assented, readily and animatedly—and then a brief echo of the colonel's words that would stay with all of us for the rest of our time at the Air Force base, and that has stayed with me to this day: "I'd say that my mom was showing me 'moral leadership' back then. She wouldn't have put it that way. She said later she was doing what was 'proper,' and she hoped I'd do what was proper, when the time came for me to prove myself—that I knew what was proper."

The colonel's face showed his pleased gratitude, even as he urged us to keep in mind what we'd heard—and so we did: we repeated that well-remembered episode in a class to others, wrote of it to friends, to parents, wives, future wives, and I would often in my daily life, later on, hearken back to those few minutes that became, actually, a long-lived lesson of big help as I talked with my own children, with the children I got to see in hospitals, clinics, and in classrooms far distant from that military base, whom I hoped to stir with the help of a memory become a constant companion. Our military leader had made mention of "moral leadership," and one of us had concurred, had returned to his childhood, to the point that a phrase used by a colonel had taken on great significance for us. Nor could we, seconds after that class with the colonel, deny him *his* "moral leadership," even as those two words would always be connected to what one of us told us—he who remarked at the end of that very day, as we sat and drank a beer or two: "I never thought I'd be remembering that trip I took with my mom to the library."

At that beer-time and others, we followed our leader in our own spontaneous manner—what he asked, we were now asking ourselves. We were revealing to one another, to ourselves through our occasional memories, what moral leadership can concretely mean in this or that life. Our friend's mother, it turned out, was not alone—though her willful act of conscience, under unfavorable social circumstances, certainly stood out as exceptional.

Creating a "Climate of Respect"

Some of my parents' remarks and actions entered our discourse; we were each calling upon our earlier experiences, learning from one another, learning the meaning of moral leadership from recalling lived instances of it—our past experiences turned into our military leader's surrogates. I hadn't for years given much attention to my mom and dad as occasionally outspoken, forceful moral protagonists or leaders, all their own. For one thing, they both tended to be quiet—more than willing to read what others had to say (especially their favorites, Tolstoy and George Eliot), rather than eager to find excuses for sermons. Etched in the back of my head, and suddenly on top of it, were some events that really held me in their grip—what my mother or father had done.

Small wonder, then, that I took notice when our colonel-leader spoke of leadership as something constantly exerted apart from the formality of orders spoken, obeyed—and talked of a "climate of respect" we owed one another there. My mom and dad sometimes spoke similarly as they took the wheel (talking about leadership!), took us where they pleased and, not rarely, where my brother and I wanted to be. Every so often, though, we got sidetracked; something happened to catch Dad's attention, or Mother's, usually to the perplexity and impatience of my brother and me—even to our apprehension.

Once we were with our father, on the way to do shopping. He abruptly brought the car to a halt, for no reason apparent to us. He parked, got out, said nothing, walked quickly toward a man who was standing in the middle of the road, hunched over, his hand on his back. Dad talked with him, took his arm, got him across to his seeming destination, a drugstore, took him inside. I recall wondering why dad had stopped, where he'd gone. At one point my brother and I were set to leave the car, take ourselves to the drugstore—no mean feat, for us then, to cross that busy highway at our elementary school age. Eventually Dad reappeared, got to the car, looked at us, and saw anxiety and reproval on our faces. I dared give expression to my alarm and my vexation by reminding him that we had to be back in an hour, for the lunch mother was preparing. But he was not persuaded by my ode to punctuality, dressed in filial devotion to our hardworking cook of a mom. "I think your mother would have wanted us to stop, if she'd been here with us," we heard. Then came a brief description of what had happened: "That man was in pain, and he needed a bit of help." No more at the time—he was a good one for whetting a listener's appetites matter-of-factly, but not killing them with strenuous language. We knew that he had made a choice, let himself offer "a bit of help"— and we were glad to be on our way to food, to possessions for ourselves.

Later, back home, we would hear Dad reporting to Mom on the street incident; and she, intuitively figuring out our confusion back in the car and more inclined than her taciturn husband to go into explanations, was quick to say something to us—tell us what she thought had happened while we were traveling to the store. I wouldn't remember her every word, but I couldn't overlook her manner of addressing us (her evident moral seriousness, I'd now say), and especially I couldn't fail to notice the personal tone she brought to her words—the mention she'd make of "respect" due various others. It was almost as if, uncannily, she had spoken *for* us as well as to us. Sometimes Dad's "worries" (I remember that chosen word well!) might be "inconvenient" (I also remember that word), but we ought to be thankful that he helps us to notice what we might be too busy to take in at all—there I paraphrase, but she very much got her moral message across to us, and Dad's as well.

Such remarks on her part, intended to give voice more amply to Dad's deed, may have lacked the vividly compelling authority of my fellow physician's library experience with his mother, but when I tried to describe my own childhood memory of moral leadership as I'd seen it enacted, heard it fitted into a parent's values, his or her take on the world as he or she met up with its hurdles, challenges, I began to concentrate upon, and thereby, understand better, an aspect of my early life.

Nor were my parents, as it goes in so many families, all alone in their moral concerns, as they informed their lives. My brother and I went to schools, heard teachers speak, observed their deeds—came home with stories we'd seen unfold. A fifth-grade teacher of mine not only read Lincoln's words, but took them to heart, near tears as she spoke of a historical figure whom she revered and wanted us to admire. When my own children were in elementary school I recall their mother taking them to her father's study in his home, so that they could see their grandfather's picture of Lincoln, whom he also admired, had learned in the early years of this century to regard as an especially able and decent American president—moral leadership as it hovers over lives, across generations and family experiences. What a teacher told me, at nine, my mother more than told me at the same age (she even showed me *her* elementary school history book, with its picture of Lincoln, and tribute to him, and her bookmark that remained in place, always on that page, even as my wife had a host of childhood memories of Lincoln, his statements, his actions told her by her dad, and told to our children by her).

Taking Aim at Complacent Consciences: Dickens and Others

In high school we all studied American history again, met Lincoln and his moral leadership again; we met others, as well, who had stood for something important in history (the abolitionists, notably) and we met writers who had tried to turn the attention of their readers to the high cost of callousness, Dickens and Tolstoy especially, in their pungent, searing fictions. Dickens went out of his way to record the misfortunes of a range of vulnerable people, and a teacher told us eleventh graders to "carry Dickens" with us, to "let his eyes and ears become yours." We wondered how to do so and whether it was desirable to do so—but an insistent instructor got a buzz going in his occasionally nonchalant, self-preoccupied class of teenagers. We were inclined to memorize names, plot structures, to recite learned literary pieties—but we were taken aback when Dickens was presented as someone who "took aim at complacent consciences," a description we were less likely to forget than the abundant factuality and the host of analytic literary propositions put before us. Our teacher hit his desk as he spoke that way about an author—he didn't pound, but his intent, his emphatic manner, got to us: he cared that Dickens cared, and he hoped we'd also care, busy and ambitious and self-absorbed though we sometimes were. This was no strident, finger-wagging moralist who had infiltrated an old high school of modest repute, but a teacher who knew his subject cold, wanted us to know it well—but who was also, like Dickens, worried about the world. In that regard, I can still see his daily newspaper on his desk, and I can see the clippings from that paper on his bulletin board, journalistic excerpts meant to call our attention to human frailty and hurt not unlike the kind Charles Dickens had given the life of affecting, enveloping fiction.

"We can learn from Dickens," we were told, but not only so that we could score well in our grade-point averages and do well in our future educational lives. Our Yankee teacher, Joseph Hobbs, spoke out with a certain moral vehemence that jolted and unnerved us but took us over: "Carry Dickens in your full hearts as well as your clever heads"—a charge of excess, we may have mused; an overwrought expostulation, our clever heads, always on the grab for new words, for "interesting ideas," may have concluded—yet those admonishing words scored with us: a rustle of cleared throats, of shuffling feet, of notebooks or paper moved on desks, as we collectively indicated an unease that had caught hold of us. When I told my parents, who dearly loved Dickens, what Mr. Hobbs, the notorious hard marker, had said, they shrewdly resisted the temptation to rush to Mr. Hobbs's side, much to my surprise. Another comment that has persisted in my memory—my dad's, as he wryly shook his head: "I guess Mr. Dickens has worked his way into Mr. Hobbs's heart, and he [Mr. Dickens] also wants the company of your class." I wasn't so much told, given a hearty *yes* to a teacher's remark, but rather, reminded that reading can reach within one, make a person anxious to share with others what he or she has come to know or feel, kindred readers if not kindred souls. Today I clutter up that fast, fatherly aside with interpretive weight, but Dad was trying to be helpfully clarifying rather than a hectoring moral underliner. Decades afterward, in my teaching life, as I struggle to connect college students to Dickens, I think of Mr. Hobbs and Dad—and wonder how to do spoken justice to, say, *Great Expectations,* to the moral possibilities such a novel can offer us, its readers.

Perry Miller: Connecting Wartime Experiences and What We Read to Lived Life

In college I would meet another teacher of English literature, Perry Miller, who wanted to make connections in his life between what he'd read and how he acted, as well as thought. He urged extensive reading lists on us, asked for papers, gave back grades, showed delight in demonstrating his informed erudite reaction to "texts," to the questions we posed in a seminar—but every once in a while he'd do an end run around our procedures and our notions of what he aimed for us to make of this weekly segment of our education. We'd have read, courtesy of him, the "New England divines"—the three thundering Mathers: Cotton, Increase, Richard; Anne Bradstreet, Nathaniel Ward—the Puritan writers who struggled to make moral sense of this new country they were helping to build; but Miller didn't want the matter to end with his, with our, on-target interpretive commentary. He kept bringing Pascal, a favorite of his, into our discussions. He wanted to know, as in *Pensées,* what "the heart's reasons" are for us; and he told us of times in his life when he'd been "floored," when he'd wondered about life's meaning with no satisfying success—such as when, in the American Army, during the Second World War, he'd helped "liberate" a German concentration camp, and so saw what the Nazis had done to the hundreds of thousands of men, women, and children they'd taken to such places.

He was an officer. With others in command, he was leading troops;

but he became "numb," aghast at what he'd seen. Beyond that emotion, he felt "frightened for all of us, for mankind." We could right away accept, comprehend his "horror" (that well-known word of Conrad's in *Heart of Darkness*) but we weren't prepared for his lasting, personal response to what he'd come to see in central Europe—the intensity of his moral inwardness as it exerted itself on him during the rest of his military stay abroad. But far harder for us to grasp were the concrete, daily consequences of such reflective thinking for his postwar American life, and very important to him, to us, the "shadow" (he called it) of that wartime experience on his academic life, his neighborhood and social life in a university and its environs.

We heard much from Professor Miller about the moral and political compromises that played their enabling and ultimately decisive role in the emergence of Nazi rule over Germany. We learned of Dietrich Bonhoeffer and his fate, and by the time our professor had taught us his many lessons we were unlikely to forget Bonhoeffer (whose story follows in this book), and so much else—the history of hatred, I suppose it can be called, that has by no means been confined to central Europe, but figured in America, even in the university we were then attending, which had its own past of quotas, restrictions, its own indifference to the plight of others nearby, even as it accumulated money and power over the generations. It was "really something," to draw on the vernacular, for us students to hear our professor speak of the gratuitous, mean-spirited remarks that he had heard in the very faculty club where our professors dined regularly; to hear of highly educated individuals not being completely immune to prejudice, to gratuitous and glib dismissals of others by virtue of race, religion, creed—even as Miller, in some Augustinian admissions and self-indictments (we were studying St. Augustine's *Confessions*) chose not to stand loftily apart from his colleagues, from so many others, as he shared off-the-cuff comments he heard from time to time, sometimes the noise coming from within his mind: "unspoken voices," he called them, that can connect us to arrogance, to one or another kind of felt exclusivity, superiority.

"How might we be more honorable and decent to others?" So he kept asking us, not only rhetorically but because he wanted us to embrace personally a certain spiritual and literary tradition. To be sure, he wanted us to memorize the contents of those texts, know them cognitively; but he wanted them to find a place in our hearts—so that we connected what he once called "the moral dissent" of a Thoreau to our own lives as we went about them: the young writer's skepticism, for instance, aimed at an unexamined materialism, its consequences for the environment. Miller wanted us to take note of whom we routinely respected, whom we ignored or patronized—and he wanted us to remember what a colleague of his, Professor Werner Jaeger, whose course just about every one of us in the seminar was also taking, had done in Germany in the 1930s—stand up to the Nazis, hence his exile to America.

Always the questions posed were meant to rush us toward empathy, true, but also toward a willingness to take candid stock of ourselves, imagine our own decisions were we ever to face the terrible moral quandaries that visited the lives of Germany's professors and students under the Nazis, but that were nearer at hand than we may have occasionally realized. "Who says what, hearing what, and when, where?" He raised his voice to that sweeping question, but I couldn't forget the muffled choking as he spoke, nor could we fail to notice the flush of his face, the slight bending downward of his head, eyes staring at the floor and then directly at us.

A few days later, when two of us saw him chatting amiably with a janitor, then helping him carry some objects out the door of our lecture hall, we "made connections" (he'd often asked us to do so with regard to books and our lived life) between what we'd heard him say and what we saw of him as he went about his work.

When a classmate noticed Professor Miller helping one of those nameless "university employees" move a car out of the way (it was blocking traffic) he was quickly ready to tell us that news, though we were no less ready, I have to remember, with psychological interpretations: our teacher was always trying to be different; he didn't dress like most of his colleagues, or talk like them—he was a rebellious character.

Werner Jaeger and Greek Virtues,
Human Failings

Miller's moral counterpart, Werner Jaeger, was no less a difficult challenge to us, however formal and reserved he was, a contrast with
Miller's provocative outbursts of folksiness. Jaeger wanted us to think
about the Greek "virtues" that he, a classicist, pressed upon us, but he
also kept bringing us back to the Nazis and the implications of their
rise, and to our "human failings," which he freely admitted were not
necessarily diminished or abolished by intellect, including its extensive
use in his ambitious, time-consuming course, its reading list long with
references to the philosophers and playwrights of ancient Greece.
"Those two guys," some of us were wont to say, "are out to get you, always throwing monkey wrenches," or other words to that effect. I remember so clearly our slangy irritation or bafflement, our moral
exasperation.

Dr. Loeb and Dr. Kneeland:
Learning from Patients

A short couple of years afterward, in medical school, I happened on
two others in that teaching (and reflective) tradition, both internists:
Robert F. Loeb and Yale Kneeland, each stalwart in a resolve that we,
their students, not only learn "signs and symptoms," as the phrase went
in the medical textbooks, but how to learn gratefully, even humbly,
from our patients. All the time Dr. Loeb was warning us, lest we become "too taken" with ourselves—after which he'd warn us, further,
that our white jackets set us apart, elevated us all too much in the
minds of our patients, and worse, in our own minds. "Learn from your
patients," he kept saying, "let them become your teachers; then you'll
be learning to show them the respect they deserve." All to the good, we

agreed as we listened, but he was prone to such platitudes—and, very important, some of us felt, he could be very tough on us, no matter his doctor's compassion for the sick; he even mobilized sarcasm to bring us up short, make us study harder so that we'd answer his questions promptly, exactly. Woe to the student who failed to give a wanted answer to one of his incisive medical queries—some of us, accordingly, joked that the only way to get along exceedingly well with Dr. Loeb was to get sick and become one of his ward patients, of which there were no small number.

After one class, when he'd been especially tough on us, we accompanied him on his patient rounds, and were surprised at the shift in his mood and manner. He was gracious, kindly, deferential to those in his medical care—a side of him we were not privileged to experience first-hand. Some of us, yet again, joked about that seeming split in a teaching doctor's manner; we wondered whether we might all somehow become victims of an epidemic, then really enjoy our professor. Eventually we understood that he wasn't being gratuitously cold or indifferent to us, his students; he wanted each young would-be physician in the classroom to learn and learn and learn, and he made clear to us his reasons one day when he spelled out an analogy between his work, as he saw it, and our future work as he envisioned it to be: "This is a war against illness we're fighting, and we have to be armed with all possible weapons."

We weren't at the time impressed by those words, though they did come back to me as I heard another physician, that colonel, talk in the Air Force base to which I was assigned five years after graduating from medical school. In any event, we learned so very much from Dr. Loeb about medicine in the abstract, and about the "delivery," he called it, of such acquired knowledge to the patients we increasingly got to meet, know, and try to heal. We also learned, at his side, how a gesture on his part, on ours, could help establish trust, could build up confidence and hope in men, women, and children medically down on their luck, indeed in danger of dying. We watched our teacher shake hands, touch the arms or shoulders of the sick as he conversed with them; we heard him trying to be friendly, reassuring—and we observed him observing others, taking note of their difficulties but also asking after their families, even asking how he might be of help to husbands and wives and parents, explain things to them. His was a constant solicitude extended sensitively at the bedside on wards, even as hours later, in his office or in the classroom with us, he could glower at us or be bluntly critical of what we'd said or written on paper.

Members of the White Rose:
Yale Kneeland and Wartime Resistance

Perhaps we were helping our teacher in our own relatively defenseless, obliging way—taking it on the chin from him as recipients of his frustration and anger, which his work with patients surely generated. But this kind of interpretive psychology was denied us by another of our teachers, Yale Kneeland, who overheard us complaining, and had by his friendly nature earned our trust. In fact, we were handed psychology as a reply to our own try at it: "Your teacher is very hard on himself— harder by far than he is on you. He tells us [his colleagues] that we have to hold ourselves to the highest standards, even if it hurts, and he doesn't hesitate to call himself to account, severely!" Told that, our faces fell, though our minds had been cleared. Again and again Dr. Kneeland would come back to that explanative remark—and tell us how deeply moved Dr. Loeb constantly was: "He wants with all his mind and heart, with every ounce of strength in him, to do right by his patients; and though he may be hard on you folks sometimes, he wants to do right by you now, so that you'll be able to do right with *your* patients down the line when you're docs, and have them, the full responsibility for them."

A description of a fellow teacher's strenuously exerted moral leadership—and, actually, Dr. Kneeland's own moral leadership—being put on the line for us harried, apprehensive medical students, occasionally inclined toward self-pity. But Dr. Kneeland wanted us to take leave of ourselves—stop wallowing in our laments with respect to the "stresses" of medical education, and stop bellowing about the sometime strain of satisfying a teacher's ever-impending request for answers. We were asked by Dr. Kneeland to look beyond ourselves, to travel with him in our minds to Germany. He told us of his medical friends who lived in Munich (and elsewhere across Hitler's Third Reich) during the 1930s and 1940s, when "monstrous evil," as Kneeland called it, ruled. A group of medical students, at great personal risk, had dared take up a collective struggle against a regime set upon the wanton slaughter of millions.

Those students called themselves members of the "White Rose." They often wore that flower as a badge, an emblem of a moral purpose: to protest and resist Nazism in all possible ways. The medical students wrote newspapers and leaflets, established an underground network of publication, a political opposition and resistance to Hitler and his henchmen. The leaflets were mailed, placed in classrooms, in public locations; the medical students who dared do so had become a morally awakened cadre who chose to risk their all in order to stand apart from, stand up to, a Nazism that, alas, had gained control of colleges and universities as well as Germany as a nation. These were so-called Aryans, who might have rationalized their relative helplessness, gone about their regular busy ways, with no danger to themselves from the police, the military. These were "mere medical students," Dr. Kneeland let us know, his resort to the word "mere" a means of emphasizing a considerable irony: those on the bottom of a hierarchical society well-known for its embrace of class and caste, for its levels of power and now for its denial of rights and even personal safety to millions, were at the same time those willing and eager to fight hard and long, as students rather than big-shot professors, no matter the consequent danger, on behalf of a nation's growing population of the persecuted and endangered.

We listened with rapt attention as Dr. Kneeland spelled out the above—and then this terrible blow of information: the youths were seen stocking pamphlets in piles, handing them out; then the Gestapo caught them, confined them, and killed them. Medical students, we realized, had become moral protagonists—martyrs who dared resist viciously punitive dictatorial power being used to kill wantonly.

Dr. Kneeland, we would later understand, knew better than to follow that narrative with a sermon, or an implied remonstrance whose gist was that we were pretty damn fortunate medical students ourselves, for all our often declared complaints. But we were not without our own voices of conscience. We knew how blessed it was to live in the United States, as opposed to Nazi Germany—and we wondered, during days that followed, what *we* might have done had we been there in Munich, in a distinguished school, with much to occupy our time, much to preoccupy us (and therefore, incline us to overlook what was happening around us, to others, in that case the thousands of Jews who were being round up and, too, all those who regarded with alarm and horror what had enveloped a country known for its first-rate medical institutions, among its various educational and cultural achievements).

As we were leaving Dr. Kneeland's presence at the end of that class, our heads troubled and bowed, he moved toward us, toward the door, and did speak, quietly, four words, which we would hear resounding after we'd gone back to our rooms: "Let us remember them!"

He wasn't chasing after us to conclude a message intended to awaken us morally. He was letting us know by the lower tone of his voice, his near-whisper, that he was, in fact, talking to himself, addressing a side of his life very much like that in us—we were all, in that room, of a similar lucky circumstance, as compared to what had confronted those who had organized, joined the White Rose group of medical students, and, too, their few but important physician supporters. Months later, when some of us happened to be with Dr. Kneeland on a social occasion, the members of the White Rose were mentioned, and I remember Dr. Kneeland's terse remark: "I think of them, those medical students, when I am wondering what we hope to do as instructors of medicine." He said no more, but we obviously wanted to hear more, and he must have sensed that, as we all stood there, suddenly quite solemn. He shook his head, a notable way of registering his melancholy dismay—and then, with more silence remaining, several of us tried to thank him for what he'd told us, given us, even as we realized awkwardly the substantial irony: the willful moral life of others, their torture and their deaths, their terribly foreshortened lives, became fodder for our moral thinking, a source of inspiration, a warning, maybe, all to our advantage. It was as if our teacher knew the foregoing in his heart, rather than in his conceptualizing head—and so he did say this, his eyes looking right in our direction: "It is an honor for us to honor them."

We were ready to agree without exception—though we pulled back a bit from the brink of that mournful statement with our own private ruminations, eventually shared in retrospective, querying contemplation: what had we ever done to deserve such an honor—who are we to be such recipients? Such a line of questioning is specifically unanswerable—perhaps is best addressed by keeping it alive, a constant moral challenge posed by an enormous collaborative act of moral leadership that became known as the White Rose, and was, for us, a quite hard-to-forget spur to inwardness handed us by a teacher who embodied "moral leadership" in his storytelling classroom life.

The just-described time spent with an especially kindhearted and winning person came back to me, for obvious reasons, when I heard "moral leadership" given explicit discussion by another physician (though a colonel, a surgeon) in his seminar with us new "inductees," a word every now and then slapped on those who first came to that base's hospital. I was almost set to speak of the White Rose, but had by then forgotten names such as Hans Scholl and Alexander Schmorell, and Sophie Scholl, Hans's sister who rallied to her brother's aid, and Willi Graf and Christoph Probst, also medical students. They were names on a piece of note paper, left at home back North, and I hesitated to speak of them anonymously. Still, belatedly I came up with an abbreviated summary of what Dr. Kneeland had told us—only, I must admit, to hear our colonel say a brief "yes." He had heard about that act of moral defiance, and he wished that we all could read about what he called, with clear feeling, "the tragedy of Germany under Hitler." There was little chance, at the time, for us to repair to summary reports, newspaper clippings that would tell of the White Rose. For our colonel, ever anxious that leadership of various kinds be considered, and among them, the moral leadership he'd repeatedly mentioned, the White Rose resistance of young German medical students was a lesson to be studied—and his take on one of the more important moments, it can be considered, in all moral history, was surprising to us at first, though on second thought unsurprising: "It took *discipline* to do what they did, to fight a police state." None of us disagreed—perhaps *we* were disciplined enough to hold our tongues, if not our breath.

I wanted for a second or two to argue, to say that "discipline" was not the essential trait to explain what those young men and women had done—anyway, I was sick and tired of hearing that word "trait" summoned at the drop of a hat, and I had persuaded myself by then that arguments were pointless in that particular class. Maybe, so thinking, I wasn't that far away, in mental set, from the "reality testing" (that mix of conformist compliance, obedience, and subservience) that worked so compellingly to keep so much of Germany still, while a handful of students dared speak up, defy the guns and jails of the Nazi thugs who had the pervasive Gestapo at their every beck and call.

Yet those who wore white roses, who knew what the cost for so behaving might be, most certainly must have had a measure of discipline in them. They had to be careful, circumspect, well-organized for a while, in the hope that stealthily, cleverly, watchfully, they would be able to outwit their almost omnipresent would-be persecutors, the police become an army of arbitrary murderers set on building concentration camps aimed at the destruction of millions of lives; and they had to restrain fear, constrain the temptation to protect their lives for the sake of a long life—and so doing, subdue ordinary and expectable impulses and wishes ("normal," we call them, using a normative psychology), however scary the world had become in 1930s and early 1940s Germany. Under such conditions, discipline was not as inapplicable as we in that military bastion of discipline were tempted (by our own rebelliousness as not quite indoctrinated, newly made officers) to keep believing. Our colonel, more intuitive (less rigidly rule-obsessed) than we, for our own reasons, wanted to recognize, stopped himself in his tracks, and us in ours, by making mention of a new "trait" (Lord save us, a few heard their heads say), and by calling it "moral discipline"—a phrase that, unforgettably, seized us, leaving in its wake our stunned, staring faces, which soon enough displayed a gratefulness that had arrived in us: *yes,* that could well have been how a group of students, in their twenties, against such overwhelming odds, managed to form an idealism of conjecture, of wishful thinking, then turn to another kind of idealism, one of carefully planned and executed activity, that in fact spread across an entire, lawless nation, brought to its abject knees by "*seig heils*" heard everywhere and enforced by an internal army of hit men, of ever-on-the-prowl butchers become slayers of their country's one-time citizens, now deprived of their elementary rights as human beings. From Munich, white roses (and the rallying words that they were meant to symbolize) spread brazenly, to Berlin and to Hamburg, and even to Vienna, absorbed into Hitler's growing empire in 1938. The more the story of that "movement" came to our minds, the more we had to hand it to the colonel, accept his astute analysis, judgment— and consequently, come to another kind of acceptance: an understanding of how hard it was for us, unchallenged, untested, unlike those German youths had once been, to put ourselves in their shoes, to appreciate the mental qualities (all right, the traits) that had made for their moral leadership.

Qualities of Moral Leadership

No wonder, back then, that we began to "zero in" (the phrase our military if not moral leader used) on the various qualities that make for leadership in general, and certainly for moral leadership. No wonder that, over the years, as I became involved in the civil rights struggle in the South, and up North, too, I'd think back to some of those qualities we discussed—I was seeing moral leadership put into deeds, given voice. It was, of course, one thing to discuss such leadership in a class, make lists of qualities that make for that particular aspect of our humanity, recall memories and hear others do so—our personal answers to our teacher's suggested inquiry. It was quite another matter to observe firsthand the moral leadership of ordinary fellow citizens, some of them school-age children rather than founders of social or spiritual or racial or political movements. But the analytic consideration of our class in that Air Force hospital back in the late 1950s did help me to make sense of what I'd heretofore experienced (at home, at school, as a volunteer in a Catholic Worker Movement soup kitchen), and of what I'd thereafter see and hear, go through amidst certain efforts I worked with friends and colleagues to initiate.

All in all, then, moral leadership has to do with "finding a way for oneself, pointing a way for others," or so I once heard Dorothy Day say as she looked back at what she'd tried to do in the 1930s—"We were building places," she amplified modestly, referring to a moral leadership that had to do with the establishment of places where the poor, the hungry, and the homeless might receive food and shelter, the helping hands of others. But to find a way, to point a way, to work with others, start actions, see them through to completion, is to be the moral leader she was and others have been in various ways.

To be a certain kind of moral leader, as Day was, as some who faced down sheriffs in the Mississippi Delta during the 1960s were, as those who tried to change America politically have been, is often to see what needs to be done or changed and then to *exhort,* to *remind* others of what was, what needs to be or ought be; to *criticize* what is, even *reprimand, reprove* those who won't see it or acknowledge it, who uphold the conventional, the established, at whatever cost to people in trouble. To be a moral leader is to see and to provoke, to *stir* others, *teach* them, *persuade* them, *move* them to *reflection, inspire,* and *inform* them, *dramatize* for them the particular issues, matters at stake in a given struggle, *emphasize* for them (for oneself, too) those issues, those matters—to *lecture, hector* even, *invoke* (calling, for example, upon moral traditions, beliefs, teachings), to *evoke* (give expression to those learned values, pieties that have been passed by parents, teachers, and clergy to the young). To be a moral leader is to *reason,* directly or indirectly, with others, to *expand* their sense of the possible, the desirable, the undesirable, and so at times to *restrain* others, *warn* them of dangers, even as one is *alerting* them to possible gains, achievements: to *uplift,* to try to help *enable* ideals, give them the life of a personal and social reality. To be a moral leader is to *tell,* to *announce* and *pronounce,* to *spell out* plans, programs, to *engage with* others so that what is *proposed* is taken to heart and connects with the consciences of listeners, leaders, or viewers. To be a moral leader is to *will,* as already indicated, and as the instances ahead indicate: stories of moral leadership realized, examples of such leadership as exemplars of it have won their various victories, breakthroughs, achievements, and accomplishments.

Moral Passion

To be a moral leader is, then, to call upon moral passion within oneself, set it in motion among others, and do so resourcefully, pointedly—here I return to Dorothy Day, speaking once of what she hoped to do when she began work in the morning at a particular soup kitchen: "Oh, I don't always know exactly, but I gird myself for any difficulties ahead. I guess you have to be determined yourself, if you're going to ask others to stand *with* you, stand *by* you! I speak to the Lord, through prayer, and I speak to my conscience. I hope I'll be able to speak to others successfully—that I'll make sense to them, and they'll want to work with me. I guess, if you want to figure it all out, what we try to do—it's *affiliation,* it's your *conscience, addressing* it, and it's *getting to* others, *touching* them, *reaching* them. If you want to be cynical, you could say we 'sweet-talk' some folks, but I hope with the Lord's will in mind, not just our own!"

So she let the matter drop, in her own upbeat fashion—as she hinted at her wish at times to *entice* and *incite* others, *coax* and *cajole* them, *urge* them on, *talk them into* this or that angle of thinking, line of doing, *win them over.* But she always made mention of a certain *reciprocity* that took place: herself excited by others, stirred mightily by them, "turned on," as her granddaughter would put it, not cynically or glibly, but devotedly, even as she herself "turned on" those others. So it had gone with her, and for others; so some of us who had watched, attended her words, attended meetings where they were spoken, and would conclude with our own generation's language ("she got them all worked up") or with that of a new generation ("she turned them on")—moral leadership as intellect calling upon the energies of conscience, with the loyalty of others a signal that such a call has been contagiously successful.

The Thin Red Line

"There is a thin red line," Dorothy Day once told a few of us, "between asking and trying so hard to get something done that you're near ordering, handing out requests that people take to be orders." Now we all have Terrence Malick's movie version of James Jones's novel (*The Thin Red Line*) written with just that vernacular expression for its title, even as Dorothy Day often summoned those words to remind us (remind herself, we'd finally understand) of the subtleties and shadings of human relatedness, how one can connect with others in a range of ways, with various degrees of intensity, with a shift of emotions that may not be explicit but sure come across (are felt, recognized) as real, as defining in their intention and expectation.

In the movie, moral leadership gets closely examined, rendered—its workings and a substantive version of it. In the military, and at war especially, obedience is all, the chain of command a link that holds everyone together, so our colonel kept telling us in the Air Force base hospital. But obedience has to contend with instinct, as *The Thin Red Line* makes abundantly clear—this is its central psychological exploration. American marines are in far off Guadalcanal Island to win a decisive battle with Japanese foes who have established themselves in a commanding position—below them the jungle's wilds and the desirous newcomers, whose landing we behold, and who will have to risk death in order to uphold and complete their mission. The crocodile that figures at the start and the end of the film is meant to make a point about war and conquest, about human nature, and indirectly about leadership and its sometimes driving, demanding, relentless affirmation—be it pursued up a river in Africa (as in Conrad's *Heart of Darkness*) or in the far Pacific near Australia.

But leaders, by definition, have to come to terms with followers, and so those who affirm an intention have to obtain the consent of those whose deeds (their very lives in jeopardy) will confirm the reality of what has been sought as an ideal, an utter necessity if the dreams of various planners are to be realized. (In the military, those planners are admirals, generals; in the business world, they are company officers or, lower down, entrepreneurial bosses, such as Conrad chose to give us in his tale of greed come to naught.)

What Malick wants to consider, through his camera's exploration, is the risks attendant upon greed or desire as they get worked into a particular course of action, in this case a military one—with all the human consequences of a moral and military leadership implemented in a particular setting, that of a battle for height. Those with the height of leaders who claim a military vision that is being carried out in the name of a nation's survival and strength (a moral outlook) ask others to fight for a height—so that the loftiness of a country, a fighting tradition (that of the Marine Corps), may be won yet again, secured inch by inch on a selected then directed battlefield exertion. An ideal becomes an ordeal; moral leadership (developing a strategy for military victory, national success) has to be followed through, followed up—followers now sacrificed, sufferers who pay the highest possible price, even as their buddies, their friends hitherto at their side, must persist, or risk the wrath of leaders quick to garb themselves in purpose, rules, mandates, urgencies, and customs, the moral paraphernalia of wartime. Unerringly, fiercely, and implacably, as befits a military story, a movie director gives us a psychoanalytic scenario worthy of Freud's metapyschological theory-making: Eros and Thanatos live "naturally" on an island, and in the contrived or man-made or artificial ways of military engagement—even as the id of instinct and impulse, of yearning, of affection, of camaraderie with its attachments, bonds, has to meet the superego's agreeable or naysaying scrutiny (conscience alarmed or persuaded in the name of pieties) and, too, meet the muster of the ego's watchfulness, its ever-present capability of critical examination, of assessing odds and determining this or that likelihood. A moral leadership that is to work must mobilize a following in the name of a virtue, a cause, an occasion; must in life's various struggles (a battle of the more dramatic, vivid kind) inspire and coerce others, those two emotional lines of leadership and command working together intimately, even as Malick reminds us that endangered warriors are tied together by affection (the id) but also harbor the fear and grief, and ultimately the anger, that accompany us when death threatens, when it takes away those we know, have grown to love, and now lose. Yes, our marines figure out a way to win (the ego's resiliency, canniness), and yes, our marines are loyal (the superego) to their patron military tradition, to their country and ours (we who watch the film and root for them, grieve with them and over them) and that being the case, they take orders, stick their necks out, stare clear-cut, noisy, almost certain death in the face.

The Thin Red Line tells of moral leadership that ultimately won't give ground (officers have to shout, make evident their steady conviction, no matter what), and tells concomitantly of obedience, compliance, assent: what happens when what is proclaimed or ordered gets taken to heart, gets believed, even when the clatter of a machine gun threatens not only bodies but the willing minds of followers that are essential for a victory. True, the jungle's law opens and closes the movie—the alligator's appetite; but military law, the moral constraints of leadership as it gets passed down the ranks, also pervades the film, is its central subject of investigation. Fighting men, who must take orders, must also contend with "mourning and melancholia"—to mention Freud's way of evoking a universal and inevitable human experience becoming so immediately omnipresent in a war. The abstraction "mourning and melancholy" has to do with the vulnerability of human connection, and when that becomes thoroughly apparent, when ties are sundered, it is then that moral leadership gets threatened by hearts broken, ears becoming deaf, eyes looking for a way out rather than the way ahead (up the hill, up to physical conquest, but also to the satisfactions of moral conquest, whereby danger has been overcome, survival secured, albeit the uneasiness of death felt, lives remembered). No question, wars persist, recur; no battle is the last one—and so we are left at the end with the alligator's always unappeased hunger. Yet we are movie-goers who have had or will have our own fights to try winning.

Small wonder that we are able and even anxious to immerse our-selves in a chronicle of wartime moral leadership, its doubts and decla-rations as expressed by those who mobilize moral reasons, legal (or corporate or military) necessities, and by those who, on the other side of things, are fighting followers. Every day is a battle *for us,* we know, even as we hope to prevail, while heeding those voices within us, about us, that tell us to move ahead, notwithstanding the tricky and precari-ous terrain—our own moral leadership as it can guide us, pull on us, even as we know full well that grim chance and sorry circumstance may await us.

Walker Percy

Speaking of those who sit watching as *The Thin Red Line* unfolds, the novelist Walker Percy, in *The Moviegoer,* makes clear the power of words and pictures, of a story on film, to draw us in, draw us on. His central character, Binx Bolling, is on a "search"—a morally energetic attempt to find his bearings, to find the point of things. Binx knows well what it means to be alone, lost, yet he finds himself through another's growing attachment to his sometimes stumbling self—hence his poignant avowal of human connection as a kind of guiding deliverance. "There is only one thing I can do," he lets his beloved Kate know toward the end of his "search," and he spells out the matter with these words: "Lis-ten to people, see how they stick themselves into the world, hand them along, and for good and selfish reasons. It only remains to decide whether this vocation is best pursued in a service station or—"

With that concluding inclusiveness an author suggests the length and breadth of moral leadership as it gets affirmed, amid the detours and dead ends of our days. We do, indeed, no matter who we are, what we do, hand one another along, give one another various reasons to be, to take a stand, to act—as a philosophical storyteller, Percy, beholden to

Søren Kierkegaard, knew, as did the Memphis mother mentioned earlier in this chapter know in her heart, mind, soul when she took her son's hand in the library, in the face of racial exclusion. Her son was to remember that moment always, and to tell others: a saga of moral leadership in ordinary life handed along, handing us all along.

IX

Dietrich Bonhoeffer: The Will
and Moral Transcendence

I was first introduced to the writings of the German theologian, pastor, and, ultimately, martyr Dietrich Bonhoeffer by my college professor Perry Miller, whose research (already mentioned in earlier pages) it was to explore the provocative wisdom in the sermons and essays of the New England puritan divines of the seventeenth and eighteenth centuries. To this day I recall Miller's account of Bonhoeffer's willful stand against the Nazis—a singular, voluntary opposition to tyranny that culminated in his execution in a concentration camp only weeks before the end of Hitler's regime. Miller himself was obviously haunted by Bonhoeffer's life—this Lutheran, this "Aryan" of great social, economic, and educational privilege, who refused to embrace the führer and his henchmen, as the great majority of Germany's ministers all too evidently did, many of them even wearing the swastika as they went about their so-called spiritual duties. To this day, also, I recall Miller's emphatically put challenge to us in his seminar: *"What would you do under such circumstances, under Hitler, if you were there, back then?"*

By the time that question had been put to the class, not one of us was able to answer with any moral confidence. A remarkably vigorous and knowing teacher had immersed us in the Germany of the early 1930s, in Bonhoeffer's personal life: his family background, his religious training, his early career as a scholar—and we had thereby come to realize that by no means was the outcome of his life (death at thirty-nine) predictable during many of the years that preceded it, even the late 1930s, when he had made quite clear his principled, energetic opposition to the Third Reich. Bonhoeffer's life, like that of so many idealists, took shape gradually—a growing response to a growing evil whose contours time and events only gradually revealed.

In medical school, at Columbia's College of Physicians and Surgeons, I followed Miller's advice and took a class (mentioned in the introductory chapter) given by Reinhold Niebuhr, a seminar on Bonhoeffer's life and work given by a friend of Bonhoeffer's—twice in the 1930s Bonhoeffer had come to study at Union Theological Seminary. Niebuhr was no stranger to irony, and he was at pains for us to realize how concerned many at Union were for Bonhoeffer when he decided, in 1939, to leave America (after being here only a month or so) for his native land. By then Bonhoeffer's explicit, brave resistance to the Nazis was thoroughly established. He might have stayed in the United States, helped awaken a still strongly isolationist nation to the great threat fascism posed for the Western democracies. But he wanted to take his stand amidst his own people—though in 1939 he emphatically did not have imprisonment and a martyr's death on his mind. Some of his friends at Union, however, had his choice of a return to Germany very much on their minds, as Niebuhr let us know: "It was tempting for many here to regard him as in trouble psychologically, as depressed. It was tempting to recommend that he see a psychiatrist—*then* he'd become more 'realistic.' "

As I read Eberhard Bethge's biography of Bonhoeffer, and his own words, I gradually understood how shrewd Niebuhr was to remind us of the potential disparity of thought and assumption between modern psychiatry, and yes, even certain precincts of contemporary religion, with its emphasis on "pastoral counseling," on the one hand, a viewpoint that stresses social adjustment, which soon enough can eagerly accommodate political power, and on the other, a traditionally biblical viewpoint that is skeptical of "power and principalities," even adverse to them. Eventually, with reluctant yet unyielding realization, Bonhoeffer concluded that his position in society, his personal safety, and, if need be, his very life were not to be defended at all costs, were not to be his bottom line: "the cost of discipleship," to use his phrase, the cost, that is, of a loyalty under great duress to Jesus, to His example, can be high indeed—beyond the imagining of some of us who get called "normal," and who surely would have known, in Bonhoeffer's situation, to be "realistic," as Niebuhr put it so bluntly.*

"This is the end, but for me the beginning of life"—those last recorded words of Bonhoeffer's, in one of Hitler's concentration camps, on his way to death, remind us how topsy-turvy a certain kind of moral and spiritual life can be, how utterly indifferent, even contrary, to various received secular pieties, not least the psychological ones that offer us the "reality principle" and "normality" as conceptual judgments of our behavior. "Rebuked and scorned," as the biblical phrase goes, Jesus did not play it cool and cagey, did not temper His message or His behavior in order to avoid "conflict" or "anxiety" or "depression," in order to "work" on this or that "problem"; rather, He pressed on, acting on principles that to others seemed incomprehensible or dangerous, even life-threatening: the essential "madness" of a kind of ethical determination that won't settle for the rewards of social conformity. Similarly, while others (many who called themselves Christians, attended church regularly) cannily cut their views and actions to suit the political power of the day, Bonhoeffer realized that, in the poet Paul Celan's words, "death is a master from Germany"— hence the requirement of standing up to it, even if to do so defied all that others deemed to be practical or a matter of common sense. No wonder a young Jesuit who teaches in my undergraduate course recently wished, wistfully, that the Catholic Church would one day make

---

* I tried to summon the range of Bonhoeffer's thinking in *Dietrich Bonhoeffer,* Modern Spiritual Masters Series, Orbis Books, 1998.

Dietrich Bonhoeffer its "first ecumenical saint"—a Lutheran theologian who lived as if Jesus were a concrete, nearby presence, constantly insisting that deeds, not clever-spoken or written words, not practiced rituals, are the test of a particular faith's significance in one's life.

Some institutions, some nations and churches as well, have their ways of singling out leadership. For that young Jesuit, Bonhoeffer was a compelling moral and spiritual leader whose life deserved immemorial recognition, whose life was a reminder of an unyielding opposition to evil—his stand against Hitler's criminals even more trying than Dolci's against those of the Mafia: both men were seemingly immune to the fearfulness that tugs at so many of us. On the very day Hitler took power, in January 1933, Bonhoeffer was on the radio, warning his fellow Germans of the danger ahead—Nazi leadership was an invitation to the devil, of criminality become state power. Soon enough a brilliant theologian would be an enemy of a ruthlessly murderous totalitarian state, and soon enough a modern martyrdom would be lived—a moral witness steadfastly pursued. "None of us could forget him during those years [the 1930s, early 1940s]," Niebuhr told us, referring to an extraordinary witness, one sustained bravely, courageously, without letup. "His life," Niebuhr remarked once, "became for many of us a contemporary moral challenge—we looked up to him as if he'd been sent to inspire us, to serve as a reminder of what truly matters: to assert, to live, day by day, our principles, our beliefs."

Bonhoeffer's witness turned into its own kind of leadership. He called upon his fellow ministers to speak up and out—to refuse the authority of Nazism, to take it on as the enemy. He refused for himself any number of convenient exits, refuges—he said no to a gangster regime, even if death was to be his certain fate, so he knew as he took the measure of a lawless state determined to kill by the hundreds of thousands its own citizens. An intellectual's life, a theologian's, gradually became a daily embrace of a faith (as it had to be, for him) worked into remarks, friendships, and deeds of various kinds—all elements of a growing martyrdom unselfconsciously assumed.

Will and Martyrdom

The psychology of the martyr, of a certain kind of moral leader who won't be frightened by obstacles and opponents large and vindictive, is the psychology of will—of a decision made and its consequences be damned. In this age of determinisms, emotional and social and historical and economic, there is little room for "will" in the vocabulary we summon when we try to understand human affairs. Sometimes first things get overlooked in our rush for the less obvious. Erik Erikson, talking about psychoanalysis (and his study of Luther) once observed that "willfulness often is regarded as a secondary trait—we rush to explain the reasons for it. I believe some people have learned to be willful about their beliefs—their willfulness is a big part of them, and it is summoned by them in pursuit of whatever it is they want to uphold. Perhaps that is what 'leadership' is all about—the person who won't take no for an answer: he believes something and he'll do everything it takes to get across what it is he believes, and why. Others with the same outlook—well, they aren't as committed to their ideals, or they don't know how to stick to their guns, live up to their words, 'so help me God,' as it's put." We were, needless to say, as Erikson's students, colleagues struggling hard and long with the matter of human particularity—what makes for a singular moral distinction that becomes for others a gladly noticed, summoning signal, a beacon that inspires even distant strangers to thought, to decision.

In the words of David Roberts, a theologian who knew well of a witness that began in America as well as Germany, "Bonhoeffer was a solitary person, and often by choice he was reclusive. He kept his distance from many of us at Union, and later in Germany, we all know now, he kept his distance from the Nazis in a manner few others could quite dare emulate." As I look back at those remarks, which I heard in Roberts's class, I think of Dolci as well as Dietrich Bonhoeffer. Both were stalwart moral leaders; each of them stood his ground fast, almost fiercely so, against the constant threats of fascism, of gangsterism around every corner. Dolci has told us that he had to remove himself from so very much around him in order to be able to turn away from dozens of invitations, seductions, possibilities—a society ready to absorb him, and thereby rob him of his resolute intent, intentions; and hence his loneliness, which he described not with maudlin self-pity, or as evidence of a mind endangered or vulnerable, but rather, and ironically, as the consequence of a spirit strengthened by a canny watchfulness, wariness: all that (and them) I must keep at a distance. So, too, with Bonhoeffer, whose witness was more strenuous than Dolci's, and more solitary—one affirmed, even so, by judgments constantly made. Such a witness, an extended moral vigil, required a mind's constant critical activity—until at last the one at a decided remove is the one held deep in the minds and hearts of others: moral leadership that comes from afar (like religion itself) to those who are caught up in, tied to, the rhythms of ordinary life, and yet who hunger for the encouragement, the guidance, the relief and release, the example that a leader's chosen moral transcendence, embodied in years of commitment, can keep offering during his or her life, but in some instances, long afterward as well.

X

The Bond Between Leaders and Followers: Erik Erikson, Gandhi, and Albert Jones, a Boston Bus Driver

These people are making their own kind of history, and we need to know that side of it, how people 'on the bottom' can take the lead—and make followers out of their leaders." So said Erik Erikson to me about a group of African-American children in Boston in the late 1960s, and their bus driver, who was driving them to and from previously all-white schools.

I often thought of Erikson's words "make followers out of their leaders" as I rode on that bus and talked with those children, and especially as I listened to the volunteer bus driver, heard his story of how he, a janitor in a block of apartment houses, had found the time and will to get some thirty elementary-school children to and from schools "across the big divide," as he called it—from "an almost all-black Roxbury" to "the white streets yonder."

Erikson was himself trying to understand another kind of protest, and leadership, both displayed earlier in the twentieth century—the deeds of India's Mahatma Gandhi, a man who was quite well-educated and became known, celebrated across the world.

Erikson on a Bus Driver as a Leader

In 1967 in Boston, a group of African-American parents organized themselves into the Boardman Parents Group—an effort on their part to find less crowded, more adequately staffed schools for their sons and daughters to attend. I started going to their meetings; and when those mothers and fathers, with the help of private funding, secured a bus to take their children out of a ghetto neighborhood (Roxbury) to schools elsewhere in Boston (the Back Bay, and eventually South Boston), an initiative allowed by an "open enrollment" rule long on the books but rarely used, I ended up riding that bus myself every day. I wanted to see how the children saw things—to learn from them firsthand what it meant to leave one world, travel by bus to another one, stay there for a few hours, then return (in a city once known for its abolitionist sentiments).

I was also, at the time, teaching in a course at Harvard offered by the child psychoanalyst Erik Erikson. His work had come to mean a lot to me, not only *Childhood and Society,* with its acknowledgment of influences on the mind other than those arising in a particular family's life, but his attempts to understand the nature of moral leadership—as in his studies of Luther and Gandhi. His own moral leadership, for many of us trained in psychoanalytic psychiatry, would be decisive, and I would spend a good deal of time in the late 1960s and early 1970s not only teaching with him and learning from him, but learning of him. As I wrote a biography of Erikson, an intellectual leader who had been interested in a religious leader (Luther) and now a political leader (Gandhi), I was talking with and observing poor families attempting their own kind of collective leadership. Erikson listened to the tapes I made of conversations with that driver, those children, two of whom were his sons, and connected them all and their story to the work he was doing on the life of Mahatma Gandhi.

"It's a fantasy, for sure, but I can imagine Gandhi listening to this tape, and clapping and smiling," my psychoanalytic teacher once said. Then he explained why: "When he really liked something he often clapped—and I'd guess that he would be very impressed by this man's determination to teach his sons, and their friends and neighbors on the bus—teach them how it matters to stop and think about ethical questions, and once you've done that, and decided where you stand, how it matters to take action, thoughtful action, but action. Here is a man who has plenty to do, more than enough, taking care of all those buildings (menial work, you and I would call it, but not Gandhi, he'd call it valuable and necessary and even exalted work!) and yet he finds time to drive children on a bus, an old one, way across the city, and he comes to pick them up, and both times he's teaching them, giving them lessons on leadership, and then he works into the night to make up for the time he's 'lost' on the job. The children know what he's doing, not just his sons but all of them—he's to them what he tells them to be, down the line, to themselves: people with convictions, moral convictions that they're ready to uphold ('come what may,' the saying goes). For Gandhi, it would be a privilege to meet this man, I know—he was always on the lookout for such people, and was always aware of his relative 'luck,' his 'high position' in life, compared to this fellow, this Al you've gotten me to know. He's not only driving those kids, he's leading them someplace, and it's not only a geographic place, it's a place in their minds, and needless to say, in his, first: they don't want to be with whites so much as they want *to be,* period. Or am I getting too dramatic here?"

"Let's Go"

Al Jones's leadership had emerged through an accident and by instinct, he once indicated: "When I went to the first meeting in the church, I heard people talking about whether they should send their sons and their daughters over to 'whitey territory.' One man shouted *no,* and some agreed. But others said *yes*—and I began to understand that we all were teetering, that's what: mothers and fathers, not sure of ourselves, what to do, and let me tell you, scared, scared out of our minds, and when you're scared you tremble, and you're afraid you'll make a mistake, and here were our children, and they'd be the ones to suffer, to pay for our errors, for all the mistakes we made.

"The noise got louder, and I could see what was happening—I said to myself, sitting there: hey, Albert, don't you see, there's a crowd of people here, and they're talking about themselves and their kids, but they're going one way one minute, and the next way the next minute, and they're headed for trouble and more trouble, for a fight and another fight, and this won't stop until someone starts telling it like it is, and speaking big, speaking the truth, speaking above himself and way beyond himself, even if he's scared, like anyone else (but everyone is!) and he's decided to roll the dice, not to make dough but to put his heart on the line, no matter what, and his soul, too—and that's being a leader. 'What's a leader?' I asked myself that, right in the church, so help me God. I asked myself: what should you say now, Albert? But I heard nothing, except my heart beating hard, and I saw my fingers moving, my right hand shaking, and I could feel my toes, ready to go—get out of there, rather than take a chance and stay and say what seems right. I knew, I knew—if you open your mouth, in no time flat you've got people naysaying you, and giving you a look that says you've fallen flat on your face! Who wants to take risks, when if you keep quiet you're not 'out there' and hearing yourself bad-mouthed! I was in the middle of that, thinking like that—and then, my God, I heard myself!

"You keep asking me what I said, but it wasn't much," he insisted modestly. I had, for sure, leaped when he spoke of his comment, delivered amidst a spell of silence. He had been intent on listening rather than speaking. He had heard the noise we all make when we are sitting somewhere and getting ready to up ourselves and take leave. He had heard the consequence of his feet moving, his arms as well. He had noticed what his ears had heard, and what his eyes had picked up, bodies in motion while time passed, the drifts of time now on the loose amidst the apparent demise of a meeting, a planned presentation of thought and feeling, of expectation and apprehension. His eyes reached for the faces of others, but no one seemed interested in looking at anyone else.

In church, he remembered, people turn to those near them—the felt reassurance that a shared time together provides. But now he felt alone, and surmised that others were also cut off, each from anyone near or far. No authority on "crowd behavior" or "group psychology," he nevertheless had taken a social pulse in a place, and his mind had become alert, alarmed: "I've gone to church all my life, and I know when a meeting is going to end, when we've all been together, because of the faith in us, and the music—but there, at that discussion about school, it was different, I realized: this is going to be over in no time fast, that's what I realized—that's what came to my mind, and I don't rightly remember that I thought much of anything, until I heard my very own voice, and it wasn't spoken long, because I was short and to the point. 'Let's go,' that's what I said, just two words.

"A man in front of me turned around to look, and I could see he didn't know what I meant—if we should leave, or get ourselves together and make some decision. I could tell he wasn't sure; I could see it on his face—so I decided to make myself better understood. That's when I raised my voice and really spoke up. That's when I pitched it to the folks—like my wife says it, I 'had my say.' I started low, in my voice, talking with the man [in front]. I said, 'We should *get going,* and *take charge*—get things under control.'

"I could see that guy wasn't out to argue with me, but he was wondering: okay, buddy, but how do you (should you) go do that. It was written all over his face, and it was running all through my head: hey, Mr. Albert, it's time to 'go,' all right, to let go with an idea, a *proposal,* that's the word. Say it like you believe, I told myself, say it so others will get going themselves, in their minds, like it's going in your mind. So, I started myself up again—I was talking high, talking loud. I said, 'Listen folks, this is important.' I said, 'It really will make a difference, what we do.'

"I said this: 'Don't you see, Mr. Charlie, he's out there, and he'll decide what happens to our kids, whether they go here or there or some other place—he'll decide according to what suits him. But these are *our* kids, and we can forget that, and let them become Mr. Charlie's, his property, or we can say *no,* nothing doing—it's up to us to stand up and speak up and take the lead, that's the difference now: we're going to be the ones who make the decisions, or we're going to sit back and be—*theirs, their* people. They're used to owning us, and we're used to being owned, and now we're talking about our children, our sons and our daughters, and I ask you right now, that's what you have to figure out: will you stand up for yourself and your own, your flesh and blood, your kids, or will you hand them over to those big shots—you know: Mr. Charlie?'

"Next thing I knew, I was out of breath, huffing away, and as my momma would say, 'scared, mighty scared.' But no one took me on, to argue. I sat down, and all I could hear was that the folks were leaning and shuffling their shoes, and the man in front of me, he was still staring, and he didn't seem upset. All of a sudden, a big surprise; he got up himself, and he was standing like I was, and he was talking: 'I heard the man's words, and I'm one hundred percent with him. Let's go, like he said.'

"For a second, I was with him, like he was with me. It was like a reversal—me staring the way he stared! He told everyone they should realize that it's 'now or never.' He told them that he'd heard me, and so now it's time to 'come up with an answer,' and 'the answer should be yes, yes, let's go and take the lead, and tell all the Mr. Charlies that we're on the move, we've taken our step for ourselves, no matter what they all want to happen to us—it's for us to stand up and take our stand.' That's when I joined with him. He'd had his say, and he was stopping, and I stood up, and I said, 'Yes, sir,' and I said, 'Let's go,' again, and then he said it, too, and then people were repeating themselves, and it was amazing, because we were all together, united.

"Afterwards, as we were leaving, people were hugging and smiling, and that's when a man came up and said, 'You get this going, but then what . . . ?' It was then that I thought to myself, all right: if you start something, you're part of doing the starting, then you'd better not disappear. You owe it to what you've begun, to the kids, your own and everyone else's here. That means you volunteer, you drive, you go, you go with them. So, I said that, I told the minister, as we all were talking, walking to go home. I said, 'I'll go with the kids, and drive the bus, if it comes to that.' He laughed; he said, 'First you're telling us "Let's go," and now you're saying that you'll go, too, and that's a big step you're taking.' I answered him: 'Yes, sir, Mr. Minister, reverend.' He laughed and told me I was becoming a leader, because I had the 'impulse' of one, and he was following—but I said, 'No, just offering to drive, that's all.' I guess if you drop the usual in your life, and start speaking, and making your offer, then you're out there, out of the everyday things you've got to do. If that's what 'leading' is, I think I understood, then and there, what the reverend was getting at, and what I'd be having to face myself, one of these days—so when I went home and talked with my wife, I was more savvy than usual. Usually I let her know some-thing, and she'll try to get me straightened out in my thinking, but that night I was being as clear as I could, and she could tell. She told me my mind was all 'set,' and she was with me, and she'd do all she could to back me up. 'I'll walk with you,' she promised—and I admit it: I was scared for both of us."

Crossing Boston

By the next week he was the bus driver who took African-American children into white neighborhoods and previously all-white schools. At first he did so without pay, at the behest of northern activists who had dared take advantage of a city's rules and laws. In a sense, he was the one who took a group of African-American children from a ghetto, with its overcrowded schools, to genteel white neighborhoods whose schools offered plenty of room (and solid educational circumstances) for those children. Eventually, he would travel with them when they went on a regular city bus (as opposed to the one a group of civil rights activists initially secured, which he drove). In time, as well, when African-American students began going to South Boston—a tough or-deal indeed, for them and for the city, which had to endure a full-fledged racial conflict, one very much out in the open—there was another bus to be driven, no easy task, as he learned quickly: "I never thought I'd hear the language those people used when we arrived [at South Boston High School]: it's up on a hill, that place, and those people are down in a sewer, that's what I thought when I heard them and saw them lifting signs. I wished I could get out of the bus, and start a conversation with them all, but I knew they'd never give me the time of day, and it wouldn't be long, I was afraid, that I'd be on my way to the City Hospital—they'd bash my head in, and there'd be nothing left of me, before I got out of their hands, unless I got killed."

He stops. He hastens to remind me (to remind himself) that "the North is the North," and "the city of Boston wasn't going to let people go wild and become a mob." But he often thought, at first, that mobs might indeed be let have their sway—that being so, he poured out his worries and apprehension to his wife: "We began to ask ourselves: *why,* why take the risk? I always answered in my heart with one word (no long explanations): *because.* I was using shorthand, I was telling myself that I knew the score, knew what was at stake, and so I couldn't turn my back on myself—on my own knowledge, you could say. If you can trick yourself, maybe you avoid some troubles, but hey, you're giving up on what you know is right, and I'll say this: I'd rather go through a neighborhood mob cussing away at me for being a 'dirty nigger' than sitting in my own chair here or lying on my own bed, and realizing that I'd 'chickened out' and let those haters rule my mind. That's the victory they want, and that's the victory I won't give them. The ministers, they told me I've been a 'good man,' and I've been a 'leader'—well, I don't know. It's not for me to call myself fancy, uppity words. I know my faults. But now I can sleep, and if I'd backed down, back then, over this integration thing, I think I'd be wasted by now, for lack of sleep. So when I asked myself (and my wife asked) *why,* why I got into all this, and spoke up, and kept showing up to drive the bus in the first place, and later, to go to South Boston with the young people—the answer was to get my sleep, and so I could look at myself in the mirror and not want to run away in shame: that's the explanation, for sure."

"A Person of Stature": Gandhi and Mr. Jones

He had edged into the driver's seat, had become a person of substantial daily significance to a particular neighborhood's children and their families. On the way to school he made his remarks, sang a song (such as "Dixie" or "The Battle Hymn of the Republic"), and became for boys and girls, for their mothers and fathers, "a person of stature," so his own minister described him.

I still remember mentioning that phrase to Erik Erikson, who immediately pointed out that "early in Gandhi's life" he was characterized as "a person of stature" by some who knew him. Well, yes, obviously and understandably, I recall thinking in connection with the Mahatma, and yes, with this thoroughly obscure janitor and now sometime bus driver.

"Why don't you ask others what they think of him?" Erikson's suggestion struck me as an unnecessary one. I was often on that bus he drove, could see and hear for myself how he helped shepherd a flock of youngsters from one part of a city to another, amidst considerable social and racial stress. Indeed, I'd mentioned him in some early writing I'd done about "bussing in Boston," a melancholy moment in a northern city's political and educational struggle. But Erikson's suggestion, defensively rebuffed by me as unnecessary, exerted itself as I met with those who would qualify as individuals worthy of the kind of inquiry he had indicated as desirable.

I sought the pastor of the driver's church, heard Mr. Jones praised as a "leader," as "the one our children most admire and trust," heard him extolled as "a man of moral conviction, who will put his life on the line, even, if his conscience dictates he do something." Such words struck me as excessive, and the minister quickly picked up a restrained but evident skepticism on my face and in my questions. At one point, I heard in the church's vestry an echo of what I'd heard from Erikson in a university's library study: "Hereabouts, we're all just plain folks, the Lord's little people, but you've got to remember who *He* was—just a carpenter who spoke the truth that came to Him, and besides, He was willing to stand up for what He believed to be true, one hundred percent true. I say it every Sunday [in church]; I say, Jesus will be there for you because He was where you are now. I say, if there's a test, and it's going to be yours, whether you stand up for what's right, then the Lord will take notice, yes, He will. That's why I think Mr. Jones, our brother Albert, is doing so well—he's got the Lord watching over him and smiling."

I tired of that religious rhetoric. I wondered how to get beyond it— even as I was thinking of what to report back when I saw Professor Erikson. I concluded that I should say my good-byes, make my way back to my car. Yet this polite and spiritually impassioned pastor had already figured out what my face and body registered, an intention of immediate departure. Suddenly, a remark was made: "You're a busy man—and you know, that's what Brother Albert told us once, at a meeting we had in this church: 'You all are busy,' he said, and no one spoke, and he could tell he should keep going, try to circle us in. 'It's important to be busy,' he went on, 'but if you don't find the time to change the world, then you're busy keeping it the way it is, and that's the truth Jesus knew, and that's the truth we've got to find for ourselves, right here.' He kept saying that every day counts, and true, we have to keep busy and keep going, but sometimes, there comes a time, when here and now everything counts, and you have to be here and stay here, because there's no choice—'not if you want to do right, be on the Lord's side.'

" 'Powerful,' a man said, and then his wife, she said 'right,' and then everyone was nodding, and saying 'right,' and 'one hundred percent right,' one man said, and his wife upped it, and she said 'a thousand percent,' and a man went for broke, he said, 'two thousand percent,' and I'll tell you, we all were up on the ceiling, that's where we were, that's where he had us, and that's when I thought to myself, Brother Albert, he's got us wide awake, our consciences, and he's moved us a good distance, a good one, and he's a strange one, and he's got his nerves bothering him, but he's being God's servant, that's who, a leader doing what *should* be done, what's correct—a correct person standing for the correct, that's who Brother Albert is, and that's what those children he drives to school know, and that's what we all have known, since he began coming at us."

Erikson listened with concentration to this tape with his own kind of nodding approval, but to my surprise, with an insistence that he come meet this pastor, and especially Al Jones, the bus driver. At the time I felt a bit of exaggeration at work—Erikson's willingness to connect his moral hero, Gandhi, with the pastor's newfound one. At the time, as well, I was busy at work holding high the children whom the driver took to school and returned home from school. No wonder Erik Erikson, hardly a stranger to the virtuous possibilities in children, which he'd evoked, rendered in his breakthrough book *Childhood and Society,* resorted to a polite and wry kind of indirect remonstrance with me! "I hope you won't mind," he remarked, "if I try to connect the great moral figures in history to those children you're meeting, and to the man who drives them on the bus. That's the 'problem,' you could call it, of teaching history, and becoming a student of it. You can become impressed with what you're learning, with the people whose lives you're studying, but it doesn't take long for you to be removed, courtesy of this education, from the world and how it actually works, the world that may truly resemble those distant worlds of the history books and the biographies."

Informants: Ones Who Help
You Learn About Yourself

"You know," Erikson continued, "when I spoke with a man and his wife in India—they were both friends of Gandhi—they kept telling me how *amazing* his life was. You can imagine—I picked up on that word right away. I wanted to know what they had in mind, of course—but they used that word to indicate a proper awe, while at the same time they let me know how surprised they were by 'all that happened' to Gandhi. I was surprised by their surprise! I took the liberty of reminding them of Gandhi's long struggle to realize his ethical ambitions for his people. After all, if they knew the young Gandhi, why should they have been surprised by what happened to him? But they kept going back to the man they knew, to his ethical side. At one point the wife referred to Gandhi's difficult, aloof side, and declared him 'very much like others' in their 'social circle.' Yes, he was 'tough and determined,' and 'hard to get along with if you disagreed with him and very critical of anyone who didn't follow him.' But that was, finally, her point: where others were more or less like him, or not so different, he was stubborn and determined, and where others were stubborn and determined, he had something on his mind, something that really mattered to him, something that wouldn't let go of him, and something that he wouldn't, couldn't let go of.

"It's true," Erikson resumed after suddenly stopping: "I'm the one speaking here, but that must be familiar to you in your work, that word 'informant'! The informant can be the one who helps you learn about yourself, your own ideas—the one who 'informs' you that way! You're learning from those informants nothing less than how a leader helps make history in a city, makes it more moral!"

A shrug now, of the professor's shoulders; a raising of his eyebrows, a lowering of his head, then a direct glance at the one sitting opposite him: "We both have to be careful when we 'apply' psychoanalysis! We can turn Gandhi into someone 'obsessed,' and your [driver] friend into a troubled eccentric—this minister and his neighbors are getting ready to do that, I sense from what you've heard. That's what caught the imagination of the [Indian] couple—they were amazed at the way a *situation* can turn a seemingly ordinary person into someone bigger than he was, a leader, a moral leader. Yes, that's it [I had commented that an ordinary one becomes extraordinary]. But there's an unusual side to a Gandhi; he's waiting for that 'situation,' even trying to bring it about so that he can move further, and others will be more responsive or attentive—the human chemistry of the leader and the led."

Much more discussion of that—of the bond between the one who leads and the ones who follow—an Eriksonian formulation that had informed *Young Man Luther* and would give essential shape to *Gandhi's Truth:* psychoanalysis as respectful to, appreciative of, history and sociology, both—what an "event" in a neighborhood or a nation (in India or in our United States) can prompt in a particular person, hence Gandhi's moral thinking and concerns become newly charged, his demonstration of moral leadership, and hence that driver's driving force in his community, his city.

Put differently, as Erikson said, weighing carefully a certain step he was taking, and asking me to take: "We're not prepared, often, to call a man like your friend Albert Jones a 'leader.' But he *is* a leader of yours—in the sense that he's helping you see a lot; he's 'leading' your mind to understand how a 'plain guy' becomes outstanding, a figure-head in his community during a time of challenge and trouble—a leader, we do have a right to call him. You're trying to figure out his 'psychodynamics,' and I respect your wariness! But a leader gets attention, even yours, someone from way 'outside' our society. If we emphasize those psychodynamics we turn them into an explanation, and there you have a right to be careful, to resist the interest so many people have in psychology as the answer to everything, and the explanation of everything.

"People want to know about 'the psychology of leaders,' our Gandhis and our Albert Joneses, or others you met down South in the civil rights years, or now up here; and you and I are tempted by our profession and by its role in our culture (the use people make of us)—we're tempted to come up with something that's reasonable, and yet we meet people like that couple [who knew Gandhi] or the men and women you tell me are now 'in awe' of someone's leadership, and then we have to do the best we can to reply to them when they speak their surprise or wonder or amazement, even as we try to find out for ourselves how to approach the riddle of leadership—as you say, the 'mystery' of who becomes a leader—when and why, for what reasons personal and social and political and historical."

Soon enough Erik Erikson was sitting with me in that bus as it hurtled onward through residential areas and stretches of shops—the children musing and watching, or playing around, and occasionally horsing around, hence the driver's raised voice, his reprimand, and always a plea, an exhortation, often begun with "Come on, you kids," followed by the gist of the speech, the heart of the bussing matter, as in this exclamation, which Erikson heard and later made much of as we hearkened back, together, to our ambulatory moment: "Stop and think while we're moving, all of you! Hear me? You're on your way to school—but you're on your way to the head of the class! You're leading your people! For a long time we were kept outside, outside America. Now we're going inside, inside America, and you kids, you're our leaders. We're following your direction. You go in there, that school, and learn what's right. You get 'correct' on all your tests. You *be* correct! We'll learn from you! You'll make us better, better off. *We'll* become correct, too, on your account."

For us those words were obviously stirring, as they were for the children who heard them—some of whom, one could notice, sat up exceedingly straight as they were told to "be correct," as if their bodies wished to comply forthwith, to fall in line with the speaker's firm suggestion, his command made credible and appealing by virtue of each day's journey, on his part, with the boys and girls who now seemed ready to offer him an earned assent.

Leadership of Ethics in Action

"There's leadership in action," Erikson enthused in his office back at Harvard, and then he claimed more for what he heeded closely, as closely as the children being addressed: "We saw 'a leadership of ethics in action,' a driver driving home a moral message to young people— and all of them leading: the adult sharing leadership with his young charges, reminding them of the importance of what they're doing, and of their own importance." For this student of Gandhi's "truth," Gandhi's "leadership of ethics"—a phrase I often heard in that office— a day in Boston's black (Roxbury) neighborhood, a bus trip across the city to a white neighborhood that the children kept calling "downtown," had become an encounter of sorts with a lived affirmation of moral leadership, the driver's as it had informed the responsive behavior of children on their way to and from school.

At one point the driver had reminded the children of this: "You're carrying 'the right thing' on your shoulders for our people." Both Erikson and I weren't quite clear what "the right thing" specifically meant, nor were we convinced that the children, then and there, quite knew—yet they surely knew that the driver in his mind definitely knew, and he had for some time been making his concrete, storytelling case. Indeed, days later, when I talked yet again with some of those youngsters, they made clear to me that they understood quite well his message, that it had also become theirs, as Erikson would conclude while he listened to tapes, looked at drawings done in "interviews" I'd done: "I suppose we could speak, in general, of a 'leadership of the good'—all those young people and their driver friend on their joint way to 'freedom, freedom now.' " He was, in that last regard, summoning the song, the chant he'd heard on the bus, a powerful music on the lips of the driver and all those being transported. Such words, such a cry of the heart, of the soul, such an affirmation of hope and expectation, amidst still persisting vulnerability (even, in some instances, social and economic exclusion, hence bondage) echoed powerfully in the ears of Gandhi's biographer, as he tried so earnestly to do his own kind of traveling: "I felt in that bus that I was being carried to moments and events that Gandhi knew and observed—how it goes when people try to assert themselves and become their own leaders, and that way find their beliefs, their principles."

We were, of course, approaching, with the help of some children and their driver, an existentialism of sorts—the good enacted knowingly in life, and the good worked into a ride that became a big step: leadership as a shared move, a trip the driver both casually and fervently graced as "blessed by the Lord," after which, inevitably, the warning that "He is watching us," and the suggestion that "we be on our best behavior": a moral leadership at the wheel that soon enough got carried into the lives of young people who were impatient to make a new school their own, and worried lest in some way, at some moment, they falter.

When I mentioned the latter to Erikson, told him of some of the fears and anxieties I'd heard put to word by some of the children, he smiled broadly, jested with me about ourselves, *our* times of apprehension, even agitation, then dared bring his spiritual mentor into the company of those children and the rest of us—and did so in his own distinctive way: "Even a moral leader is entitled to moments of doubt—and maybe a moral leader is doing the best he can, or she, if there's some trouble or alarm eating away inside at him or her, in the course of the work of leadership that's being done. Gandhi—he knew how to be uncertain or alerted to danger, the same way these kids feel at times during the week!"

We were down to the obvious, the relationship between demonstrated, affirmed moral leadership and the ups and downs a life can present, and especially the ramifications of a social, political, and historical crisis. Moreover, Erikson was quick to remind himself and me that adventuresome children such as these, and boldly imaginative, morally awake adults such as the driver, are "entitled to company"— hence a professor's interest in that Harvard office not only in the many Gandhi met, confronted, and took pains to persuade, but any number of individuals in the schools visited by those African-American children, and soon enough, other schools across Boston as it tried more broadly to come to terms, like the South, with the desegregation demanded by the federal courts.

Mary Ann and Alice: Acts of Contrition

At the height of racial conflict in Boston (prompted by a federal court order that African-American students be admitted to schools across the city in the interest of a better education), I got to know a group of highschoolers who also lived in Roxbury and were bussed to South Boston, to a mostly Irish Catholic neighborhood. In no time people were at one another's throats. Those who lived in Roxbury were, like their younger predecessors mentioned earlier, anxious to break out of poverty and, too, the long-enforced isolation that had been the fate of their ancestors: slavery, then segregation down South, and up North attendance at neighborhood schools commonly overcrowded, understaffed, and educationally inadequate.

But those who lived in South Boston, so-called white working-class families, also regarded themselves as victims. "Their" school was now under the control of a judge who himself lived outside of the city, and that was the bottom (residential) line—if you had money, you could buy your way out of the uncertainty and tumult of a court-supervised social and racial crisis. Indeed, if you had money, you could live in some of Boston's swankier neighborhoods, send your children to private schools. At the time, though, the "class" side of the issue was buried under the outburst of anger, on both sides, connected to "race"—and, of course, it was not lost on people in either Roxbury or South Boston that many of those most in favor of this version of integration were white people who lived outside Boston, untouched by the strains of such a struggle.

I was visiting that high school, talking with young men and women coming there by bus from Roxbury and with those who had always come there from the streets of South Boston. As one who had studied school desegregation in the South, I was now in my native region as an observer of a city where I'd been born and grew up. One African-American student I got to know, Mary Ann, was a remarkably stoic and farsighted person who kept telling me she could "understand" the evident anger of some of the white people of the city. "It's new, and they're scared," she said tersely.

As I listened to her I often wondered whether I would be able, under such circumstances, to summon for myself that kind of understanding—put myself in the shoes of others who weren't being welcoming to me. I chalked up some of Mary Ann's generosity of spirit to her good-natured, hopeful temperament. She was a cheerful, bright young lady, and she was determined, as well, to outlast the cold, unfriendly reception she was all the time receiving. In her own way she was, of course, a leader, and one with an unpretentious but evident moral sensibility—her willingness to extend empathy and understanding to those who feared or disliked her presence among them.

But four months into that experience, Mary Ann's grandmother suddenly died of a stroke, and the girl was devastated. The grandmother had effectively been Mary Ann's mom, because her mother worked hard and long cleaning rooms in a Boston hotel and had to contend, as well, with rheumatoid arthritis. The grandmother's sudden death, at only fifty-eight, stunned everyone in her family—and Mary Ann was more than tempted to leave school, get a job, try to take care of her ailing, hard-pressed mother and her younger siblings. Yet she stayed on, though obviously saddened. She had usually worn bright clothes; now she dressed in black. She had usually tried to smile, to answer questions eagerly and spiritedly in class; now she was slow to respond, distracted. *She* should be in that "fancy hotel cleaning up after those rich folks," she told me once.

One day when I came to talk with Mary Ann, she had an "incident" to report: "A girl came up to me in the hall; they never talk to me, and a lot of times they whisper swearwords, so I was surprised. She asked if I was 'all right.' I said yes, sure. She said she noticed I was wearing black all the time. I said yes, my gramma died. She said she was sorry. Then she told me her father died a year ago, and she knew what I was going through. It was nice of her."

Nicer still, that the girl, Alice, dared break with her many South Boston school friends and kept talking with Mary Ann—not the kind of behavior likely to earn her applause from her friends. Alice asked Mary Ann if there was anything she could do to be of help. No, there wasn't. Finally, Alice asked for Mary Ann's address—so she could send a sympathy card.

Mary Ann was touched but skeptical: "She's still upset because of her father, that's why she's trying to be nice to me." Once more I took note of the psychological acuity, the capacity to figure out others with a certain thoughtful detachment. But a month or so later, Mary Ann found herself less readily comprehending—puzzled by what she heard.

Alice told her that she was sorry for all that had been happening there at South Boston High School—and told her she personally regretted her outspoken disapproval of earlier days. Then this from Mary Ann: "She told me she owes us [the African-American students] an 'act of contrition,' and I didn't know what she was talking about. So I asked her, and she said the priest told her, if you do something, and you figure out it's wrong, then you should recognize that you've made your error, and try to make up for it some way. You face up to what you've done and pray you won't do it again. I think that's why she sent the [sympathy] card to us, 'an act of contrition.' I didn't know what to say—so I joked, and said I've learned a new word, contrition! I told her I'd never have heard of that word if I hadn't come here to this school!"

The black girl, Mary Ann, was puzzled by a spoken gesture of a white girl, by Alice's chosen word, only to learn from another of her white classmates that the heart of "contrition" had to do with "regret." For those students "contrition" was familiar—"something priests say when they want you to apologize and admit you've made a mistake." For the black child "contrition" conveyed a certain elusive mystery: "I think it means you've done something that can get you in trouble, but whether you meant to do the wrong thing, that's up to God to decide, so you can't be sure, and He's the one who is watching, and He knows."

God As a Moral Companion

I was intrigued and stirred mightily when I heard that remark of Mary Ann's, which struck me as powerfully suggestive in its implications— the notion that God is a moral companion of sorts to us, that He observes us and comes to conclusions about our episodes of wrongdoing, no matter our claims, excuses, self-justifications. A heavy weight, I recall thinking in my psychoanalytic mode—the very idea that we can err, and that our missteps are noticed. In contrast, I began to remind myself; the word "guilty" predominates for many of us today, but with a subjective emphasis. The black teenager put her finger on me and my kind, and then another matter as well, when she favored me with an ironic gesture: "You see, if you go and do a bad thing, your conscience will make you sweat and you'll feel down in the dumps, my gramma would say, so you'd better behave, or you'll lose your appetite and you'll toss and turn right through the night. But Gramma said it's more important what you do than whether you're upset because of what you did. She said we should go check in with our minister, and let him tell us the right and the wrong, whether we're on God's side or we've gone and strayed!"

There it all is, and here we are—on many talk shows and sometimes in churches, in an occasional school, and in certain homes: guilt as a problem, something to be addressed through a conversation that aims at awareness, if not (Lord, save us) "insight." Interestingly, at that Boston school a convergence had occurred: the black girl had heard echoes of her religious background, her family background, from her white peer and classmate, had heard thoughts about regret and remorse, about sadness as a felt response to deeds acknowledged and recognized as thoroughly bad, as malevolent in nature—such as the heckling of newcomers through a resort to racial epithets and scornful personal comments. A priest had intervened, called those taunting words worthy of contrition, and several black students who were the recipients of such language had, in turn, worried whether their hostile critics might be soon enough feeling "guilty"—even as those critics, too, struggled with that word, and with another one, as a Catholic child, Maureen, a friend of Alice's, told me: "I should have kept quiet. I think the priest wants us to be nicer to them, but I'm not sure what he thinks we should do—maybe he thinks we should be sorry. That's what contrition is, to be sorry. I asked the priest: 'Should I feel bad, and take my sister's advice?' She says, 'You either go on a guilt trip or you don't.' The priest said, 'No, you go visit God, you go that way and you'll know.' But my sister says you should get guilt off your back. The priest says God gave us backs to carry things. He said, 'If you've gone down the wrong road, you need God to get the right road directions.' My sister says, 'It's *you,* you should help—get your head cleared, so you're not overloaded with guilt.' I think I should vote for the priest!"

Her explanation, her moral, self-scrutinizing story, rang in my ears—a jolt almost: that when we err, we ought feel regret, sadness, remorse (as opposed to talking and talking about our "guilt"). Here was a girl able, like Alice, to stand up to her friends, to resist, finally, their heckling boycott of African-American fellow students, and so doing to assert unselfconsciously a kind of daily leadership, a moral independence. I also kept remembering a moment's unselfconscious act by that white girl, Maureen—she lowered her head briefly as she spoke, and then raised it, her eyes still looking at me. She seemed strangely at peace with herself and in no need of speaking, her sister's pressing, ever so contemporary psychological advice notwithstanding. Later, as I tried to understand what had happened to Maureen, how her mind had worked, I began to realize that her head had, in fact, spoken to me—a child who knew that misdeeds deserve an expression of regret, and a child willing to embrace melancholy and affirm an intention to make public her awareness that the Lord who sees mistakes will also see something quite real and important: contrition expressed and conveyed through a head's movement, through eyes widened in silent, knowing penitence.

All of the above, for me, was immensely interesting, yet perplexing. The more I heard about these children and their connections, involvements with one another, the less I understood what was actually happening to them, the African-American children and the white children, both. The white girl, Alice, and her friend Maureen were willing to talk about matters religious and psychological, and the African-American girl, Mary Ann, was not quite sure, for some time, why Alice had approached her, even as she had heard a lot about Alice's personal and spiritual life. My work with these children, and with others who were their friends, was obscured by my less than clear comprehension of them, my inability to understand what was actually taking place in the embattled school they attended.

One day, as I prepared to present the new work I was doing in South Boston and Roxbury, I heard in my mind what I anticipated Erik Erikson might find worthy of comment. He would ask this or that, I was sure; he would stress one line of inquiry, turn away from another. We were far away from the Mahatma then, and I wasn't anticipating a discussion on leadership that resembled ones we'd had earlier. Yet Alice had already told me that her friendship with Mary Ann, relatively muted and by no means ostentatious, had been costly to her, even as

Alice's priest let me know that he himself had his "concerns" about the "implication," as he called it, of his conversations with Alice, and with Maureen, too. He had encouraged a familiarity between Alice and Mary Ann that put the former in jeopardy: "Don't think it was easy for her to cross that racial line at Southie [South Boston High School], and I have to admit it was easier for me to do the right thing by saying the right thing than it was for her to—well, deal with me and my priestly advice, and its effect on her as she struggled with what went on every day in the rooms and corridors of that school!"

Erikson on a City's Young Leaders

In fact, Erikson and I managed to have a thorough and satisfying discussion of what was happening at South Boston High School and elsewhere in the city across the Charles River from his study, where we tried to figure out what was taking place, especially in the minds of certain young people and, indeed, among them as they went about their daily lives. "You are, I think, trying," he once said, "to learn about the 'psychological adjustment' of children, and you're trying to do it as an observer, through your interviews. Now, you're immersed a bit in religion and theology, just as the children are when they find themselves grappling with that word 'contrition.' (It's tempting for you and me to follow them, and their priest—to go further than conventional psychology will let you or me or all of them go!) Maybe we should take a step back. Maybe we should stop (only for a few minutes!) being child psychiatrists or psychoanalysts—or even social observers, versed in a knowledge of 'group dynamics' and 'social stress.' There's no question that those children are going through a lot of personal turmoil, and that there's plenty of that turmoil out in the open, on the streets with people shouting, and inside the school with people keeping their distance from one another, the whites versus the blacks. But why not look at what this school crisis has done—at the emergence of leaders, young people who go beyond the 'society' around them, and become moral leaders!"

We talked about those youthful moral leaders at some length, about the strains in their personal lives, in their everyday educational lives, and in their religious lives, as they struggled to reconcile *faith,* as it was enunciated to them, with *being,* with each day's tasks and challenges and possibilities. Here was, we realized, an occasional moral leadership as it gradually took shape—one moment's enactment, then another. In Erikson's words: "I wouldn't try to formulate this [the above mentioned chronicle, the behavior noted and its origins, consequences] with too much emphasis on either the mind or religion and the Bible! I'd think of what these young people are doing for the rest of us as well as for themselves: they are showing us—showing that priest!—what happens when moral values are really put to the test, when someone has to 'take the lead' in life, live up to what is said in church or at home or in a classroom by a history teacher or a literature teacher or a Sunday school teacher. If you live up to values, you're doing that, taking the lead with regard to them: that's moral leadership—what Gandhi tried to find 'doable' for himself. It's important for us to remember this— that moral leadership as we study it in history and politics (from the distance of time and events we never get to see or learn about in any detail) is also moral leadership that can happen right in front of us or not far away." With that he was ready to stop, and with that I was somehow more aware of where I was headed in my work (I was handed along, in Walker Percy's sense, in that work, given direction in understanding it). And these children I was getting to know were finding a moral direction for themselves, and exerting it, living it out, for the city that was now theirs to lead.

XI

High and Low Places: Two Presidents
and American Children

Even as I began working on this book (the writing of it, of course, but also the review on my part of notes and tapes, of research done over a thirty-year stretch of time, and of fiction and essays written on the subject by certain novelists I admire) the news was filled, as mentioned in the first chapter, with reports of an American president's sexual indiscretions, his vulnerability to charges of wrongdoing—and so the words "impeachment" and "censure" became increasingly used in accounts of his prospects, not to mention his place in history. From the students in the classes I teach at an elementary school, a high school, and from the teachers in a seminar I offer every autumn in a graduate school of education, I heard a chorus of references from pupils and their instructors about an American president, about his personal life as it connects with his work.

Albert Jones, the "handyman," as he still calls himself, and janitor, and one-time volunteer bus driver who appears in the chapter on Boston's desegregation struggle, kept bringing up this book's concerns as he and I and millions of our fellow citizens, in the waning months of 1998, tried to make sense of what was ceaselessly and thoroughly confronting us as we glanced at newspapers, turned on radios or television sets in our homes. "How can that guy lead, do his business? That's what I want to know," I heard during one visit to the African-American church where Albert and so many others paused weekly to pray, but also, as he often reminded me, to mull things over: "I thought to myself the other day, that fellow [President Clinton] sure is in bad trouble, and he needs all the hard praying any of us can do for him! Some people say he's a no-good, and some people say he's on our side, so we've got to stick with him—but I'm not sure he's all bad, no sir; and I'm not sure we should stay with him just because he'll be trying to do us favors—that would be swapping a pat on his back for a handout to us!"

Is a Good Leader Ordinarily a Good Person?

A thin smile from him ended that moment of political commentary, a declaration of sorts—then a polite and generous shift on his part, in which my long-standing interests were explicitly and with evident kindness acknowledged, culminating in a pointed question: "Do you think a leader who does wrong (he cheats on his wife or tells lies) can still be a good leader—I mean, a leader who does good?" I'm not, at first, sure how to reply to him. I end up saying that in the long history of humanity there have probably been leaders who have made plenty of mistakes, even on occasion behaved quite badly, yet also done much that I suspect he and I would consider quite impressively worthwhile. I also begin wondering out loud whether a good leader is ordinarily or expectedly going to be a good person.

We were dealing there and then with ambiguity, complexity, even irony, and this often quite thoughtful man, who had no claim to money or power or a "higher education," and whose moral leadership came to him out of the accidents of a humble life rather than as a perquisite of electoral office or a career's achievement, took the lead (as he'd done in his neighborhood's life) in talking about kinds of leadership: "Like I've said before [in our conversations] there are times when you go and do what you believe is the right thing to do, and you know you may be paying a price, because, let's face it, good things don't come easy a lot of the time, and the same for *doing* good things, there can be a stiff price you pay. I know that about 'leading' in life (in my kind of life), but I don't know what to say about how it goes up there, for a president living in the White House. I've told you lots of time what my pa, my father, used to tell us—that you have people in high places and people in low places, and that's how the world is. But you know, because a guy is president, down in Washington, doesn't mean he isn't a plain old human being, like anyone anywhere across America. I know that's not very smart of me, what I've [just] said, but he must be weighing stuff, the President, like we all do—kicking himself one minute, trying to get the best deal he can the next. If you're a leader, and you're up there in some high place, you better know what you're out to do, and what you can do, and what won't work. That's the right side of being a leader— you know what's important, and what you've got to do to see it happen. If you're down here, in some low place, there's still God, asking of you, and there's still your conscience, telling you a lot, saying you're all right, but every once in a while giving you a little jab so you don't slip up, whistling Dixie, and end in a real bad mess. That's where our president is, but a lot of folks, they want him out of there, that mess, so *we're* leading him, you could say, these days! My gut says: who is going to buy that sour guy [the special prosecutor] scratching after him, poking like an all-time back-alley busybody hustler, looking for something that'll boost himself?"

Leadership in a Democracy

He had, of course, with no claim to special knowledge, hinted at the mystery of leadership in a democracy, the manner in which people stake out their own claim to authority, even power, and leadership—a president (and Congress) then awaiting a public decision, a public verdict: the people's responses, attitudes, opinions, their own kind of leadership, with distinctly moral aspects to it.

In the elementary school, and in the high school, where his children and his neighbors' children learned to be with classmates of different racial background, I listened at that time to many reflections on the President and his moral, his political, predicament, from children under ten and those in the midst of adolescence. I had taught those young people in class. I have elsewhere described the possible extent and depth of certain morally introspective talking times in classrooms, in homes, on the street, near playing fields—in books with titles that aim to tell of "the moral life of children," their "moral intelligence," and how it develops. Indeed, as I heard a president's love life being discussed by children whose moral energy I had worked at documenting over the years, I understood, yet again, how the young connect with news as they do with the immediate world around them, in accordance with who they are, what they bring out of their own lives to what they are reading, hearing, and contemplating with others at school or in a neighborhood.

With so many people, I wondered what the much and constantly reported personal behavior (and misbehavior) of a man who occupied the constitutionally designated, mandated position of primary leadership in the United States of America would mean to our younger Americans, for whom the president is the leader among leaders. "He's on top of the other people who are in charge," an eleven-year-old boy, his dad nearby, told me, and then a child's amplification of that job in its present-day import and meaning: "But even if you're way, way up there, you can take a big fall, and then you're in bad trouble, and you have to watch your step."

I nod, and ask whether that description fits Bill Clinton, the president now in office. "Yes," I'm told, and unsurprised I nod again. Yet, this sixth grader wants to explore not only the future, what might well happen, what does happen, eventually, "when a leader forgets what he's got to do," but the moral implications of such failure of memory—and accordingly, the effect, really, of a mental and moral lapse on an office, and a person in that office: "A guy running the whole show, he can't slip and no one pays any attention, because everyone is busy. This guy, the President, he's the big show, a real strut, he's got to be. A leader, he wants everyone watching, he's got them—but if he goes and falls flat on his face, he's still got all of his people, everyone looking, and that means he's going down, down—no one to tag after him, no more of that."

Abruptly the father, hitherto silent as his son has talked, makes this observation: "He's *out there* all the time, the President, but he must be worried that he'll end up *out here,* standing somewhere with the rest of us, looking for direction—that's what he's supposed to *give* folks, direction, tell them the right way to go. It's too bad for him that all this mud is on him—[it] gives folks reason to question if he's president right or president wrong, and when that happens to the one you're supposed to think is number one, then that's bad for him and it's bad for us. A guy who's telling you where to go, you've got to feel in your heart he's the one you'll follow, you'll believe, no matter what. Hey, I heard my boy [a smile is thereupon directed at him] talking with his pals, and he said, 'The President must be afraid everyone is laughing at him,' and his friend Chris said, 'For sure,' and then he said something real smart, and I think he may have heard it at home, because his daddy was in the Army for a few years, he did real well there: 'A general whose soldiers are snickering away at him—he's not the one to lead them into a battle. They'll turn on him—turn away from him. A soldier, he has to believe in the general, or he'll sit on his hands and won't go out there for him.' "

That remark of a boy who listened carefully to his soldier father gave pointed and powerful expression to the dilemma a certain kind of leader constantly has to know (somewhere, somehow in his or her mind)—leadership as it connects with, affirms the faith of followers, and so, leadership the recipient of moral passion, a home of sorts for the seekers who have to do the fighting in this or that struggle. When I heard of that child's casual street aside, related to me with a grown man's obvious conviction (his faith in a boy's explication of faith as a necessary fuel if followers are to be stirred favorably toward the actions required of them) I felt fully informed: an unpretentious characterization of moral leadership as others look for it, take it in as the precondition of their commitment, as followers, to its purposes, its calls to allegiance first, and then, to action. I also felt my mind carrying me back in time to moments mentioned, evoked in the earlier parts of this book. I remembered Robert Kennedy reminding a few of us doctors that we'd better "hold on to our credibility." At the time we weren't sure what he was trying to get at—and were unsettled (maybe our pride was provoked) by the suggestion that we needed to prove ourselves believable, keep doing so self-consciously, lest we not be heard with any favor. He sensed that we didn't grasp his meaning, intent—or that we were offended by what we believed he was urging on us. Thereupon he tried to make his case, in a lively and winning show of emotion and, too, through an instructive account of how governing in America works, or can fail to do so. While he acknowledged his own past mistakes, errors of judgment, we followed him, as it were, came to fathom his remarks as honestly, even graciously meant, rather than as an indirect reproval. We fell in line with someone whose awakened conscience, willingly and disarmingly (our defensive self-importance undone!) put on the table, drew us all together: he and his aides were now the ones guiding us, because we believed they knew what we needed to know—their sense of what was appropriate, necessary, right, at last became ours.

As I talked with that father, with his son, I remembered Ruby Bridges and others I've mentioned in this book. "We're doing this," I once heard the Boston bus driver tell the boys and girls on that bus, his voice raised high—and then his "punch line," he later called it: "You're going to teach some kids a lesson, and teach Boston a lesson. Don't you forget it, your country needs to learn what's right, and what's wrong, and you're the ones to do the teaching—take us all down the road to God's truth. Remember, 'the Lord is my shepherd,' it says in the Bible, and that's what you are, shepherds—you'll steer us to doing the right thing, the way God does all the time." A little nervously, dramatically overwrought, I have to admit I thought then and there—forgetting what the Bible and a recitation of it meant to those young churchgoing children, to their mothers and fathers, to this man, very much in loco parentis, himself their morally voluble shepherd, leader.

Nor did Ruby, in New Orleans in December 1960, after a few

months of walking by threatening mobs on the way to school, fail to say her own biblically connected prayers, in which, of all ironies, she asked the Lord to "forgive" those heckling, threatening her, even as she called for His help. At one point I heard this from her: "I guess I'll be all right, and I'll try to be. My mom and dad saw the President [Kennedy] on the TV, and he said he was on our side, because it's fair and right. I was asleep, and the teacher told us [the next day] that the President spoke for us kids [she and other African-American children going through the severe stresses of southern school desegregation] and that means the country will be for us, even if those people keep shouting every morning [in front of the William Frantz School she was attending]—because he's the leader, and people pay attention when he speaks."

Yet she would learn otherwise, would learn through her own experience the occasional limits of presidential leadership: "Some of the [white] kids said [in the hall afterward] that presidents make mistakes [a white boycott of the school had ended]. The teacher heard them and she said we should all go back to our seats, so we did. She said we're Americans and we have the right to say anything we want, but she wanted to hear what we thought, really, really about the President. No, a lot of kids didn't tell her, but a few whispered; I could hear they didn't like him because he was on the side of the colored. I knew they said bad words against us. I guess I tried to forget, but I do know it was something about 'niggers'—I heard a boy call the President a 'nigger-lover.' I tried not to show them I was upset, or that I heard. I looked at the map the teacher has [on the wall] for us, and I looked at her—she was watching us, I could see. She told us that the President has to be ahead of the country; it's his job, to say what's right and to stand up against the wrong things, when people break the law or they want to hurt other people. She gave us one of her 'long talks' (that's what she calls them), and no one said anything until she asked us what we knew about the President—where he comes from, and why he spoke the other night about where we live, here in New Orleans, the trouble we're having. A girl said he was for the federal judge who 'ordered the colored into the schools, where they never were before,' and another girl said it was 'the federal courts,' and the President, 'he was agreeing with them.' 'He has to,' she said. That's when there was an argument: some kids shook their heads and said no, if he was 'tough and honest,' they said, he'd fight the courts, but he isn't, he's just a coward, a politician, that's all he is. But the teacher she didn't like that. I could tell, I could see it on her face: she wrinkles her forehead when she is upset, just like my grandma."

So it went for a child whose endeavors a president had declared morally and politically important, even as a class to which that girl belonged tried to come to terms with its split opinions, assumptions, values. Ruby's father, in that regard, told her this: "You've got the President on your side, and he's the tops." Ruby, in turn, came to this conclusion: "He's already in the history book, so he's right, even if a lot of people don't agree with him. We can help the President, the teacher said, even if some people don't like him. He's making enemies, Daddy says, because he's trying to speak what he really believes is the right thing to do. If it was a different president we had, it would be different—I wouldn't be where I am in school, my daddy is positive, and my momma. My granny says there's been a few presidents in her life, and she doesn't 'rightly recall a lot of them,' but she thinks this one, President Kennedy, she'll remember all the rest of her life, because he's a friend of our people, so that means he's cheering for us, not swearing at us the way a lot do."

She was comparing a white New Englander, John Kennedy, with the white grown-ups who cursed away at her each day she went to school. She was responding to her parents and grandparents and uncles and aunts: all of them exceedingly attentive to a president's nationally broadcast words with respect to what she and others like her were experiencing; and as well, all of them careful to take note of what their fellow (white) citizens were saying. "My daddy works in a gas station," Ruby reminded me, and then this bit of information: "He hears them saying bad words about the President, about Mr. Kennedy, he says we should call him. Filling up the tank, he'll hear people cussing: they want Mr. Kennedy 'to go take a vacation.' When Daddy comes home he says Mr. Kennedy is strong, even though he's losing lots of people here who say they voted for him, but *never again.* 'He stands up for what he believes,' and 'that's why he's a real good president,' Daddy says. Granny cut out a picture of him, and she has it on the wall—she says he's cared more about us than some of the others, the rest. It's because he spoke up for us, that's why. If you're a president, you have to make a decision—my daddy said, and our teacher said it also, just like Daddy. In church our minister said we have a friend up north in Washington, and he lives in the White House. Maybe he'll have some colored to visit him there, the minister said, and that's why we have to make our decisions, just like the presidents have to 'step one way or the other,' my daddy says."

President Kennedy and
Southern Children: The 1960s

In her home, in so many homes like hers I visited across the South during those civil rights years of the 1960s, an American president figured constantly, his picture in a place of honor, often near (and reverentially, above) photographs of family members. Even today, some of those pictures are still there for the seeing, for the remembrances they stir, for the respect they prompt—a wistful glance, a few words of gratitude. If anything, President Kennedy's unexpected, untimely death, in late 1963, strengthened a felt bond between him and many families like Ruby's that embraced the Mississippi Project of 1964, initiated by SNCC and implemented by college students from all over America. Those pictures of a fallen American president occasioned much conversation among the activists and the families they visited, tried to know and understand. In Greenville, Mississippi, a twelve-year-old African-American child watched three northern college students looking at a picture of a man once president and now gone, and then the boy declared, "He tried for us. In school [a segregated, all-black one] the teacher said he wasn't perfect—no one is; but he had a chance to do good by us [the colored] and it helped us, when he told the others [the white people] that he was going to do what was right for our country, for everyone. Coming from him—they had to listen, the white people. He was on the top, so they did." Then this brief, wry comment: "He be the only white man we have here [in his home] all the time. He be our kin, my grandpa will say."

That reference to a picture and its place told of someone from a very high place becoming, thanks to historical circumstance and his response to it, part of the daily life of those countrymen of his in a lower place. Not that a president's decisions weren't a collective aftermath of guile and calculation, of a stated morality used to conceal, and certainly burnish, any number of political needs, requirements meant to win personal advantage as well as further the nation's practical interests, maybe even its craven ones—so President Kennedy in his own way plainly made clear, when he reminded his fellow citizens that they were engaged in a worldwide effort to win the allegiance of others, in the name of "freedom," and therefore could hardly be seen over the continents as belonging to a nation that denied some of its own people such (personal, civic) freedom.

That young boy's dad, a full-grown man but called a "stock boy" in a supermarket, made the matter clear back then: "You can't sell freedom to others if you show you don't like it for anyone but yourself." When those college students from well-known northern universities heard the speaker, they praised him with admiring faces, and with words that began with the respectful "sir"—its use, then and there, a blow for freedom, as the man's head showed, through an appreciative bow. *He,* now "sir" several times, should be the President's speechwriter, one of the students eventually insisted—a bow, thereby to a savvy statement about the highest of lives, about presidential power as it is executed, for which reasons and in what manner. "We be only ordinary," that working man modestly said; as for the President, "he be the top man there is"; and as for his moral leadership, "he be smart enough to know that if you sell the best, you win, because people come to you and they're glad for what they get"—the social ethics of the marketplace became in a worker's discerning mind a means of political and moral analysis: leadership examined, metaphorically, with an ethical nuance, as well.

A few years later the intimacy some of us saw unfolding between President Kennedy and some impoverished, politically beleaguered Americans in Louisiana's riot-plagued New Orleans, in Mississippi's small-town bastions of segregationist resistance, got put on a lasting record, in the documentary film *Eyes on the Prize*, which is an aesthetic and substantive rendering of what took place, among other events, in those early 1960s, with Ruby Bridges and President Kennedy both presented, side by side, through film footage juxtaposed: astute editing itself a statement, and because of the influence of television, an act, an event, whereby culture could open eyes, open history's doors, and, too, reveal the occasional dimensions of moral leadership—a child's fate, her daily school experience, becoming an aspect of a president's fate, his daily experience as he went about his work. Rather obviously, as any number of African-Americans let some of us know back then (and continue to say, even today, out of memories handed down through families), it took a particular president to make those particular remarks, to send the particular moral message that *Eyes on the Prize*, thanks to technology, can keep transmitting across the generations.

As that store clerk, now an elderly retiree, still in Greenville, would say three decades later after looking at that documentary film: "Someone else could have turned his back on us—people find their excuses, their 'reasons' if they want to be fancy—but he'd figured that he should stand there, like he did, stand up for us, and that way, he nudged the whole country, you could say, into standing up, along with him, and along with our kids, 'the colored'—they still call us [that] here, but they do watch their step, and what they say, more and more every year."

Such a recall, given the flesh of direct, bare-bones language in response to a series of visual images on a television set (in a church's school building) goes a long way toward an evocation, an elucidation based on a life's experiences, of a concept, moral leadership, as it gets asserted, as it gets recognized, and felt in low places after being affirmed, demonstrated in a high place with an enabling historical moment the provider of a particular possibility: the exceptional and the ordinary, in a film, become kin, compatriots, or in the vernacular I kept hearing back then, "the President, he's a brother to us, Brother

Kennedy." Then, with shrewd candor: "the Klan people hate him, and they're right, according to what they believe."

Leadership, morally enacted, had made for a felt intimate connection given everyday expression, and indirectly stated in home pictorial arrangements, in casual kitchen asides, or on-the-job intuitions put to word ("I saw the white people looking at President Kennedy on the television and their faces told me what they were thinking, that he's looking out for us, the colored folks"). Not that President Clinton has had such an intense relationship with large numbers of Americans, even as his personal life prompted episodes of moral consideration (and mockery) across the land, and as well, across social and racial lines, generational divides—while, also, news of his predecessor's (President Kennedy's) personal, sexual life was made known in ways unavailable, even unthinkable over thirty-five years ago, when he lived under a different kind of allowable scrutiny. I heard, in classrooms and homes and neighborhood playing lots, children snicker at a president (they were daily recipients through newspapers, radios, television sets, of news that told of his private life, his habits, his confessions, his waywardness); I went back in my mind to President Kennedy, increasingly known now as flawed morally, personally, who was long regarded as a moral leader. President Clinton, similarly flawed (charged and self-described as such) nevertheless tried hard to place himself in a certain tradition of moral leadership, to find his place of eminence in history, to establish himself as someone of deserved renown. But I also thought about the presidency as it connects with the inner life of children, stirs them to thought, gives them considerable pause.

In a ninth-grade classroom whose members had shown quite a range of responsiveness to their president's reported doings in 1998, I heard a youth, usually shy of much public talking, make this point during our civics course: "When a person way up there, like President Clinton, falls down, it can be trouble for us, even if it's [trouble] for him—we get dragged with him, we go that way, too." I kept thinking of what she had said as I couldn't help noticing, in that class and others, how children accommodate themselves to an American president, take note of his failings, regard them through recourse to their particular sense of right and wrong, learned at home and school. In a sense, by their way of thinking of his (errant) way of being, acting, they were unsurprisingly speaking of themselves: the boys who roared with bemused or belittling amusement at a grown-up's publicly announced sexuality, bravado; the girls who looked down at him, *or* at his young paramour—their own sexuality renounced, criticized, considered in its possibilities; the boys and girls who were themselves quite in control of their impulses, and quite sensibly under the sway of reasonable consciences that had come to mean much to them, to be respected by them, and who therefore knew to distance themselves from a public figure and his young White House intern, even as they suspected, so their words indicated, an inability of those two to have a desirable control over certain impulses, and in both of them, a conscienceless side to their psychological makeup.

The foregoing, of course, has to do with the moral imagination of children (and of the rest of us called adults) as it engages with public events, as they in turn are relayed in a given society at a given moment in its history. So it goes, a president and his relationship with a particular woman, a prosecutor and his inquiry—all of that the stuff of high places as it gives daily shape to ideas expressed in the low places millions inhabit as a consequence of their particular lives. So it went with (and for) President Kennedy, as during the civil rights era he entered the minds of others, their words and daydreams, their introspective lives, their consciences as they affirmed themselves in the manifold manner that characterizes such mental (moral and spiritual) activity in so many of us. So it has gone in our time, alas, for President Clinton, for us Americans—as what he has done and said, or not done or not said, has echoed in our various heads all over: a contemporary leadership, the relative or clear-cut absence of its moral aspect, becomes for the rest of us a big puzzle, a troubling instance and example to ponder, as many children have come to know, and we grown-ups with them.

Yet even as irony so often abounds in life, the children in my elementary school class and in my high school class kept reminding me how hard it could be for many of them to make sense of a president's moral leadership, its increasingly known failures, but also, how curious they had become, prompted to think and ask and wonder about a range of oughts and naughts: a nation's flawed moral leader became, indirectly and by happenstance, a moral "case" of sorts, his misstep a prod for the moral thinking of many. One afternoon, during an eleventh-grade history discussion, a young woman spoke of her Rhode Island grandmother's response to a newspaper story—a columnist had written that "our children imitate a president who lies," and the girl's grandmother had become upset reading those words, had sent the clipping to her granddaughter. "I told Granny not to worry," we in the class were told—and then a big argument, as some students agreed, affirmed that citizens young (and older, as well) might well take their cues, sometimes, from a president's, a leader's example, whereas others disagreed, insisted that "events in Washington," as one young man put it, "don't count, not in a big way, not really." He went on to explain why: "Hey, you're who you are, and if some guy does some hanky-panky down in D.C., you'll still be who you are, and either you couldn't care less, or else you think it's okay to go and do like he does, but that's because of who you are, that's how I see it."

A prolonged, heated response. One youth after another tried to take up personally and argumentatively the matter of moral behavior as it is (or is not) shaped by the news, and in particular, by a president's reported deeds, words. None of the young people were willing to say that a wayward president's publicly described, acknowledged sexual missteps, or indeed, personal wrongdoing of any kind, had directly come to bear on their lives, or ever would. Expressions of indifference, of thoroughgoing boredom, yielded, however, to sporadic, surprising exclamations of scorn, contempt, and outrage, which prompted interesting queries or sardonic observations. One student asked, "Why are we paying so much attention to that one guy! Who cares about him!" Another student offered an answer, showed her unqualified lack of interest in a subject matter, gave voice to her disgust: "He's the President, that's why, but I don't think he stands for anything but himself—he just wants to be on top and have people clapping when he talks, so we're wasting our time, the American people, when we get so interested in someone who's (my mom called him) 'a good-for-nothing.' We should talk about someone who has lived good (been good), and not be saying over and over what the President did in the White House with that girlfriend he had there." A quick retort was immediately sent that speaker's way: "Well, he's the President, so everyone pays attention to him." In reply: "Well, I don't." But the one so addressed was unbelieving: "You say you don't, but you've got your opinions, so you've been watching the television, like everyone else." A pause, and then a comment from a young lady who claimed to be a friend to both of them, to others who have spoken—and who wanted us all to attend to more important topics: "Everyone is talking about the President, because he's the President, but it doesn't make any difference—he doesn't mean all that much. He's just one more guy who got caught doing bad! My parents know other people—they've gotten themselves into trouble (the same kind, just like he did, Clinton). My mom said you have to pity him: he's 'gained the whole world,' but he's lost his soul, like it says in the Bible. My dad says, if you pity him you should pity a lot of people who have gone walking down the same road he took. I guess you have to be careful—look where you're going, you're headed!"

At that point the free-for-all banter, exchange of opinion, abruptly stopped on its own—it was if the class took those words just mentioned quite seriously, and collectively wondered about its own destination. Some seconds of silence—during which I wondered what to say. A hand was raised. I nodded. A young man spoke forthrightly, at considerable length, his bemusement apparent on his face: "You have got to say that the President has got everyone talking about what's right and what's wrong. I think you should try to be fair: he's done a lot of good for the country, a lot more than some of the people who are going after him, and call him bad. You can make a mistake, but if you're going to judge a guy, like the President, or anyone, you should look at the whole record, everything he's done, my dad says. The other presidents—people didn't know much about them; but this one's slipped, he's fallen on his face, and we all know, so we can all decide whether he's really disgracing the country, or only himself. Me? I'd want to go hide. I'll bet some of the presidents, they could hide what they did—this poor guy, Clinton, he can't."

A long spell, thereafter, of personal commentary: young people putting themselves in a leader's shoes, considering what he might now do, might have done, and what they might do, should do, were they somehow, for some reason, in a situation like the one confronting this particular president. "Maybe it's good," an optimistic young lady averred. "Maybe we'll all learn a lesson from him." Many at once say, "Yeah!" Some, so speaking, cast a glance at me, a not rare effort to figure out what I think, and so, where they stand in relation to the one up front, behind that large desk in front of the blackboard. A young man takes a risk, declaring himself without asking permission: "He's the big boss, and he got himself in a big mess, and now we're all learning a big lesson." No further remarks—heads poised in obvious contemplation, even as some eyes come my way. I express my agreement, notice a few youths catching on to the possible irony—that a fallen leader can be an inadvertent moral instructor-at-large. The bell has rung, telling us to move along. We prepare to oblige, arrange ourselves, shift our thoughts—but a young lady raises her voice over the din; asks me directly "whether a president who makes a big mistake, a leader, can end up being good, a good teacher, even if he's done bad things—I mean, because he has!" I answer guardedly: "Sure, it seems so." I have in mind the very class we've just had. Others say so to one another with a similar vein of thought, as they mill around—and there it is, I muse, a president and some schoolchildren amidst a nation's unfolding history: moral leadership paradoxically becoming immediately, intensely discussed, despite its distant, notable, regrettable lapse.

Afterword

The last part of the previous chapter gets to the heart of this book's subject matter—I mean it to illustrate what moral leadership is, how it takes place in our everyday lives. Presidents, by word and deed, take us in certain directions, influence our assumptions, our expectations or worries; so do others, however—at home, in school, at work, through remarks made, actions initiated. We look up to those who hold high political office—presidents, senators—or to those who have become their own kind of important political figures, as community activists, as organizers (Dorothy Day, Peter Maurin, Danilo Dolce). We revere those whose moral energy inspires us mightily (Bonhoeffer), prompts thought, even moves us to statements, actions that go unrecorded in books but inform the everyday life of particular individuals. But we also constantly look to one another, to uphold for one another various suppositions and ideals, to hand one another along, morally as well as psychologically.

The students in this book who spoke of the lessons they had learned in connection with a moment in history were themselves exploring moral leadership, its possibilities and potential flaws—and in so doing, were furthering in one another a shared consideration that would stay with them, be in their heads, cause this one, that one, to "perk up and watch," in the words of another of their classmates. A classroom's moral moment can become a moral memory for those speaking and listening to one another, and in turn, an aspect years later of students' lives as men and women trying in turn to lead one another along to that "right track" they knew early on to mention.

"You have to keep your eye on the track, the right track" a girl kept insisting—and then her reminder of a fearful possible consequence: "otherwise, you'll get confused and you'll be lost, and everything will go wrong." Silence, as her listeners contemplate with evident seriousness what might happen—and then a fervent exclamation: "If you're not careful someone could come along, and he'd have the gift of gab, my dad says, and clean you out, so you'd have nothing!"

The class was taken aback by that prospect of evil leadership. In no time, "good" and "bad" were being addressed—posed one against the other. An alert had been sounded about *immoral* leadership, a threat to keep in mind as one thinks of the psychological qualities that make for the leader—the Hitlers and Stalins and Mussolinis of this midcentury who demonstrated a terrible and terrifying capacity to rise to the top, to take control, to persuade and win over others, to command hundreds, then thousands, then millions, all accomplished by a personality at work, true, but all done amidst favoring, if not enabling social, political, historical circumstances: leadership and the directions made possible for it by fate, chance, circumstance. Similarly for the humble or ordinary as well as for those who walk (if not strut) the pages of a nation's chronological life.

The teacher and the bus driver, of earlier chapters, taught certain southerners and Yankees up North how leadership, an intensely moral kind, could stir things, help shape the way a community, an entire city comes to terms with its laws, its educational practices—the "right track" found and followed because a person knew or felt or believed what truly ought happen, and knew also how to speak up and out, how to reach and touch others, call on them and round them in: an inwardness of conviction becoming an arresting example for others; a happenstance in a person's life becoming a command persuasively heeded by others, who had ears and eyes with which to notice hard and long, who had hearts and minds with which to follow suit with eagerness and determination. So it goes: one moral will, exerted in such a way as to be embraced by others—moral leadership thereby affirmed, felt, accepted, made part of a people's neighborhood's life.

Throughout our stay on this planet we have chances to take hold of our lives morally, give them shape—to become our own moral leaders as well as ones eager to take note of others, fall in line with them as participants, voters, family members, neighbors. As I concluded this book I recalled some of the individuals mentioned, known or unknown and of modest circumstances. I thought, also, of the time when I heard an African-American mother say a fervent, loud *yes* to school officials who asked her whether she'd still send her children through angry mobs heckling them on their way to a desegregated New Orleans school. "Yes I will, I will," she amplified, and then her terse further amplification: "I will because it's up to me to lead my child, so she can lead others by showing she'll do the right, come what may."

Those last three words became part of a child's moral call of sorts: "come what may, I'll do what's right," said that girl—her mother's moral leadership now her own to accept with vigorous assent and to uphold on each weekday's school visit. I thought, too, of a white man and woman, a husband and wife, the parents of four children, longtime segregationists, who were angered by school desegregation in Louisianna but who one morning abruptly stopped heckling that child, faced their fellow mob members, said, "No, enough!" Silence followed—and then a further remark of the mother's: "The Lord is watching us. Let us be followers of His goodness! Let us smile and not hate!" Such moral leadership, suddenly and surprisingly given voice, turned into an act that stopped others in their tracks, gave them pause, hence a mob became, finally, quieted for a full morning, a mob that thereafter had trouble screaming its hate with the kind of abandon previously demonstrated.

Maybe some of us won't have such a dramatic chance to realize our values, live them out, but the days do offer their moments, as the mother said when she observed, years later in retrospective reflection, "You can't always plan ahead in life; you have to do some thinking with yourself, and hope you'll come to your senses sometimes and be ready to do the right thing." Moral leadership, she was indicating, can be something one yearns to see enacted by oneself, by others—contingent circumstances become the enacted occasion for a kind of personal providence: life's daily possibilities, now and then, turned to good account.

———

As I put together the last part of this book I remembered listening to Martin Luther King, Jr., address a small group of youths, African-American and white, on their way to yet another civil rights project in Mississippi, where hatred and danger awaited them. Dr. King told of a time when he and some of his friends were being heckled in Alabama, threatened with death: "We wanted to run for safety's sake," he said, but then he added this: "The more we heard their hate, the more we realized we had to stay, take the hate on, for their sakes as well as ours. We fell on our knees before that crowd. We prayed to the Lord to protect us, but even more to watch over those men and women. They weren't born to hate like that. They wanted to make us victims, but *they* were victims—of all the malice, the meanness of mind and heart they'd been taught to feel. So we prayed for them, for all of us—we thanked them for the lessons they were teaching us, and we asked God to help them learn what had happened to themselves."

Thereupon, Dr. King sighed, shook his head. Then he called upon himself for more: "We have to find our way toward others, toward family members and friends, but also toward strangers—that was the moral call of Jesus, and before him Isaiah." We sitting, listening to him, looking at him, had heard moral leadership expressed, had seen it enacted—by a minister who had left the conventions and routines of his church to stand witness elsewhere. An unusual moment in the South's political struggle, yes—though each of us, wherever we happen to be, as Dr. King kept insisting, can "find our way toward [various] others."

As I remembered Dr. King speaking of his time down South, I remembered Erik Erikson talking about his friend and teacher Anna Freud: "In her own way she took on the whole psychoanalytic world— even her father, whom she admired and loved so much. At the time when psychoanalysis was the property of the privileged, when patients with money commanded the full time of doctors who needed and wanted money, she said 'Fine, nothing wrong there,' but she worried about the poor, the troubled children, who might also be helped by psychoanalysis, by its insights, and she spoke her mind. She worked to get a clinic going, and she even claimed that it would help psychoanalysis if more of us knew a broader range of people than we were then seeing in our offices."

Erikson was describing moral leadership in action: the assumptions of a profession challenged ethically and intellectually, and for its own sake. Like Dr. King, Anna Freud looked toward others, realized their moral significance to her and her colleagues. But moral leadership asserts itself in ordinary circumstances, and among those whose work is quite humble, even precarious—as many of us were reminded at the end of 1999 when we learned of the fate of five men in Worcester, Massachusetts, as they fought with their lives to contain a roaring blaze, and so doing, died. As I read of those fallen firefighters I remembered a pediatric patient of mine: a ten-year-old boy who had polio, and struggled mightily to use legs becoming paralyzed. I heard in my mind the words of his dad, a Boston fireman: "There's bravery for us to admire—a boy who won't give up and who thinks of us, for all his troubles. He gives us a big smile, even though he's down, and can't walk. He worries about us—all the time it takes to visit him, and the money it takes to keep him here in the hospital. He's afraid for himself, but he keeps thinking of others!" A father was referring to a vulnerable child's willingness to find his way toward others, to regard them as well as his own threatened situation. So it was for that boy and his parents, their mutual regard and respect for one another given daily expressions, given life; and so it can be for more and more of us, one dares think, hope—circles of human moral connectedness growing, touching, informing the lives of individuals and of the communities to which we belong.